International Federation of Library Associations and Institutions
Fédération Internationale des Associations de Bibliothécaires et des Bibliothèques
Internationaler Verband der bibliothekarischen Vereine und Institutionen
Международная Федерация Библиотечных Ассоциаций и Учреждений
Federación Internacional de Asociaciones de Bibliotecarios y Bibliotecas

About IFLA
www.ifla.org

IFLA (The International Federation of Library Associations and Institutions) is the leading international body representing the interests of library and information services and their users. It is the global voice of the library and information profession.

IFLA provides information specialists throughout the world with a forum for exchanging ideas and promoting international cooperation, research, and development in all fields of library activity and information service. IFLA is one of the means through which libraries, information centres, and information professionals worldwide can formulate their goals, exert their influence as a group, protect their interests, and find solutions to global problems.

IFLA's aims, objectives, and professional programme can only be fulfilled with the cooperation and active involvement of its members and affiliates. Currently, over 1,700 associations, institutions and individuals, from widely divergent cultural backgrounds, are working together to further the goals of the Federation and to promote librarianship on a global level. Through its formal membership, IFLA directly or indirectly represents some 500,000 library and information professionals worldwide.

IFLA pursues its aims through a variety of channels, including the publication of a major journal, as well as guidelines, reports and monographs on a wide range of topics. IFLA organizes workshops and seminars around the world to enhance professional practice and increase awareness of the growing importance of libraries in the digital age. All this is done in collaboration with a number of other non-governmental organizations, funding bodies and international agencies such as UNESCO and WIPO. IFLANET, the Federation's website, is a prime source of information about IFLA, its policies and activities: www.ifla.org

Library and information professionals gather annually at the IFLA World Library and Information Congress, held in August each year in cities around the world.

IFLA was founded in Edinburgh, Scotland, in 1927 at an international conference of national library directors. IFLA was registered in the Netherlands in 1971. The Koninklijke Bibliotheek (Royal Library), the national library of the Netherlands, in The Hague, generously provides the facilities for our headquarters. Regional offices are located in Rio de Janeiro, Brazil; Dakar, Senegal; and Singapore.

IFLA Publications 126

Continuing Professional Development: Pathways to Leadership in the Library and Information World

Edited by
Ann Ritchie and Clare Walker

K·G·Saur München 2007

IFLA Publications
edited by Sjoerd Koopman

Bibliographic information published by the Deutsche Nationalibliothek
The Deutsche Nationalbibliothek lists this publication in the Deutsche Nationalbibliografie;
detailed bibliographic data is available in the Internet at http://dnb.d-nb.de.

Printed on permanent paper
The paper used in this publication meets the minimum requirements of
American National Standard – Permanence of Paper
for Publications and Documents in Libraries and Archives
ANSI/NISO Z39.48-1992 (R1997)

© 2007 by International Federation of Library Associations
and Institutions, The Hague, The Netherlands

Alle Rechte vorbehalten / All Rights Strictly Reserved
K. G. Saur Verlag, München
An Imprint of Walter de Gruyter GmbH & Co. KG

All rights reserved. No part of this publication may be reproduced, stored in a retrieval
system of any nature, or transmitted, in any form or by any means, electronic, mechanical,
photocopying, recording or otherwise, without the prior written permission of the publisher.

Printed in the Federal Republic of Germany by Strauss GmbH, Mörlenbach

ISBN 978-3-598-22034-0
ISSN 0344-6891 (IFLA Publications)

TABLE OF CONTENTS

Foreword 9
Ann Ritchie and Clare Walker

Introduction to the Conference 11
Jana Varlejs

THEME I: INTERNATIONAL, NATIONAL AND CROSS-CULTURAL PROGRAMS

Library Leadership Development: Institutional Commitment, Increasing Underrepresented Populations and Impacting the Information Profession 20
Prof. Karen Downing, Dr Camila A. Alire, Jon E. Cawthorne, Tracie D. Hall, Jerome Offord, Veronda J. Pitchford, Prof. Alexandra Rivera, Alysse Jordan

Developing an International Library Leadership Institute: Thinking Outside the Borders 40
Barbara J. Ford, Susan Schnuer, Debra Wilcox Johnson

International Partnerships and Leadership Development: African National Congress, University of Fort Hare, University of Connecticut Partnership. 1999–2007 57
Betsy Pittman, Yolisa Soul, Deborah Stansbury Sunday

Leading Modern Public Libraries: A National Development Programme for England 68
Tom Forrest

Efforts in Leadership and Succession Planning, Large and Small 85
Mary L. Chute

The Leadership and Management Development Programme in the French National Library 100
Michel Netzer

Le Développement des Compétences Managériales à la Bibliothèque Nationale de France 106
Michel Netzer

5

Table of Contents

THEME II: WORKPLACE LEARNING & LEADERSHIP TRAINING WORKSHOPS

E-learning: one path to leadership development 112
Marilyn Gell Mason, Rachel Van Noord

Which Leader Are You? or: Three Functions for Leadership, Linking With Strategic Goals 126
Dr Marielle de Miribel

Quel Responsible Êtes-Vous? ou: Les Trois Fonctions du Leadership, en Lien avec les Objectifs Stratégiques de Votre Bibliothèque 139
Dr Marielle de Miribel

THEME III: LEADERSHIP INSTITUTES

Research Library Leadership Development: Creating a Best Practice 152
James Neal, Victoria Owen, William Garrison

A Question of Confidence?: Developing Future Leaders and Managers for Library and Information Services – A Case Study of a Tailored Approach to Personal and Professional Development 166
Sue Roberts, Coral Black

The New Jersey Academy of Library Leadership: What Impact Has It Had? 183
Dr Jana Varlejs

Leadership Needs of Asian Librarians: An Account of an Asian Library Leadership Institute 199
Peter Edward Sidorko

The Observant I: Self-Assessment and the Evaluation of Library Leadership Development 216
Janelle M. Zauha

THEME IV: GENERATIONAL DIFFERENCES & SUCCESSION PLANNING

Leadership Skills: When Are They Taught, When Are They Used 233
Blanche Woolls, Nancy Zimmerman

Table of Contents

Developing a North/South Leadership Dialogue: Building on the Experience of the Northern Exposure to Leadership Institute (NELI)............253
Ernie Ingles, Karen Adams, Mary-Jo Romaniuk

Location, Location, Location: A Librarian's Guide to Isolation......................271
Liz Burke

Two X'ers tell whY and how: Succession Planning for the Future................288
Perri-Lee Sandell, Susan M. Vickery

Developing the Concepts of 'Leadership for All' in Library and Information Services: Exploring the Rationale and Making It Happen..............................307
Dr Graham Walton

FOREWORD

This volume represents the proceedings of the Seventh World Conference on Continuing Professional Development and Workplace Learning for the Library and Information Professions. The conference took place in the southern hemisphere, for the first time since it was established 22 years ago, and was held in Johannesburg, South Africa, from 14–16 August 2007. As the title suggests, the papers presented at this IFLA satellite conference provide a panoramic view of the current state of continuing professional development activities for leadership in the library and information world. And as the title also suggests, there are different pathways to leadership, and there are different approaches taken in different countries and different contexts.

The proceedings, and the conference programme, were structured into four themes. Theme I established the context: papers reviewed international, national and cross-cultural programs and issues. Theme II focused on the individual, and the learning about leadership that occurs in workplaces. Theme III looked at leadership institutes: presentations described programs from different countries, and current approaches to, and perceived problems of, effective evaluation of these costly events. These papers provide the evidence base for what does and does not work in this type of leadership development program. Finally, Theme IV explored generational differences, notably Generation X and Generation Y, and their expectations of leadership as well as implications for developing and training our next generation of leaders.

Throughout the proceedings, a number of issues recur, common to any discussion about leadership. Are leaders made or born? Can leadership skills be learned, and if so, what are the most effective methods of teaching these skills? The scene is set for this discussion in the paper by Woolls and Zimmerman, which provides the research data from a survey of the management and leadership content of library school courses. Lists of the characteristics of leaders not surprisingly include: vision, honesty, strategic thinking, ability to motivate, compassion for others, responsibility, and so on. A succinct, working definition by John Kotter sets the scene for the debate on differences between leadership and management: "Good management controls complexity; effective leadership produces useful change."[1]

All abstracts and papers in this volume were submitted to an international refereeing panel that comprised Ann Ritchie (Department of Health &

Foreword

Community Services Library, Darwin, Australia), Clare Walker (University of the Witwatersrand Library, Johannesburg, South Africa), Paul Genoni (Curtin University, Perth, Australia), Susan Schnuer (Mortenson Center for International Library Programs, University of Illinois at Urbana Champaign, U.S.), Ian Smith (La Trobe University Library, Melbourne, Australia), Jana Varlejs (Rutgers School of Communication, Information and Library Studies, New Jersey, U.S.), Graham Walton (Loughborough University, UK) and Blanche Woolls (School of Library and Information Science, San Jose State University, CA, U.S.). In addition to the papers in this volume, a number of others were presented as papers, round tables or workshops, or in the Section's session at the IFLA World Library and Information Congress, Durban, 18–23 August 2007, or were not available at the time of going to print; some of these will be published through other channels. The full conference program can be found on the Section's website http://www.ifla.org/VII/s43/index.htm.

Ann Ritchie and Clare Walker (Eds)

[1] Kotter, J.P. What leaders really do. *Harvard Business Review* [reprint of May–June 1990 article] 2002, 79 (11), 85–96.

CONTINUING PROFESSIONAL DEVELOPMENT: PATHWAYS TO LEADERSHIP IN THE LIBRARY AND INFORMATION WORLD: JOHANNESBURG, AUGUST 14–16, 2007

INTRODUCTION TO THE CONFERENCE

Jana Varlejs,
Chair, Continuing Professional Development
and Workplace Learning Section

We are proud to present the Seventh World Conference on Continuing Professional Development and Workplace Learning, in conjunction with the 2007 World Library and Information Congress of the International Federation of Library Associations and Institutions, with the theme of "Libraries for the Future." Our focus is on developing the leaders for the libraries of the future, because we believe that libraries and their related organizations can be only as effective as their leaders.

This conference is indebted to the leaders in CPDWL who have made it possible and are responsible for putting the published proceedings in your hands: Ian Smith, Clare Walker, Ujala Satgoor, Ann Ritchie, Susan Schnuer, and other members. We also congratulate all those whose papers have been selected for publication, and all conference presenters and facilitators. In addition, CPDWL recognizes the sponsorships of WebJunction/OCLC and Emerald—their support has enabled us to minimize attendees' costs, for which we are deeply grateful.

Why a conference devoted to leadership development?

For some years now, there has been much hand wringing about the coming shortage not only of professionals to replace retiring librarians, but also of successors to the heads of libraries, library education programs, associations, and other key institutions in our field. As the current generation of leaders exits stage left, who is waiting in the wings to take the spotlight with a show of new ideas and energy? Where are the ambitious, talented, and eager troupes of understudies?

There is a perception of a looming crisis in leadership in the profession, at least judging from the explosion of leadership institutes, succession planning workshops, and similar efforts designed to solve the problem, real or not. Interestingly, about twenty years ago, there was a similar worry about "Where have all the leaders gone?"[1] The American Library Association president's theme for 1987–1988 was leadership development, and did inspire new attention to training future leaders.[2] That attention seems to have peaked in recent years, with well over a dozen leadership institutes offered regularly in all parts of the U.S. (http://cjrlc.org/leadership.htm). It is too soon to know whether all this activity will have the desired effect of producing a corps of new leaders who will be ready and willing to replace those who are retiring. It is not too soon, however, to take a look at the recent spate of leadership training, and to ask what *should* be the role of continuing professional development in producing the next generation of leaders.

First, can we agree on what is meant by leadership?

Informally, many of us will say, "I know it when I see it." We have in mind individuals who have impressed us by their ability to articulate a mission and to inspire others to rally in support. They are individuals who not only have strong feelings and bright ideas about what needs to be done and how to do it, but are able to persuade us of the rightness of their views and to mobilize us to take action.

More formally, scholars who have devoted their careers to studying the phenomenon, agree that there is no single, simple definition. Some have argued that group and organizational effectiveness has little to do with leadership, but the concept continues to exert fascination. The third edition, 1182-page Bass & Stogdill *Handbook of Leadership* states that it

> ...has been conceived as the focus of group process, as a matter of personality, as a matter of inducing compliance, as the exercise of influence, as particular behaviors, as a form of persuasion, as a power relation, as an instrument to achieve goals, as an effect of interaction, as a differentiated role, as initiation of structure, and as many combinations of these definitions.[3]

A distinction can be drawn between leadership and headship, with "headship as being imposed on the group but leadership as being accorded by the group."[3] Thus, leadership can be exerted by members of a group, not only or even necessarily by the titular head. The *Handbook* definition states that

Leadership is an interaction between two or more members of a group that often involves a structuring or restructuring of the situation and the perceptions and expectations of the members. Leaders are *agents of change*—persons whose acts affect other people more than other people's acts affect them. Leadership occurs when one group member modifies the motivation or competencies of others on the group.[3] [emphasis added]

Some pithier definitions depend on contrasting leadership and management:

"Leadership focuses on doing the right things; management focuses on doing things right"[4]

"...management produce[s] order, consistency, and predictability ... Leadership ... creates change and adaptability"[5]

"Good management controls complexity; effective leadership produces useful change"[6]

"The manager administers; the leader motivates"[7]

A favorite definition—"agents of change"

The Bass and Stogdill phrase above, "agents of change," is one that resonates, particularly in these Library 2.0 days, when we are faced with so much that is new that merely keeping up is more than most of us can manage. We look to colleagues who can identify what is most useful and can show us the way to put it to work, whether it is a new technology or a better way to advocate for libraries. In the current crop of leadership institutes, there is a strong focus on managing change, and it is clear that leadership from within the ranks is as vital as leadership at the top of the organization. The assumption is that change is good and necessary, and that it happens whether we are leading it or just being dragged along. An institution is likely to achieve greater success if it has agents of change throughout the organization, and not just at the top. If this is true, then it is a good idea to offer leadership development even for the youngest professionals and for those who do not want to be heads of organizations. In my evaluation of the New Jersey Academy of Library Leadership (see Theme III) it was revealing how often participants admitted that they did not really want to become directors: Leadership was attractive, headship not.

But we still need "titular heads"!

Since it seems that the headship avoiders outnumber the strivers, we may want to pursue two questions during this conference: (1) Why do librarians tend to duck the executive level, and (2) Can formal professional development create the "fire in the belly" that it takes to reach for the top? Is this just another way of asking the old question, are leaders born or bred?[8]

There is some evidence that librarians tend not to be born leaders. As part of the evaluation of a leadership institute that used coaches from outside librarianship, the coaches were asked about differences that they saw between our field and other professions. Their comments were:
- Librarians tend to be more conflict averse;
- Tend to shy away from power and influence;
- Express the desire to have power and influence, but do not know how to proceed;
- Have less self-confidence;
- Are less likely to take risks;
- Find it hard to have authority and claim it.[9]

Librarians themselves admit to a lack of leadership aptitude. A study conducted by Outsell found that only 29 percent of corporate librarians consider themselves to be "very adept" at leadership.[10] The fact that librarians tend to be introverts rather than extroverts has been a constant in studies of the profession's personality characteristics.[11] It is reasonable to expect leadership to be more closely linked with extroversion, and therefore to go against type for librarians. Does this mean that our profession is never going to have a sufficient cadre of born leaders? More to the point of this conference, if leaders are born and not bred, are leadership institutes a waste of time and money?

In looking at the follow-up reports on the many institutes held recently, the typical conclusion is that while there is no way to prove that they do produce leaders, there is evidence that they do benefit the participants and their organization, and are not a waste of time and money.

The current U.S. model of leadership training

In the United States, the various institute descriptions show a great deal of similarity in content, with many based on the original 1990 Snowbird Institute.

Notably, there is "a strong component of self-analysis ... addressing potential fear of creativity, risk taking, and change."[2] This continues to be a characteristic, as does the inclusion of mentors. The development of self-confidence is a major objective, as is the formation of a network of peers across different types of libraries.[12] As already mentioned, there are a dozen or more regional and state institutes held at regular intervals across the U.S., quite a few of them modeled after Snowbird and employing the same team of trainers. The model has been successfully exported to Canada[13] and Australia.[7] Of course there are variations in the format and the details, even within the same institute. Connie Paul, the organizer of the New Jersey Academy of Library Leadership, describes the different formats that are possible: one-week residential, monthly meeting, and two-to-three days repeated over several months. Each has its advantages and disadvantages, but she claims that the overall process is more important than the particular format or content.[14]

Typically, the institutes include the following:
- Change agent behavior;
- Communication styles;
- Conflict management;
- Styles of leadership;
- Mentoring and networking;
- Motivation;
- Coaching and developing others;
- Risk assessment and management;
- Self-awareness of strengths;
- Establishing personal goals;
- Developing a shared vision of the organization;
- Understanding group dynamics;
- Team building;
- Workplace values.[15]

This is a long and varied list, typical of the content of most leadership institutes. Even institutes that depart from this model cover what might be seen to be the core curriculum of leadership training: understanding oneself, shaping and articulating a vision, and motivating others.

In whittling down the list of leadership qualities for use in a performance survey, a team at one university library decided to inquire about vision, collaboration, communication, fairness, and leading by example—not too far removed from the core.[16] The fairness characteristic is not one that is usually a training component, but could be seen as an aspect of ethics, which is a component in Canada's Northern Exposure to Leadership Institute (NELI).[17] Also touched on by NELI but less so by the traditional U.S. model is advocacy, which is emerging as a major concern in professional associations, including IFLA (http://www.ifla.org/IV/ifla72/papers/106-Lux-en.pdf). Surprisingly, little attention seems to be given to political skills.

How effective is leadership training?

Looking at what has been written about the various institutes, one gets the impression that most participants find them both inspiring and reassuring.[18,19] Institute attendance may not be the salient factor determining whether someone will become the head of an organization, but for many it does raise self-confidence, build relationships, and teach some skills that are useful regardless of future career trajectory. If the measure of effectiveness is the number of "graduates" who become top tier leaders, the evidence is not strong, or is still out. It should be remembered, however, that leadership from within the ranks is also an important goal, and that followers as well as leaders are vital to innovation.[19] The real question is whether the current very large investment in leadership training for the relatively few is justified, given all the other needs for professional development for the many. A serious issue is the selection of participants, which is highly competitive in some cases, though much less so in others.[20] There has not been a compilation of nomination procedures and selection criteria across institutes, which would be interesting to see. There also has not been an attempt to determine whether it is better to direct training to early or mid-career librarians. It is reasonable to expect that those possessing leadership potential to begin with will be more likely to make the best use of it, but how are the "born-to-lead" to be identified? Resources for paying for these institutes are limited, which also affects who gets to attend and who does not. There is a daunting number of variables involved in evaluating leadership training, so it is understandable that assessment is seldom undertaken, especially the kind that tries to determine the ultimate outcome, i.e., stronger library/information organizations.

If leadership training is not the best solution, what are the alternatives?

A recent book makes the case that leadership is intrinsic, and not something that can be taught.[21] If that is the case, then special efforts to identify and train

Introduction to the Conference

leaders are not the best use of resources. Presumably, the individuals who have the drive and talent to become leaders also have the ability to learn on their own, and to attract mentors and champions who will give them opportunities to grow. Beverly Lynch, a library/information science professor whose specialty is management and leadership, and who has led the UCLA Senior Fellows Program, emphasizes this last point:

> Kotter ... says that one way to develop leadership is to create challenging opportunities for young people ... New librarians are graduating from our schools of library and information science with solid technical knowledge, good theoretical frameworks, and an ability and desire to work in stimulating settings reflecting the service goals and values of our libraries. The challenge for libraries is to give these new librarians those jobs—not after a three-year apprenticeship in a setting that is not technologically sophisticated, not fast paced, and not intellectually stimulating, but right away. Libraries must first find and create jobs that will continue to challenge these graduates so that these new employees will be able to manage change, which they already embrace.[22]

What *should* be the role of continuing professional development in producing the next generation of leaders?

This is the question posed at the outset of this introduction, and one that will continue to be explored throughout the conference. Formal leadership institutes are certainly a part of the answer, but they cannot be the primary engine of leadership development. Their efficacy is not proven, and despite their popularity, they are not readily accessible to all the individuals who could benefit. Just as with professional development in most other spheres of librarianship and information work, the responsibility to continue to learn and grow rests primarily with the individual. Secondarily, it is incumbent on employers and supervisors to nurture and encourage development of their staff, not only through in-house training and support for external education, but also through providing the challenging jobs that Lynch refers to. There is a need to create environments in organizations that foster learning through experimentation and through tackling problems in groups where fresh ideas are welcomed. Internal efforts can be more easily supported now by the many online learning opportunities available. As connectivity improves across the world and as more courses are mounted in a greater number of languages, we can look forward to just-in-time learning for library and information workers, including those who aspire to leadership positions. An ongoing challenge for those of us who advocate for professional development across the board is how to link the learner with the right learning opportunity at the right time, and how to promote quality in continuing education, including leadership development.

REFERENCES

[1] Gertzog, A. (ed.) Leadership in the Library/Information Profession. Jefferson, NC. 1989.

[2] Bonnici, L.J. Creating the library leadership institute at Snowbird: an exercise in leadership. Library Administration & Management 2001, 15 (2), 98–103.

[3] Bass, B.M. Bass & Stogdill's Handbook of Leadership 3rd ed. New York: the Free Press, 1990, p. 11.

[4] Leadership development in libraries: theory and practice. Illinois Library Association Reporter 2001, 19 (5), 6–8.

[5] Holcomb, J.M. Learning to lead: debunking leadership myths. Law Library Journal 2005, 97 (4), 729–34.

[6] Kotter, J.P. What leaders really do. Harvard Business Review 2001, 79 (11), 103–111.

[7] Barney, K. Evaluation of the impact of the 2003 Aurora Leadership Institute—'the gift that keeps on giving.' Australian Library Journal 2004, 53 (4), 337–48. URL <http://www.alia.org.au/publishing/alj/53.4/full.text/barney.html>

[8] Nichols, C.A. Leaders: Born or bred. Library Journal 2002, 127 (13), 38–40.

[9] Sullivan, M. Urban Libraries Council—Evaluation of the Executive Leadership Institute (ELI), 2004 (unpublished ms), p. 7.

[10] Outsell trend alert: renewing, recruiting, refueling—hiring and developing staff for information management roles. Info About Info Briefing 2006, 9 (June 23)

[11] Scherdin, J. & Beaubien, A.K. Shattering our stereotype: librarians' new image. Library Journal 1995, 120 (July), 35–38.

12 Maurer, M.B. & Coccaro, C. Creating a more flexible workforce for libraries—Are leadership institutes the answer? Technical Service Quarterly 2003, 20 (3), 1–17.

13 Ingles, E. Northern Exposure to Leadership Institute—some personal reflections. Feliciter 2005, 51 (1), 38–40.

14 Paul, C. Just do it! Leadership training builds strong networks. American Libraries 2004, 35 (9), 44–5.

15 Berry, J.K. Texas Accelerated Library Leaders: Tall Texans. Public Libraries 2000, 39 (6), 311–3.

16 Turrentine, C. G., Lener, E.F., Young, M.L. & Kok, V.T. A qualitative approach to upward evaluation of leadership performance: pros and cons. The Journal of Academic Librarianship 2004, 30 (4), 304–13.

17 Hook, D. & Palmer, T. The sixth Northern Exposure to Leadership Institute. Feliciter 2002, 48 (3), 108–9.

18 Nicely, D. & Dempsey, B. Building a culture of leadership: ULC's Executive Leadership Institute fills libraries' biggest training void. Public Libraries 2005, 44 (5), 297–300.

19 Gjelten, D. & Fishel, T. Developing leaders and transforming libraries: Leadership institutes for librarians. C&RL News 2006 67 (7), 409–12.

20 Byke,S. & Lowe-Wincentsen, D. Following to the top and leading from the bottom. Paper presented at nls2006, The Joint Niland Scientia Building, UNSW, Sydney, Australia. URL http://conferences.alia.org.au/newlibrarian2006

21 Zauha, J. Leadership training for all: providing opportunities for degreed and non-degreed librarians in a regional institute. In: Genoni, P. & Walton, G. (eds.) Continuing Professional Development—Preparing for New Roles in Libraries, a Voyage of Discovery. Munchen, K.G. Saur, 2005: pp245–55.

22 George, B., with Sims, P. True North: Discover Your Authentic Leadership. San Francisco: Jossey-Bass, 2007.

23 Lynch, B.P. Theory and Practice. Library Administration & Management 2004, 18 (1), 30–34.

LIBRARY LEADERSHIP DEVELOPMENT: INSTITUTIONAL COMMITMENT, INCREASING UNDERREPRESENTED POPULATIONS AND IMPACTING THE INFORMATION PROFESSION

Prof. Karen Downing, MILS,
University of Michigan Foundation and Grants & Executive Research Service Librarian, kdown@umich.edu

Dr Camila A. Alire, Ed.D,
University of New Mexico & Colorado State University, Dean Emerita, calire@att.net

Jon E. Cawthorne, MLS,
San Diego State University, Associate Dean, jcawthor@mail.sdsu.edu

Tracie D. Hall, MLS,
Dominican University, Assistant Dean, Graduate School of Library and Information Science, thall@dom.edu

Jerome Offord, MS, MLS,
Association of Research Libraries, Director of Diversity Initiatives, Jerome@arl.org

Veronda J. Pitchford, MLS,
Urban Libraries Council, Program Officer, vjpitchford@urbanlibraries.org

Prof. Alexandra Rivera, MSI,
University of Arizona, User Services Librarian, Riveraa@u.library.arizona.edu

Alysse Jordan, MS,
Columbia University, Social Work Librarian, aj204@columbia.edu

Abstract

Like many African nations, the United States has a shared history of colonialism, the effects of which are still with us today. Because of continuing inequalities between the races, in the U.S. people of color are vastly underrepresented within librarianship, and even less visible as library administrators. At the same time that librarians' skills are gaining in importance, there is an urgent need to prepare the next generation of library leaders. According to Robert S. Martin, former director of the Institute for Museum and Library Services (IMLS), "Our nation faces a quiet crisis: a critical—and burgeoning—shortage of librarians" (IMLS, 2001). To address the looming shortage *and* demographics that do not reflect growing non-white populations in the United States, a variety of U.S.-based programs has been developed to illuminate future library leadership options for early to mid-level career librarians.

This paper describes the necessity for such programs in societies where inequalities exist, discusses several model programs from the perspectives of program developers, participants, and content providers. The paper also provides both theoretical and practical aspects of developing leadership programs to increase the numbers of underrepresented/disadvantaged people in leadership positions.

Open access to information and knowledge is vital to any open society. Libraries can and should be a starting point for access to information for all its citizens.

South African Library Leadership Project

Our nation faces a quiet crisis: a critical—and burgeoning—shortage of librarians.

Robert S. Martin, former Director of the Institute
for Museum and Library Services, 2001

INTRODUCTION

The twenty-first century will belong to those who can find and use information strategically to their individual and societal benefit. With the volume of information doubling every three years, "the greatest challenge facing us today is how to organize information into structured knowledge ... to assimilate it, to find meaning in it and assure its survival"[1]. In this changing and challenging information landscape, the role of librarians who are charged with developing collections and services for scholars, students, and the public-at-large becomes ever more important to educational and life-long learning as well as societal success.

Libraries help us organize information into knowledge, something we can use. They are also important cultural and educational organizations that help to counter some of the educational and technological inequities in society. Librarians are important, yet within U.S. librarianship ranks, there exists a critical and growing shortage of professionally trained information scientists[2]. At the very time that the skills of trained librarians are becoming more important—as we switch from a manufacturing-based society to an information-based economy—there is an urgent need to prepare the next generation of library leaders. Soon to exacerbate this problem are looming mass retirements. Researchers have estimated that "58 percent of professional librarians will reach the age of 65 between 2005 and 2019"[3]. Since 2000 in academic libraries alone, approximately 52,000 of 186,000 in the United States were 55 or older[4].

This paper describes four unique programs within the United States: The American Library Association's (ALA) Spectrum Initiative, the oldest and largest of the minority leadership programs; the Minnesota Institute for Early Career Librarians of Color, which develops leadership potential in early career academic librarians; the Association of Research Libraries' (ARL) Leadership and Career Development Program, targeted to developing mid-career academic librarians of color into leadership roles; and the Urban Libraries' Council (ULC) Executive Leadership Institute, which focuses on individual coaching of librarians from urban settings. Each program targets early to mid-range career librarians, and all have been in existence for multiple years. These programs were designed to create future library leaders and meet the information needs of minority communities. It is imperative that as a profession, we move to educate and develop a large, dynamic corps of racial, ethnic and ethno-linguistic minority librarians and library leaders if our libraries are to remain relevant to our changing user demographics. Each of these programs has lessons for the future of library leadership.

DEMOGRAPHIC CHANGES AND THE FUTURE

The United States has a long history of exclusion, inequity and deeply engrained institutional racism toward people of color. Despite some progress since the Civil Rights Act of 1964, which outlawed discrimination on the basis of race and gender, our history still touches virtually every aspect of modern life for persons of color. Whether it be inequitable access to health care, housing, employment or education, the historical legacy and current culture of racial discrimination is still a daily reality for many minorities within the United States[5].

Like the country as a whole, librarianship has not always been hospitable to the ideals of diversity. The lack of library professionals of color mirrors the presence of leaders of color in corporate America. Glaring inequities are not limited to the library profession, but also stand as a professional microcosm of the impact that institutional racism has on diversity in the workplace. Teresa Neely observes

> The practice of librarianship, in the aggregate, mirrors the lack of diversity that is reflected nationally, everyday, in media representation, news and sound bites and by major players in the political arena. It reflects the national dominant culture and therefore, has the tendency to share and echo similar ideologies and biases about diversity, race and affirmative action.[6]

With a legacy of racial discrimination the United States, like many countries across the globe, is barely ready for the coming demographic realities. By the year 2050, demographers predict the United States will become a "nation of minorities."[7] Population increases among African-Americans and Native-Americans, and particularly among Asian Pacific-Islanders and Latino/Hispanics, have resulted in a society more racially, ethnically, and linguistically diverse than ever before.

Are libraries ready to respond to these changing demographics? Almost certainly they are not. Among large Research I university libraries, the lack of racial and ethnic diversity is an issue. The *ARL Annual Salary Survey 2004–2005*[8] reports that there are only five minority library directors at these 123 libraries. Within the ARL, minorities comprise only 13.1 percent of professional staff. Specifically, Asian/Pacific Islanders comprise 5.9 percent of librarian staff, African Americans 4.6 percent, Hispanics 2.4 percent, and American Indian/Native Alaskan 0.3 percent. While this percentage has increased slightly over the last several decades, it is still not close to representing the college-aged populations of the United States. As Adkins and Espinal write

> Librarianship's whiteness impacts the publics we serve. When people of color do not see themselves represented in libraries, they may not approach the librarians. They may not even approach the library.[9]

So pervasive is the culture of exclusion in libraries that the International Federation of Library Associations and Institutions (IFLA) was moved to list among its eleven goals for 1998–2001 the following objective:

> work toward the integration of multicultural and multilingual services into the general management of libraries, combat racism among library workers and management, and promote an enlightened approach to racial matters in the library services."[10]

Grady and Hall write

> In 1991, racial and ethnic minorities comprised 9% (344) of the 4,032 graduates receiving accredited MLIS degrees. In 2001, they accounted for less than 13% (504) of the 4,109 MLIS degrees awarded, an increase that fails woefully to reflect the combined 152% growth increase experienced by these populations between 1990 and 2000."[11]

Despite the proliferation of library and information science (LIS) diversity recruitment initiatives, there is also growing evidence of higher than average attrition among ethnic minorities in the profession due to limited opportunities for professional mobility and access to positions of leadership.[12] The rate of attrition among racial and ethnic minority credentialed librarians age 35 and under is particularly troubling.

According to the recently released Diversity Counts study, while there was a 3% loss of all credentialed librarians, and a 1% loss of white librarians in this age range, between 1990 and 2000, the loss of African American credentialed librarians age 35 and under was 47.6%, 41.4% for Latino credentialed librarians, 17.6% for Native American and 6.8% for Alaskan Natives and Asian Pacific Islanders.[13] These are sobering disparities in losses of young librarians of color—disparities that challenge us as a profession to think about, and act on what can be done to halt or decrease the departure of our early and mid-career colleagues.

As the profession grapples with developing and sustaining effective diversity recruitment mechanisms, the inability to retain the "generation next" librarians of color within our ranks is a sign that, rather than gaining headway, we are slowly losing ground. Librarians and researchers Adkins and Espinal give a compelling example of the effect of such persistent inequities in library service on one user group:

> For every Latino public, academic, and school librarian, there are about 9,177 Latinos in the population. For every white, non-Latino librarian, there are only 1,830 white non-Latinos in the population. This disparity means that whites have five times more opportunity to find a librarian with roots in their culture than Latinos.[14]

Nearly 58% of the existing credentialed Latino librarians are age 45 and over, indicating that, unless critical recruitment and retention mechanisms are put in place before this majority reaches retirement age, the service gaps Adkins and Espinal identify could become even more glaring.[15]

At a time when libraries are struggling to create relevant, resonant, and accessible services and collections for increasingly diverse populations, a startling number of younger librarians of color are leaving librarianship. These are librarians who should be in the grooming process for the next generation of library leadership, and who could serve as vital liaisons to ethno cultural and ethno linguistic communities. Instead, they are opting out of the profession; leaving before having the opportunity to assume the kinds of leadership positions that impact libraries and lead to real outcomes in services to traditionally underserved populations. Rather than tangibly multiplying the numbers of librarians of color, existing minority recruitment and education programs run the risk of simply providing for the replacement of retirees and those leaving the profession prematurely.

With an aging profession, a profession that does not reflect the diversity of its library users, and a profession that is experiencing change and strain on many levels, it is important to invest in the future of our profession by developing the next generation of library leaders.

In 1997, recognizing the symbiotic relationship between the continued viability of libraries as public-service and cultural institutions, librarianship as a meaningful field of practice, and the ability to engage the nation's rapidly proliferating ethno-cultural diversity, the first of several minority retention and leadership development programs was launched by the American Library Association. The Spectrum Initiative, a diversity recruitment and retention program was created to attract members of ethnically and racially underrepresented groups: African-American, Asian and Pacific Islander, Latino/Hispanic, and Native American to careers in library and information science.

Disseminating its first scholarship packages the following year, the Spectrum Initiative "marked a sea change in the profession's commitment to recruitment of a diverse workforce."[16] Originally intended to last only three years, the Initiative exceeded early targets in recruiting LIS students of color and raising diversity awareness in library schools and librarianship as a whole. Just two years after it had dispensed its first scholarships, noted library educator and researcher, Kathleen de la Peña McCook wrote, "new energy fueled by the Spectrum Initiative ... has been infused into the thinking about the kind of profession librarianship needs to become."[17]

Immediate and palpable results prompted the Association to extend funding for the Initiative, initially designed to disseminate 150 scholarship packages valued at $6,500 each ($5,000 cash award for Masters of Library and Information Science education and approximately $1,500 in travel funding to attend the Spectrum Leadership Institute, a three-day pre-professional career development program held the summer following the first year of study).

In addition to accelerated professional mobility, another byproduct of the program's early impact has been its growing recognition, among undergraduates and individuals still early in their first careers, as an access point to the profession. Half of the respondents to a survey of the program's first five years reported being under age 30 at the time they received the scholarship, with more than a fifth reporting being between 21 and 25 years of age. The early successes of the Spectrum Initiative, and the attention it brought at the highest levels of the ALA spawned a series of other leadership programs, each with their own unique audiences and content.

LEADERS' PERSPECTIVES: THE ROLE OF LEADERSHIP AND MENTORING IN PROGRAMS

Leadership programs offer a distinct advantage for early and mid-career librarians. In addition to professional skill building, strategic career planning, networking, and mentorship opportunities, these programs provide a particular value to librarians of color, who may not necessarily have had access to, or even been aware, of the informal social networks that exist within the dominant culture of the organizations in which they work.[18]

Cultural and generational differences in communication and management styles can sometimes serve to further marginalize the profession's future leaders, who are increasingly younger and more racially diverse than their more traditional counterparts.[19] Information professionals who are familiar with a wide variety of leadership models, and are able to be flexible in their approaches to working with others, will be the most successful in an increasingly multi-generational and multi-cultural workplace.

The programs identified in this paper have all included an essential component—the involvement of experienced minority library leaders. These programs offer enhanced development of newer professionals because veteran leaders of color are able to share their expertise and experiences, provide advice, and serve as mentors. In the final analysis, they serve as successful role models demonstrating to the programs' participants (minority library school students and librarians) that professional success is achievable in the library and information management profession.

As academic library director Camila Alire writes, "what the minority leader brings to the position is knowledge of minority history and culture; evidence of supporting services to minorities; and possible linguistic abilities." Perhaps most importantly, minority librarians "can advocate for organizational change ... serve as role models ... (and) provide the necessary linkages to minority communities—however the community is defined."[20]

Librarians from under-represented groups may also bring a heightened awareness of social injustice to their professional work. Personal and collective experiences of marginalization or discrimination often predispose minority librarians, especially those in leadership positions to "lead the efforts in looking for obstacles in achieving diversity in the library organizational policies and procedures."[21] Alire asks, "Who best to articulate diversity and provide the necessary platform to enable library organizations to align their missions with the unique realities of our growing multicultural society than library leaders of color?"[22]

Most minority library leaders view these programs as an investment in the future leadership of the profession. That is, the programs are grooming these participants to assume leadership positions in their chosen career path within the field. These programs serve as de facto minority leadership succession programs. However, it is important that the focus should first be on minority retention of the participants, before succession leadership, in the field of librarianship and information science, whether these are new or mid-career librarians.

Herein lies the role for the minority library practitioner. It is vital that the program participants are exposed to minority library leaders through program participation and through mentoring. What is most critical from the practitioner's point of view is being able to share one's professional experiences—successes and pitfalls—so that the program participants learn from them. At all times, the minority library leader is serving as a role model.

Authors Downing and Cawthorne have been involved in three of the four programs described in this paper—the ALA Spectrum Institute, the ARL Leadership and Career Development Program, and the ARL Initiative to Recruit a Diverse Workforce. Both as program participants, and now as program content providers, the authors have graduated from being mentees to becoming mentors for a new generation of librarians of color. Our involvement has enriched our professional development through curricula that have included sharing a day in the life of a minority academic library dean; scenario enactment of issues such as scholarly communication, coalition development, budget planning, and grants development; and general and specific career development, goal setting, and job search strategies. These curricular elements are designed not only to encourage program participants toward successful career paths but also to share with them the realities of becoming a minority library leader.

Serving as mentor to various program participants is another aspect in which the authors have been involved. These mentoring relationships have been both formal and informal. No matter the type of mentoring relationships, they have served to support the participants, to develop their self-confidence, and to guide them through whatever stage of their career they are in.

> In general, an effective mentoring relationship is characterized by mutual respect, trust, understanding, and empathy. Good mentors are able to share life experiences and wisdom, as well as technical expertise. They are *good listeners, good observers,* and *good problem-solvers.*"[23]

Mentoring relationships are among the best methods for successful minority role modeling, and minority mentors are gratified knowing that they are contributing to the well-being of their profession by participating in these programs. More important is that they are contributing to the library users of color who are served by these program participants. Overall, these programs designed for minority students and mid-career librarians are a win-win for them as well as for the minority library leaders involved.

INDIVIDUAL LEADERSHIP PROGRAMS

Spectrum Scholarship Program[24]

Professional leadership is a major component of the Spectrum Scholarship program, an effort by the American Library Association to increase the representation of ethnic and racial minorities in the library profession. To date, 415 individuals have received Spectrum Scholarship funding. In addition to the funding mentioned earlier, a major component of the Spectrum program is a three-day institute that occurs each year in conjunction with the ALA annual conference. The goal of the institute is to cultivate advocacy, excellence, and leadership among the Spectrum Scholars. Each of the inspiring speakers and activities encourages mentoring, networking, goal setting, and career planning among a diverse group of service-oriented librarians about to embark on their careers. A unique and long lasting professional bond fosters the acquisition and development of skills and knowledge to which these scholars are not necessarily exposed in their individual library school settings.

Spectrum Scholars benefit from participation in the institute in numerous ways. The scholarship award process is one that challenges its applicants to seriously consider their potential role in libraries. It is a competitive process and receipt of the scholarship imbues the recipient with a sense of accomplishment. Many academic institutions recognize the importance of the program and its scholars by providing matching funds for additional financial support. Receiving the scholarship is just the first of many benefits: scholars are also given a one-year membership in the ALA, which bolsters professional activity and social networking.

Involvement in professional networks seems to be a natural consequence of the program. In a survey of Spectrum Scholarship recipients 1998–2003, over half the respondents indicated they had joined a division of ALA and 52% also joined at least one of five ethnic caucuses of ALA.[25] In addition 64% of the survey respondents attended an ALA conference while they were students, and one third attended a statewide or regional conference. Over half of the respondents maintained their ALA affiliations after they graduated.

A second element of the Spectrum Scholarship Program is the three-day leadership institute where scholars participate in an intensive and interactive retreat engaging with leaders in the library profession while developing a sense of community with other Spectrum scholars present and past. The institute fosters sharing of both personal and professional experiences and lays the foundation for strong lasting friendships and professional relationships. These relationships are the basis for potential future collaborations.

A natural third element of the programs is that scholars have a keen awareness of the meaning of "giving back" to the Spectrum program and the profession. One example of this is the Spectrum Scholars Interest Group (SSIG), a committee that coordinates the efforts of all the scholars who are interested in creating and implementing initiatives that support the program and profession. Collaborative research and scholarship are just one of the many opportunities created by the SSIG. Advocacy, leadership development of peers, and continued support of the Spectrum Scholarship Program are other products of this group.

The Spectrum Scholarship Program has had a profound impact on its scholars. In addition to receiving monetary support for pursuit of an LIS education and the prestige of calling themselves Spectrum Scholars, scholars come away with a sense of their important role in the profession. The relationships cultivated in the institute are long-lasting and the ever-expanding network of scholars provides a family of colleagues that are accessible and responsive to each other's scholarly and personal needs regardless of space and time.

While the number of minority librarians is still not representative of the United States' demographics, library assistants do have a higher proportion of representation in the library profession.[26] A survey of Spectrum Scholarship recipients indicates that two-thirds of the respondents were working in a library when they made the decision to attend an LIS program. This suggests that the Spectrum Initiative has made it possible for most prospective LIS students to realize their goal.[27] The survey also reports that 29% of the respondents indicated that they would not have pursued their education without a Spectrum scholarship.

Ten years after its inception, the Spectrum Scholarship Program, has achieved the credibility and consistency necessary to warrant the shedding of its "initiative" status. Spectrum ranks as one of the LIS profession's most prominent and prolific diversity recruitment programs, having supported the LIS education of over 475 scholarship recipients. With an emphasis on leadership and peer-support, the Spectrum Scholarship Program has become noted for its high retention and the early career advancement evidenced by participants. Perhaps one of the salient and succinct assessments of the program was written by a 2006 Spectrum Scholar: "I feel like it put me ahead 5 years into the profession."[28]

Minnesota Institute for Early Career Librarians[29]

The Minnesota Institute for Early Career Librarians was designed for early career academic librarians from traditionally underrepresented groups who are in the first three years of their professional careers. This weeklong institute has a two-fold focus: combining development in leadership and organizational behavior with developing a practical skill set in key areas for academic librarians. In addition, Institute participants join a community of peers with whom they develop a support network that will continue throughout their professional careers.

For participants, many of whom are involved in library residency or internship programs at their home institutions, the Institute may represent their first opportunity to network with other librarians of color. This powerful experience can provide a positive affirmation of the unique cultural assets and perspectives that under-represented librarians bring to the workplace, while legitimizing more collaborative or collectivist leadership styles that may be less prominent in the dominant culture, which tends to value a more linear or hierarchical leadership model. Along those lines, surveys of participants since the introduction of the program in 1998, have reflected that the community building aspect of the program was felt to be one of the most influential components of the Institute.[30]

Tools for reflection and self-awareness are built into the program, so that participants often draw upon skills they have developed through participation in family, school, and community life, to harness their personal power and enhance their leadership potential within the academic library world. By inviting new librarians of color to explore their professional identities and values in a culturally supportive context, the program often has the impact of inspiring participants to pursue leadership activities such as fundraising and professional writing, which they may not previously have had the confidence or tools to explore.

The Institute encourages participants to embrace their roles as emerging library leaders, whether or not they are in an official leadership position. The peer network created by the Institute has proven invaluable; many former Institute participants have gone on to serve as co-authors and colleagues, often citing the positive impact the program has had on their careers; and most have been promoted or moved on to new positions.[31]

ARL Leadership & Career Development Program[32]

The need for support in the recruitment and training of librarians, especially minority librarians, was expressed as early as the 1960s and 1970s in funding provisions of the Higher Education Act Title II-B. ARL worked for many years to address their growing concerns about recruiting and retaining a diverse workforce in research libraries.

Two grants from the H. W. Wilson Foundation in 1990 and 1991 enabled ARL to establish the project "Meeting the Challenges of a Culturally Diverse Workforce" and hire a part-time Diversity Consultant. Demand for seminars, resource materials, and consulting services on diversity topics continued to grow. By 1993, the ARL membership recognized the need for a full-time program to address minority recruitment and retention. A grant from the Gladys Krieble Delmas Foundation in 1994 assured a stable beginning for the program.

ARL launched the Leadership and Career Development Program (LCDP) in 1997 to increase the number of librarians from under-represented racial and ethnic groups. The LCDP is an 18-month program to prepare mid-career librarians from underrepresented racial and ethnic groups to take on increasingly demanding leadership roles in ARL libraries. Over the course of four LCDP offerings, 80 librarians have completed the program and a large percentage of them have either been promoted within their libraries or have taken new positions with significantly expanded responsibility.

The LCDP design includes: two LCDP Institutes, an opening and closing event held in conjunction with national professional meetings, a career-coaching relationship with an ARL library director or staff member, and a personalized visit to an ARL member library. Twenty librarians, representing a variety of library backgrounds, years of experience, and racial and national origins, were selected to participate in the 2007–2008 program class. The Medical Library Association (MLA) and National Library of Medicine (NLM) sponsor two LCDP participants from the medical library community by providing mentors and financial support. To ensure participation in LCDP in the future, ARL has also supported grants to diversify library schools.

Today, ARL Diversity Initiatives has two major minority based programs: the LCDP and the Initiative to Recruit a Diverse Workforce (the Initiative). The Initiative received funding from the Institute for Museum and Library Services (IMLS) in October 2003 to augment member funding for the program. The Initiative grants tuition/educational funds to students from minority backgrounds to assist in the completion of their MLS degree. Grantees agree to a minimum two-year working relationship with an ARL library upon graduation. Four stipends were awarded in 2000.

In 2001, the program focused on enhancing the base fund by seeking grant funds and other contributions. In addition, four new grantees were selected for the 2002–2003 academic year. An advisory group from ARL directors/deans and the ARL Diversity Committee provide guidance and support for the program. In August 2004, the Diversity Committee selected 15 participants to serve as the first cohort of the newly expanded Initiative program.

The program enhancements include leadership training and mentoring. For the 2004–2006 programmatic years, ARL's Diversity Committee selected 16 graduate students to participant in the Initiative. The current class's composition includes:
- 13 female participants (81%) and three males (19%);

- 40% African-American (5 females and one male); 33% Latino/a (four females and one male); 20% Native American (two females and one male); and 7% Asian (one female);
- Five participants (33%) are attending library school on an ARL campus;
- Six participants are currently working in an ARL library (75%), one participant is working in a special library with a research focus, and one is a school media specialist.

Prior to receiving IMLS funding, the Initiative awarded a total of 8 awards (years 2000–2004).

Those selected to participate in this competitive program also participated in several professional skill-building courses through ARL's Online Lyceum, including Professional Writing Skills, Library Fund Development, and Power Dynamics and Influencing Skills. In the ongoing development of the program, these specific topics were chosen based on feedback from ARL Directors and from previous program participants about what skills were most essential for future library leaders.

Indeed, the vast majority of participants have found that a formalized mechanism for building upon their professional writing skills; enhancing their self-awareness; developing a better understanding of power and influence; and familiarizing themselves with issues surrounding library fund development, both in theory and at their home institutions, has enhanced their professional identities. It provided a solid foundation from which to progress in their careers, either through seeking positions of greater responsibility and potential for leadership, or through promotion at their current institutions.

Participants must also identify areas of research or particular challenges they face in their current positions, and design a project to address these issues throughout the course of the two-year program. Supporting librarians in their scholarly contributions to the field distinguishes this program from other leadership development programs.

Urban Libraries Council Executive Leadership Institute[33]

The Urban Libraries Council Executive Leadership Institute (ELI), funded by an IMLS grant for emerging middle management leaders in urban public libraries, is a ten-month program that employs a model of action learning and individualized executive coaching for participants. Dr. Eugene Schnell, a nationally known independent organizational development consultant on leadership and diversity for corporate and non-profit organizations, designed the curriculum. The action-learning component of ELI, designed by Jay Conger, gives participants an opportunity to apply the skills they are learning through the program, paired with customized and personalized executive coaching.

There are two central questions that are often asked of ELI designers: why choose a coaching pedagogy for development of middle managers, and how does it impact leadership development? Performance-based executive coaching has been long used as a means of performance-based improvement in corporate America. In a 2004 survey by Right Management consultants of Philadelphia, 86% of companies said they used coaching to sharpen the skills of individuals who have been identified as future organizational leaders.[34]

Executive coaching provides an objective, one-on-one, private third-party opportunity to deconstruct the perceived stigmas that may impact on, and be attached to professional performance and achievement. This is especially necessary for minorities in the workplace. Coaching differs from consulting and mentoring because coaching requires clients to identify and develop their own resources and skills for future success and sustainability of performance. Consultative coaching typically provides the client with 'answers', whereas mentoring, generally speaking, rarely focuses on performance-based achievement.

The Action Learning component, defined as a leadership challenge through the ELI program, provides a practical opportunity in the workplace for implementation of new skills and behaviors. These skills and behaviors are acquired through leadership development, leadership assessment tools, such as the Myers Briggs Type Indicator, and the Fundamental Interpersonal Relations Orientation-Behavior (FIRO-B), the 360 degree assessment tool and the coaching process. The ULC ELI program was not specifically developed for minority leadership (although every attempt is made to have an inclusive pool of participants) in the urban public library, but it does provide another potentially successful model for leadership training of minorities in librarianship through action learning and executive coaching.

The impact of participants in ELI has been significant. Participants not only have the opportunity to understand their own leadership style through coaching and action learning but also, as in each of the previous leadership development programs, to build a national network of peers through the program.

CONCLUSION

With the advent of the Internet, information is available to the masses in ways never imagined before. In this current and rapidly changing environment, librarians are, and will continue to be, ever more in demand. It is vitally important for globally-oriented, information-rich, and emerging societies to embrace ways to help support and nurture leaders that reflect the communities they serve. Sherman states

> The library that we are most familiar with today—a public or academic institution that lends out books for free—is a product of the democratization of knowledge ... Instead of eliminating the need for librarians, technology is reinforcing their validity.[36]

As pioneering librarian and co-founder of the Black Caucus of the American Library Association, Dr. E. J. Josey reminded colleagues in his foreword to *Diversity in Libraries*, about the importance of minority librarian leadership development to the profession as a whole. He wrote that while the profession must strengthen its collective resolve, "to be certain that the Spectrum Initiative will not die. We must be cognizant of the fact that the Spectrum Initiative in and of itself will not solve the problem. This must be the profession's responsibility..."[37]

The authors, who have been participants/beneficiaries of these programs, program directors and program content providers, agree that the profession has a responsibility to insure that the next generation of library leaders more closely reflects the populations their library institutions serve.

REFERENCES

[1] Gregorian, V. White House conference on school libraries: *Keynote address*. [online] 2007 Jun 4 [cited 2007 Jan 21]: Available from URL http://www.imls.gov/news/events/whitehouse_1.shtm

[2] Institute for Museums and Library Services. *IMLS Responds to nation's shortage of librarians funds recruitment, education and technology training.* [online] 2001 [cited 2004 Nov 12]: Available from URL: http://www.imls.gov/whatsnew/01archive/071701-1.htm

[3] Institute of Museum and Library Services. *Over $21 Million to Recruit New Librarians and Help Offset National Shortage.* 2000. Accessed on December 12, 2006 URL: http://www.imls.gov/news/2005/062805b.shtm

[4] Kyrilladou, M. Young. *ARL statistics, 2004–2005*. Washington, D.C.: ARL, 2006.

[5] National Urban League. *The state of Black America*. New York: National Urban League, 2006.

[6] Neely, T. Diversity in conflict. *Law Library Journal* 1998, 90 (4), 587–601.

[7] Grady, J. & Hall, T. The world is changing: Why aren't we? Recruiting minorities to librarianship. *Library Worklife: HR E-news for today's leaders.* [online]. 2006. [cited 2007 Jan 20] Retrieved from URL: http://www.ala-apa.org/newsletter/vol1no4/recruitment.html

[8] Association of Research Libraries. *ARL annual salary survey.* [online]. 2006 [cited 2006 Nov 7]: Available from http://www.arl.org/stats/pubpdf/ss05.pdf

[9] Adkins, D. & Espinal, I. The diversity mandate. *Library Journal* 2004, 29 (7), 52–54.

[10] International Association of Library Associations and Institutions.. *Library Services to Multicultural Populations Section: Strategic plan 2006–2007* Accessed on January 30, 2007 from URL: http://www.ifla.org/VII/s32/annual/sp32.htm

[11] Grady & Hall. Op Cit.

[12] Ibid

[13] Ibid

[14] Adkins & Espinal. Op Cit:52.

[15] Ibid

[16] McCook, K. de la Pena. Introduction. Librarianship. *Library Trends*, 2000, 49 (1) 1–5.

[17] Ibid:2

[18] Thomas, D. A. Race matters: The truth about mentoring minorities. *Harvard Business Review* 2001, 79 (4), 63–71.

[19] Mosley, P.A. Mentoring Gen X managers: tomorrow's library leadership is already here. *Library Administration & Management* 2005, 19 (4), 185–193.

[20] Alire, C. A. Diversity and leadership: The color of leadership. In Winston, MD (ed). *Leadership in the library and information science professions: theory and practice*. Binghamton, NY: Haworth Press, 2001: 95–110.

[21] Ibid

[22] Ibid

[23] National Academy of Science, National Academy of Engineering, Institute of Medicine. *What is a mentor, adviser, teacher, role model, friend*. National Academy Press: Washington, D.C., 1997.

[24] American Library Association. *Spectrum—new voices, new vision!* [online]. 2005 [cited 2007 Feb 5]; [5 screens]. Available from: http://www.ala.org/ala/diversity/spectrum/spectruminitiative.htm

[25] Roy, L., Johnson-Cooper, G., Tysick, C. & Waters, D. *Bridging boundaries to create a new workforce: A survey of Spectrum scholarship recipients, 1998–2003*. [online]. 2006 [cited 2007 Feb 5] [32 pgs]. Chicago, IL: American Library Association. Available from: http://www.ala.org/ala/diversity/spectrum/spectrumsurveyreport/BridgingBoundaries.pdf

[26] Davis, D. & Hall.T, *Diversity counts*. [online]. 2006 [cited 2007 Feb 5]; [37 pgs]. Chicago, IL: American Library Association. Available from: http://www.ala.org/ala/ors/diversitycounts/DiversityCountsReport.pdf

[27] Roy, Johnson-Cooper, Tysick, & Waters. Op. Cit:29.

[28] Carlson, T. Personal testimony. *Spectrum 1997–2000 report*. Chicago, IL: American Library Association. 2000.

[29] University of Minnesota Libraries. *Minnesota institute.* [online]. 2006 [cited 2007 Feb 5]; [5 screens]: Available from: http://sdt.lib.umn.edu/institute/

[30] Johnson, P. & DeBeau-Melting, L. *Retaining and advancing librarians of color.* [online]. [cited 2007 Feb 5]; [10pgs]. Available from: http://www.cce.umn.edu/kof/cdrom/pdfs/KOF005_RecRetAdv_Johnson_P.pdf

[31] Publications by former participants in the Minnesota Institute include: Cogell R, Gruwell C (eds). *Diversity in libraries: academic residency programs.* Westport, CT: Greenwood Press, 2001. Multiple authors. UMN Technology and Leadership Training Institute. *Leading Ideas: Issues & Trends in Diversity, Leadership & Career Development* 1998, Dec; 5, 2–5.

[32] Association of Research Libraries. *Diversity Initiatives: leadership & career program* [online]. 2006 Dec 22 [cited 2007 Feb 5]; [8 screens]: Available from: http://www.arl.org/diversity/lcdp/

[33] Urban Libraries Council. ULC Executive Leadership Institute [online]. 2006 [cited 2007 Feb 5]; [5 screens]: Available from URL: http://www.urbanlibraries.org/ulcexecutiveleadershipinstitute.html

[34] Michelman, P. What an executive coach can do for you. *Harvard Business School: Working knowledge.* Accessed on January 30, 2007 from URL http://hbswk.hbs.edu/archive/4853.html

[35] Sherman, W. *Are librarians totally obsolete?* Accessed on January 20, 2007 from URL http://www.degreetutor.com/library/adult-continued-education/librarians-needed

[36] Josey, E. J. Foreword. In Cogwell RV, Gruwell CA (eds). *Diversity in libraries: Academic residency programs.* Westport, CN: Greenwood Press, 2001: pp.ix–xii.

Acknowledgements The authors would like to sincerely thank Ms. Lynn Hawkes for her superb editing and organizational skills, as well as her support and enthusiasm for this project.

DEVELOPING AN INTERNATIONAL LIBRARY LEADERSHIP INSTITUTE: THINKING OUTSIDE THE BORDERS

Barbara J. Ford, Director
Mortenson Center for International Library Programs
Urbana, Illinois, USA
bjford@uiuc.edu

Susan Schnuer, Associate Director
Mortenson Center for International Library Programs
Urbana, Illinois, USA
schnuer@uiuc.edu

Debra Wilcox Johnson
Johnson & Johnson Consulting
johnson_johnson@tds.net

Abstract

A grant from the U.S. Institute of Museum and Library Services provided the opportunity for the Mortenson Center for International Library Programs at the University of Illinois Library at Urbana-Champaign and the Illinois State Library to develop and test modules for international library leadership institutes. Two institutes have been held, and this report details the resulting learning and the subsequent modifications to the institute's format and content.

BACKGROUND AND REVIEW OF THE LITERATURE

The Mortenson Center for International Library Programs at the University of Illinois Library at Urbana-Champaign was established as a center for continuing education for librarians and information specialists from all over the world. Over the years the Mortenson Center received a number of requests to offer a leadership institute. After some consideration and review of the leadership training possibilities in the field, it was apparent that among the many library leadership programs none focused on leadership in an international context. The Mortenson Center, working with the Illinois State Library, wrote a grant to develop an international library leadership program. The grant was funded in 2004 by the U.S. Institute of Museum and Library Services (IMLS).

A review of the literature reflects the increased emphasis on leadership in library and information science. Not surprisingly, over the past few years, many organizations have started offering leadership institutes. In a 2004 special issue of *Library Trends* on organizational development and leadership, Mason and Wetherbee analyzed the content of current training programs.[1] At an earlier date, the Association of Research Libraries developed a registry of library leadership development programs and now provides major leadership development resources on its website.[2] In November 2006 the Council on Library and Information Resources convened a meeting of leaders of mid-career library leadership training programs and discussed unmet leadership needs. From the report it appears that international perspectives were not part of this discussion.[3] A search of the library literature reveals that a number of countries are developing leadership programs, but these programs generally do not take an international focus nor bring together librarians from a variety of countries.

The need for this project became clear upon reviewing the content of several prestigious leadership programs in the U.S., such as the Harvard Leadership Institute of the Association of College and Research Libraries; the Frye Leadership Institute; the Senior Fellows Program at University of California, Los Angeles; the Urban Libraries Council; Leadership for Public Libraries; and the Snowbird Leadership Institute. There are many differences among these institutes, but it is clear that they did not focus on engaging participants in the discussion and understanding of global library issues. None of the institutes is designed to meet the needs of a diversified audience of U.S. and international librarians.

INSTITUTE GOALS, CONTENT, AND EVALUATION

Defining library leadership and its characteristics is an elusive task, especially when placed in an international context. Research by Kouzes and Posner[4] over several decades identified four skills that respondents from six continents selected as leadership characteristics: leaders are honest, forward-thinking, competent, and inspiring. Two earlier landmark studies focused on different traits. The Ohio State leadership studies identified 'consideration' and 'initiating structure' as key skills for leaders, meaning that they found that effective leaders acted in friendly and supportive ways toward subordinates and also structured work activities to achieve the goals of the group.[5]

The Michigan leadership studies identified three main behaviors of leaders: task-oriented behavior, relationship-oriented behavior, and participative leadership. Effective leaders would structure their work in unique ways and would focus not only on the work, but also on developing a relationship with their subordinates. Effective leaders would use a participative management style, involving many others in the process of sharing ideas and problem-solving.[6]

Drawing on research and personal experience, Mortenson Center staff developed a leadership institute that could navigate across cultural and linguistic differences. First, however, staff had to establish critical guidelines.

Guidelines for the Leadership Institute

- Participants would be practicing librarians, middle- to senior-level managers, and would be evenly split between U.S. librarians and librarians from other countries.

- There would be an even mix of international and U.S. speakers.

- While the institute would be in English much of the time, other languages would also be used at times.

- Topics and skills to be covered during the institute would create an even playing field. In other words, presentations and activities that would be new to all participants, were chosen.

- Content for the institute would be based on concrete concepts common to all librarians. Content developers believed non-native speakers could talk about leadership in a disaster-preparedness exercise, for example, more easily than they might in a lengthy discussion about the meaning of inspirational leadership.

- The sessions would include a mixture of lectures, workshops, large- and small-group activities, a simulation game, and a project for the participants.

- The institute would be residential, providing ample opportunity for the participants to mix in informal situations.

- The development of the content of the workshop would take place in collaboration with the international partners of the Mortenson Center.

Institute Goals

After setting the guidelines, institute developers moved on to the goals, which included the following:

- To establish common language for talking about leadership and a better understanding of leadership traits in a global context.
- To develop cross-cultural communication strategies.
- To gain deeper appreciation and understanding of the context of library operations in other countries.
- To develop problem-solving skills useful in an international situation.
- To build lasting professional relationships with librarians from other countries.

Institute Content

Having determined the guidelines and the goals, the next task focused on the content of the leadership institute, which included advocacy, cross-cultural communication, and negotiation as skills used to develop leadership traits. In addition, a component on preservation and disaster-preparedness was added for three reasons:

- Both issues pose potential, real-life problems for most libraries.
- Many librarians have little or no training on these issues.
- Both topics could be introduced in a tabletop exercise that mimicked a library disaster where participants must apply their cross-cultural communication and leadership skills in an emergency situation.

The disaster-preparedness exercise would be the last component in the institute, tying together the skills learned on previous days.

One of the greatest difficulties in designing the content proved to be identification of a leadership measurement tool that considered traits of leaders working in a global context. After reviewing many of the commonly and not so commonly used tools, the Campbell Leadership Descriptor[7] was selected. In addition to being relatively easy to administer, this instrument also listed a trait called 'multicultural awareness' that measured the following skills: has a global view; is culturally sensitive; is globally innovative; provides an effective global leadership image; and is internationally resilient.[7]

The nine components identified in the Campbell Leadership Descriptor provide a common language about leadership qualities. As described in the instrument,[7] the nine components include the following: vision, management, empowerment, diplomacy, feedback, entrepreneurialism, personal style, personal energy, and multicultural awareness.

Institute Evaluation

The funding for the project allowed for the hiring of an evaluator, who worked as part of the team to develop the evaluation strategies for the institute. By focusing evaluation on the outcomes of the institute, the following evaluation questions came to the forefront:

- What types of learning gains are made in the designated content areas?
- To what degree do participating librarians feel more comfortable working together in a global context?
- What types of activities will be implemented locally after this training?
- What type of networking will emerge among the participants?

A variety of techniques was used to gather information for the evaluation, including pre- and post-tests, observations, questionnaires, and interviews. Evaluation information has been used throughout the project to help monitor progress and refine the leadership program.

THE FIRST INSTITUTE: SEPTEMBER 2005

Participants

Thirty librarians participated in the first leadership institute: 15 international librarians and 15 librarians from Illinois. The international librarians were from the countries of Botswana, Colombia, India, Japan, South Africa, Mauritius, and Vietnam and came from public and academic institutions. The Illinois librarians came from all over the state, both rural and urban locations, and worked in school, public, academic, or consortium settings.

The Program

The leadership institute took place over four days and was hosted by the Illinois State Library in their facilities in Springfield, Illinois. Most of the participants stayed in a local hotel. The schedule was as follows:

Day 1 (late afternoon):
Reception—Welcome and Greeting
Dinner

Day 2 (all day):
Session: Being a Library Leader in the 21st Century
Session: World Library Leadership: The World Summit on the Information Society
Session: Small-Group Discussion and Reports on Issues of the World Summit on the Information Society
Session: Leadership Assessment

Day 3 (all day):
Session: Pamoja—A Cultural Simulation Game
Session: Communicating in a Multicultural Environment and Small-Group Exercise

Day 4 (half-day):
Session: Developing and Exercising Your Disaster Plan

Evaluation

Overall, participants found that the institute was 'useful' and exceeded expectations. They reported learning in all the goal areas for the institute, and made positive and appreciative comments about the experience.

Responses about the institute differed discernibly between international and Illinois participants. The most significant difference was in how the international librarians rated the amount learned in all topic areas; they tended to report that they learned a 'good amount' or 'great deal' about all topics. The exception to this tendency was international library issues, where they reported learning the same amount as the U.S. group.

At the start of the institute, facilitators encouraged participants to meet as many people as possible. This goal definitely became an outcome of the training, as nearly three out of four participants met and talked with most of the participants. Among the Illinois librarians, all but one fit in this group, but for international librarians, half fit in this group.

1. Ratings

'Usefulness' is a major criterion for determining impact of the institute. All sessions received an overall rating of 'average' for 'usefulness', so clearly there was room for improvement. The Illinois librarians tended to give the lowest ratings for 'usefulness'. The difference between the ratings of Illinois and international librarians narrowed when it came to presentation style.

The 'usefulness' scale had five ratings—extremely useful, very useful, useful, somewhat useful, and not useful at all—with extremely useful being the top of the scale (five points). The first column of Table 1 shows the combined average rating, the second the average rating from international participants, and the third the average rating from Illinois librarians.

Table 1. Usefulness Ratings for Sessions at September 2005 Leadership Institute

Combined	International	Illinois
4.3 Pamoja	4.4 Disaster Planning	4.4 Pamoja
4.1 Disaster Planning	4.2 Leadership Assessment	3.9 Disaster Planning
3.6 Leadership Assessment	4.1 Multicultural Communication	3.2 Leader 21st Century
3.6 Multicultural Communication	4.1 Pamoja	3.2 Multicultural Communication
3.4 Leader 21st Century	3.6 Leader 21st Century	3.2 World Summit
3.4 World Summit	3.6 World Summit	3.1 Leadership Assessment

Participants then rated their learning in seven topic areas using a different five-point scale: a great deal, a good amount, a fair amount, very little, nothing. The topics they rated relate to the objectives in the IMLS grant proposal. Again, the first column in Table 2 shows the combined average rating, the second the average rating from international participants, and the third the average rating from Illinois librarians.

Table 2. Amount Learned From Sessions at September 2005 Leadership Institute

Combined	International	Illinois
3.9 Leadership	4.3 Leadership	3.8 International library issues
3.8 International library Issues	3.9 Advocacy	3.6 Leadership
3.7 Problem solving	3.9 Negotiation	3.6 Problem solving
3.4 Negotiation	3.9 Problem solving	3.0 Negotiation
3.3 Advocacy	3.9 Serving diverse populations	2.9 Innovative library services
3.2 Innovative library services	3.8 International library issues	2.9 Serving diverse populations
3.3 Serving diverse populations	3.7 Innovative library services	2.8 Advocacy

2. Analysis of Learning From the Institute

The ratings show variance among participants on what they learned from the institute. To some degree, differences in how people defined the terms used in the evaluation form explains this variance, as well as differences in baseline knowledge in each of the topic areas. However, improvements in content on advocacy and innovative library services were clearly needed. 'Serving diverse populations' and 'negotiation' also seemed to need additional attention. Comments made during the institute and responses to open-ended questions also reinforced the need for these enhancements. Overall, participants wanted more opportunities to hear about library services in different settings and serving diverse populations, since this learning came primarily from informal sharing during the institute. While participants did use negotiation extensively in the Pamoja exercise, they may not have realized it. Advocacy was not a core topic of the first institute.

The response to the Campbell leadership tool indicated that eight people felt their perceptions of their leadership skills did not change, although they had a more in-depth understanding of those skills. All were, however, able to identify skills for further development. The skills most frequently listed as needing development included diplomacy (12), personal energy (12), entrepreneurialism (11), management (9), vision (8), feedback (8), multicultural awareness (7), empowerment (6), and personal style (2).

A follow-up questionnaire sent to participants six months after the institute revealed some activity or application of learning. In some cases the impact was very specific, such as a grant application or change of procedures instituted. In other cases participants reported increased sensitivity related to communication. Both Illinois and international librarians expressed regret that significant contact did not occur after the institute.

REVISIONS TO THE LEADERSHIP INSTITUTE

The evaluation of the first institute clearly identified its strengths and weaknesses. Related to the issue of what participants learned is the issue of what to add to the institute. Participants mentioned wanting opportunities for sharing and discussion of international library issues most frequently (8), followed closely by the desire for more information on library services/best practices worldwide (7). Pamoja and the disaster planning sessions received good evaluations and were used in the second institute in the same way. The sessions found least useful in the first institute—Library Leadership in the 21st Century and World Library Leadership—were changed significantly for the second institute. The session became 'What It Means to Lead in the International Library World', with fewer speakers addressing the topic and more focus on international issues. The second institute also included a session on strategies and skills for cross-cultural communication presented by an expert in the field to supplement the diversity and multiculturalism session. Emphasis on analysis and discussion of test results strengthened the leadership assessment session the second time around.

Perhaps the most interesting and puzzling finding after the first institute was the difference in the way international librarians and U.S. librarians rated the sessions. It seemed almost as if there were two different parallel sessions. Instead of bringing the two groups together on a variety of issues, the institute offered sessions that were more useful to either the international or the U.S. group. The goal for the second institute was to work on developing sessions that appealed to the group overall.

Participants in the first institute also expressed interest in advocacy, resulting in addition of a session on the topic to the second institute. The opportunity to develop advocacy plans for their local setting also provided opportunities to learn more about international library issues and library services worldwide. Some participants in the first institute (mostly international librarians) also had mentioned the need for more on leadership styles and more in-depth activities on how to lead. More directed and focused discussion of the leadership assessment tool was added to address this interest.

In addition, participants in the first institute suggested offering more opportunities for sharing and discussions of international library issues and of library services and best practices worldwide. Many participants also commented on the need for some sort of post-institute collaborative project. Suggestions included incorporating a project for small groups to be completed during the institute, or time to plan for collaborative activities after the institute. For the second institute, each participant brought two slides—one about their work and one about themselves—to introduce themselves to the group. The institute setting also allowed time to discuss issues informally and follow up with participants and speakers on topics of interest. Partners had the opportunity to develop their own collaborative projects that would continue after the institute, and to share them with the group. This revision also addressed the suggestion that there be more information about international library issues.

In response to participants' comments, facilitators made an effort to build stronger connections between and among the sessions and to connect the desired learning outcomes of the sessions to the institute goals. This component helped participants understand better how the pieces of the institute fitted together.

THE SECOND INSTITUTE: NOVEMBER 2006

Participants

Thirty-two librarians participated in the second leadership institute: 17 international librarians and 15 librarians from the U.S. The international librarians were from the countries of Argentina, Canada, Costa Rica, Dominican Republic, Mexico, Nicaragua, Peru, and South Africa. The U.S. librarians came from Arizona, District of Columbia, Colorado, Florida, Illinois, Ohio, Oregon, Pennsylvania, and Texas. The group represented both rural and urban settings, and worked in public, academic, school, and government/special libraries.

The Program

The second leadership institute took place over four days and was held at the Allerton Conference Center of the University of Illinois at Urbana-Champaign. The participants stayed at the conference center, which is in a rural setting, and had their meals and all activities together in the conference center.

Day 1 (midday):
Reception—Welcome and Greetings
Administration of Leadership Assessment Tool

Day 2 (all day):
Introduction of Partnership Projects
Session: What It Means to Lead in the International Library World
Session: Strategies and Skills for Cross-Cultural Communication
Session: Leadership Assessment Tool: Analysis and Discussion
Session: Pamoja—A Cultural Simulation Game

Day 3 (all day):
Session: Library Advocacy
Session: Diversity and Multiculturalism in Libraries

Day 4 (half-day):
Session: Disaster Preparedness
Presentation of Partnership Projects

Evaluation

The second institute clearly met the expectations of the both the U.S. and international librarians. Three out of five reported that the institute exceeded expectations. As was the case with the first institute, participants reported learning in all the goal areas of the institute.

Participants noted in their comments about their positive experiences during the institute and indicated a variety of things they took away from the experience. Many noted that developing relationships with new colleagues was one of the strongest outcomes. One person concluded that the main thing she would take back to the library would be "a new enthusiasm for networking and ongoing projects." Another librarian echoed this sentiment, noticing a "renewed energy to approach my day-to-day work."

Developing an International Library Leadership Institute

There were differences between the U.S. and international librarians' ratings, chiefly in the rating of usefulness of the sessions and in the amount learned. In both cases, the international librarians gave higher ratings than the U.S. participants. The exception to this tendency was with the session on cross-cultural communication, where the U.S. librarians rated it highest for usefulness and amount learned. Both groups reported the least amount of learning about negotiation.

Facilitators encouraged participants to meet and talk with as many people at the institute as possible. This outcome of the training definitely succeeded, as nearly seven out of 10 participants talked with most of the participants. Among the U.S. librarians, all but two fitted into this group; for international librarians nearly 60 percent fitted in this group.

1. Ratings

Determining impact of the institute depends on how participants responded to sessions' 'usefulness'. All sessions received at least an overall rating of useful, with the session on cross-cultural communication rated very useful. When asked about presentation style, the responses tended to range from 'okay' to 'inspirational and informative' for all sessions. The exception to this pattern appeared in the wider range of reactions to both usefulness and presentation style for the diversity and multiculturalism session, resulting in lower ratings for both criteria.

The usefulness rating scale had five points, ranging from extremely useful (5) to not useful (1). In Table 3, the first column shows the combined average rating for usefulness, the second column the scores from international participants, and the third from U.S. librarians.

Table 3. Usefulness Ratings for Sessions at November 2006 Leadership Institute

Combined	International	U.S.
4.2 Cross-cultural communication	4.1 Cross-cultural communication	4.3 Cross-cultural communication
3.9 Advocacy	4.1 Leadership assessment	3.9 Disaster preparedness
3.9 Disaster preparedness	3.9 Advocacy	3.9 Pamoja

3.9 Leadership assessment	3.9 Disaster preparedness	3.8 Advocacy
3.8 International leadership	3.9 International leadership	3.7 International leadership
3.7 Pamoja	3.9 Diversity/ Multiculturalism	3.6 Leadership assessment
3.4 Diversity/ Multiculturalism	3.5 Pamoja	2.9 Diversity/ Multiculturalism

Librarians rated their learning in eight topic areas. This list of topic areas differs from the first institute because of refinement in the goals of the institute. A five-point scale measured the amount of learning, ranging from a great deal (5) to nothing (1). The amount learned about advocacy clearly improved from the first institute. Learning related to negotiation rated only 'a fair amount', and the rating actually fell below that of the first institute. Overall, Table 4 shows the ratings on amount of learning, which exceeded the same ratings from the first institute. This improvement reflects the refinement of the content and organization for the second institute.

Table 4. Amount Learned From Sessions at November 2006 Leadership Institute

Combined	International	U.S.
4.2 Disaster-preparedness	4.4 Leadership	4.1 Cross-cultural communication
4.1 Leadership	4.3 Disaster preparedness	4.1 Disaster preparedness
4.0 Advocacy	4.3 International issues	3.8 Diversity/ Multiculturalism
3.9 Cross-cultural communication	4.2 Advocacy	3.8 Leadership
3.9 Diversity/ Multiculturalism	4.0 Diversity/ Multiculturalism	3.7 Advocacy
3.9 International issues	3.9 Library services	3.5 International issues
3.7 Library services	3.8 Cross-cultural communication	3.5 Library services
3.1 Negotiation	3.4 Negotiation	2.7 Negotiation

2. Analysis of Learning From the Institute

The disaster-preparedness session ranked well in both institutes, and there were minimal suggestions for improvements. The overwhelmingly positive response to the cross-cultural communication session in the second institute suggests the need to develop a module on this topic that includes the basic concepts covered by the speaker. The advocacy session was more focused and effective in the second institute and resulted in higher rankings.

One of the goals for the second institute was to find presentations of equal interest to both groups. This goal was much more successful in the second institute. Both groups rated cross-cultural communication and disaster preparedness highly, indicating appropriate content for both groups.

The leadership assessment component of the training showed clear improvement, which can provide a framework for further development of that important module. The two institutes used the same leadership assessment tool—the Campbell Leadership Descriptor.[7] Participants in the second institute rated this instrument even more positively than in the first. In both institutes, participants clearly identified areas for development of their leadership skills. At this institute, the most frequently mentioned areas for development were personal energy, diplomacy, entrepreneurialism, and management. Amazingly, these categories match exactly the same top categories from the first institute. The improvement in ratings scores may partly result from allowing more time for reflection and use of the tool in the second institute, which should be a key component in this module. While no perfect leadership assessment instrument exists, the Campbell tool does seem to work well with an international group.

The diversity and multiculturalism session changed significantly from the first institute, but the responses show that more work needs to be done to develop an effective module. The interactive discussions and exercises from this session received positive comments, which can provide a starting point for refinement. The amount of lecture, the simplistic approach, and presentation style must be examined for improvement.

The topic of negotiation did not rate well for 'amount learned' in either institute, with a drop on this rating in the second institute. The Pamoja exercise served as the chief vehicle for learning in this area. Despite effective debriefing after this exercise, the connection between Pamoja and negotiation still had not been made. This module may require a brief introduction about negotiation as a lead-in to the exercise and a revisiting of negotiation principles during the debriefing. The participants definitely exhibited a range of negotiation skills during the exercise, providing a strong basis for learning.

When asked about changes to the institute, a significant number (seven people) suggested allowing more time for sharing and interactions among participants. This response might partly explain the slightly lower ratings on learning about successful library services. However, the most frequent response (from just over half of the respondents) was not to delete anything from the institute. Five participants specifically noted the need to improve the diversity program when asked about which program to drop from the institute.

In response to suggestions from the first institute to improve networking, facilitators added a new partnership activity that participants embraced. Three out of four librarians called it a 'useful' exercise, with another 20% finding it 'somewhat useful'. Matching participants presented a big challenge for facilitators, as some participants noted difficulty in finding a common project because of differences between their libraries. While the final assessment of the usefulness of partnerships will come later, initial comments suggest some immediate positive effects.

CONCLUSIONS

Designing a leadership institute to meet the expectations of a diverse audience of librarians from the U.S. and other countries presents a unique opportunity and challenge. While today's professional literature emphasizes the need to be able to work in a global multicultural context, bringing a global perspective to library work by 'thinking outside the borders' is difficult. Many librarians have not had the opportunity to operate in a global context, so getting them out of their comfort zone where they can practice different approaches and explore new ideas is essential. The goals of the institute were developed to provide experience and tools for librarians to navigate better in a diverse global setting.

The institutes provided a variety of opportunities for librarians from the U.S. and other countries to interact, share experiences and perceptions, and learn from one another. These opportunities accomplished the institute goals of establishing common language for talking about leadership and a better understanding of leadership traits in the global setting. The institute sessions provided opportunities to develop cross-cultural communication strategies, and the presentation during the second institute on strategies and skills for cross-cultural communication provided many excellent and thought-provoking examples. Participants also practiced problem-solving skills appropriate to an international environment during the institute. Longer term evaluation of the impact of the institute on participants will be needed to see if the institute goals mentioned above have been accomplished and if the institute has had an impact on the work participants do in their libraries and communities.

The second institute provided expanded opportunities to accomplish the institute goal of gaining a deeper appreciation and understanding of the context of library operations in other countries, as there was more direct sharing of experiences and a structured opportunity to develop joint projects that should help build lasting professional relationships. More time is needed to see if participants carry out these joint projects and if lasting professional relationships develop. Illinois librarians also have the opportunity to expand their interactions with librarians from other countries through hosting librarians who are at the Mortenson Center and attending programs that visiting librarians put on at the annual Illinois Library Association conference. Of course, all librarians can seek these opportunities through participation in conferences and programs and by looking for international opportunities in their work.

One intriguing area of future research would be to examine more closely the differences in ratings of the sessions by the international participants and the U.S. librarians. While some sessions resonated equally with both groups, others did not. Was it the content, the presentation style, or the topic that caused the groups to react differently? Gaining a better understanding of what will pull an international group together is the crucial key to a leadership institute that reaches out across cultures and languages.

To test the adaptability of the institute, the state libraries of Arizona and Nebraska will conduct leadership sessions in their states in the final year of the project. These sessions will differ somewhat since the staff of the state libraries will shape the content with less involvement of Mortenson Center staff. The Mortenson Center staff also has been invited to work with a partner in South Africa to present a leadership institute there during 2008.

The leadership training modules developed in the grant will be flexible, so an entity adapting the program can select topics it deems relevant for its situation and provide training programs of different lengths. The outcome of this project will—hopefully—provide the impetus for other states, library organizations, and countries to take new approaches to developing library leaders in a global community.

REFERENCES

[1] Mason, F.M., Wetherbee, L.V. Learning to lead: an analysis of current training programs for library leadership. *Library Trends* 2004, **53** (1), 187–217.

[2] Association of Research Libraries. Leadership development [online]. 2007 [cited 2007 Jan 24]. Available from: URL: http://www.arl.org/leadership/

[3] Council on Library and Information Resources. Invitation for comments on mid-career library leadership training [online]. 2007 [cited 2007 Jan 24]. Available from: URL: http://www.clir.org/activities/details/leader.html

[4] Kouzes, J.M., Posner, B.Z. *The leadership challenge.* 3rd edition. San Francisco: Jossey-Bass, 2002.

[5] ChangingMinds.org. Ohio State studies [online]. 2007 [cited 2007 Jan 24]. Available from: URL: http://changingminds.org/disciplines/leadership/actions/ohio_state.htm

[6] ChangingMinds.org. Michigan studies [online]. 2007 [cited 2007 Jan 24]. Available from: URL: http://changingminds.org/disciplines/leadership/actions/michigan.htm

[7] Campbell, D. *Campbell leadership descriptor: facilitator's guide.* San Francisco: Jossey-Bass/Pfeiffer, 2002.

INTERNATIONAL PARTNERSHIPS AND LEADERSHIP DEVELOPMENT: AFRICAN NATIONAL CONGRESS, UNIVERSITY OF FORT HARE, UNIVERSITY OF CONNECTICUT PARTNERSHIP, 1999–2007

Betsy Pittman
University of Connecticut
Betsy.Pittman@uconn.edu

Yolisa Soul
University of Fort Hare
YSoul@ufh.ac.za

Deborah Stansbury Sunday
University of Connecticut
Deborah.Sunday@uconn.edu

Abstract

In 1999, with grants from public and private sources totaling more than $1.8 million, the African National Congress, the Universities of Fort Hare and Connecticut established formal partnerships in South Africa to accomplish[3] inter-related projects. These were: the ANC Oral History Project; the ANC archives and Repatriation project; and, the capacity building project. The major foci of the three library/archives projects was to document the historic legacy of the ANC; to develop leadership capacity by training staff to take a leadership role in librarianship, and archives organization and administration; and to establish an information exchange between peers. The resulting experience has been rewarding and of benefit to the many librarians and archivists involved in the projects by increasing their knowledge of, and giving them experience in, leading varied and multiple phases of an international partnership.

BACKGROUND/HISTORY

In 1999, with grants from public and private sources totaling more than $1.8 million, the African National Congress (ANC) and the Universities of Fort Hare and Connecticut established formal partnerships in South Africa to accomplish three projects. The projects were: the ANC Oral History Project; the ANC Archives and Repatriation project; and the capacity building project. The major foci of the three library/archives projects were documenting the historic legacy of the ANC; developing leadership capacity; and information/experience exchange between peers, that is, training staff to take a leadership role in librarianship, and archives organisation and administration.

The University of Connecticut (UConn) and the African National Congress (ANC) began discussions in 1998 regarding provision of technical training and assistance for the organisation of the ANC archives created during the apartheid era, the 'Documents of the Struggle', as well as the identification of materials associated with the ANC and the anti-apartheid movement located outside of South Africa. The ANC established an Archives Committee, chaired by the Speaker of Parliament, Dr Frene Ginwala, to coordinate the establishment of an ANC Archive while, at the same time, the University of Connecticut investigated funding options. An official Memorandum of Understanding was signed in 1999 and the University of Connecticut followed up immediately with an initial grant proposal to the Andrew W. Mellon Foundation.

Phase I of the project, the ANC Oral History Project, received $665,000 in funding to provide initial workshops and training for a team of interviewers to conduct oral history interviews with ANC leaders who played critical roles in the anti-apartheid struggle. A week-long workshop was conducted in Cape Town in 2000 by Dr. Bruce Stave, Director of the Center for Oral History at UConn. From this one workshop ten South African interviewers were trained. Over the course of the following six years, 218 individuals were interviewed, some of whom are now deceased; the tapes were transcribed and the transcriptions were approved. The first 100 tapes and transcripts were officially presented to the ANC at a press conference in Johannesburg on 12 June 2006. UConn received copies in March 2007 and an announcement regarding the availability of this important collection will be made before this article goes to press.

A second grant proposal for Phase II of the project, the ANC Archives and Repatriation Project, was submitted in 2000 and $700,000 was awarded. The proposal for Phase II involved the identification of the official records of the ANC, hiring and training of staff, purchase of supplies, transport of materials, and travel of the project partners for purposes of coordination and training. With the subsequent identification of the University of Fort Hare as the official repository for the records of the African National Congress, the three institutions embarked in 2001 on a multi-year, multi-phase project to identify, collect and make these records available for research.

The third component of the relationship was funded by a Tertiary Education Linkages Project (TELP) grant awarded by the United Negro College Fund in amount of $460,000 from the U.S. A.I.D. A separate partnership, developed between the University of Fort Hare and the University of Connecticut, and based on the belief that each institution has much to learn from the other, was established in 2001. There were natural synergies between the two Universities. Significantly, both have long-standing commitments to comparative human rights and were initially established as agriculture schools. These factors made for a good match with tremendous potential for a qualitative exchange of information and learning. In addition to the library/archives projects funded through Mellon, the TELP 'capacity building' project developed partnerships across the two universities in areas such as agriculture, education, fund-raising/development, student services, library services, and other university business processes. Capacity building included leadership development and staff and student exchanges, and followed closely defined goals set out by the University of Fort Hare in a comprehensive strategic plan[i].[1]

PHASE I: ORAL HISTORIES OF THE ANC

The new South African government took the leadership in identifying the initial project and the partners. They also exercised leadership by identifying the private funding source, the Mellon Foundation, to provide the financial support for the project, although the grant was submitted by the University of Connecticut. The project also presented the UConn librarians with the opportunity to further develop skills in grant writing and administration, as well as the opportunity to review practices and procedures while explaining them to colleagues, thus producing more efficient and up to date practices all around.

The organisations involved in this new international partnership were adjusting and changing. The ANC was settling into its role as the majority political party in South Africa and bringing to an end significant investigations into the activities of the previous administration. The Mellon Foundation itself was transitioning from U.S.-administered projects based in South Africa to local administration of funded projects. The University of Fort Hare had a new administration and a new strategic plan that identified its highest priorities. The

University of Connecticut was embarking on newly initiated global partnerships. For each of the partners, these adjustments required patience, tolerance and a firm understanding of the ultimate goals to be reached in order to navigate the inevitable changes of direction, addition of tasks, endless minutiae and daily frustrations that can so easily derail such a complex project.

The oral history project was conducted and supervised by Dr Bruce Stave from UConn and Ms Narissa Ramdhani, Project Manager. Interviewers received formal training in conducting audio oral histories in Cape Town by Dr. Stave and Ms. Ramdhani in a week long workshop covering professional standards and practices, interviewing techniques, transcription procedures and editing. The final transcription and approval of the tapes has since been completed and the first 100 tapes were handed over to the ANC and the University of Fort Hare at a press conference in Johannesburg on 12th June, 2006 by Professor Amii O'Mara-Otunnu, representing UConn.

Phase I required the hiring of a knowledgeable project manager and competent staff; developing a comprehensive and practical training programme and associated workflow; the establishment of a common set of goals; and finalizing tasks for each of the institutions. In addition, planned travel exchanges were developed to allow the principals involved in the projects to visit each others' institutions, meet with colleagues, receive detailed orientation and training, and provide opportunities to investigate other areas of shared interest for subsequent or potential projects. The Mellon Foundation also provided the opportunity for two graduate students from the University of Fort Hare to attend the University of Connecticut and study for their Masters degrees. While at Connecticut, the students would also have the opportunity to work closely with the staff of the Center for Oral History and Archives & Special Collections to gain the appropriate practical and technical skills, as well as the knowledge to serve as potential trainers and instructors when they returned to South Africa after the completion of their studies. To our knowledge, these two individuals have done exactly that—they returned to South Africa and are now employed in positions that have allowed them to guide, train and supervise others using the knowledge and skills acquired while they were furthering their education in Connecticut. The staff in Connecticut also benefited from having the opportunity to share information and regularly evaluate activities based on the questions posed by the graduate students.

PHASE II/ARCHIVES AND REPATRIATION PROJECT

The successes of Phase I led to a second, expanded relationship between the organisations. One of the early tasks of the ANC government was to gather together the 'Documents of the Struggle'. These records had been dispersed throughout the world, where the ANC had set up offices or 'missions'. The ANC leaders decided that the University of Fort Hare was the only appropriate repository for these historically significant materials. It is commonly said that the history of Fort Hare parallels the history of South Africa. The mandate from the ANC was that the records would be open to researchers, scholars, and the community, and thus act as a living collection. At the same time, it was clear to the ANC that the capacity of Fort Hare would not suffice to process the records immediately, although many related records were already housed in the University's archives. The decision was made by the ANC that the records would be processed at Luthuli House in Johannesburg and would then be transferred to the University of Fort Hare for the benefit of researchers, while Fort Hare's records were copied, processed, inventoried and returned.

Several training workshops were held with representatives from UConn, the ANC, and the University of Fort Hare. The first significant workshop was facilitated by the experienced archivist, Verne Harris, from the University of Witwatersrand, Johannesburg. The purpose of the workshops was to establish common standards for processing the physical collections, plan appropriate workflow, coordinate levels of access and potential restrictions for sensitive material and negotiate for ongoing communication amongst the principals.

The second Mellon grant provided sufficient funding to employ nine archival workers to process collections addressing Human Rights under the supervision of a highly qualified South African archivist, Razia Saleh. Interviews of all workers were conducted by representatives of the three organisations.

The project was funded for three years and during that time a number of challenges had to be faced. It was found that not all the people recruited to work on the project were trained archivists. This meant a delay in getting the project started because the new staff had to be appropriately trained. More records than anticipated were discovered at Fort Hare where the records were kept before being transferred to Luthuli House. Some of the records were in a poor condition and required cleaning and preservation treatment before they could be processed.

While the physical and intellectual work of processing the records was taking place in South Africa, Dr Katrina Greene was employed at the University of Connecticut to lead the 'Repatriation' portion of the grant. The purpose of this task was to identify and attempt to retrieve South African records in countries that hosted ANC offices during the struggle against apartheid. In her year at UConn, Dr. Greene was able to identify numerous collections in North American repositories, as well as those still in private hands. Several small collections and duplicated materials were acquired and sent to the University of Fort Hare for inclusion in the ANC Archives. This portion of the project remains unfinished as it required more time and attention to continue with the identification of ANC materials in North America, negotiation with the current holders of these materials and work to arrange for transfer or duplication of materials for deposit at the University of Fort Hare.

A singular advantage for the project was the employment of an experienced and professionally trained South African archivist to manage the project onsite in Johannesburg to serve as the ANC Archives Coordinator. In conjunction with the UConn/Fort Hare staff, the coordinator planned and implemented the employment and training of a staff of nine to work on the archival records portion of the project utilizing the materials developed in the workshop mentioned earlier. Ultimately, additional relevant ANC records were transferred from missions located in: Australia, Europe (Belgium, France, Finland, Germany, Italy, Netherlands, Norway, Sweden, United Kingdom and Ireland), Africa (Botswana, Mozambique, Namibia, Tanzania, Uganda, Zambia, Zimbabwe), North America (Canada, Cuba, United States and Asia (India, Japan). At the same time, the Solomon Mahlangu Freedom College (Somafco) records, already deposited at Fort Hare, were also processed.

Apart from the Mission records, the following personal collections were also included in the processing and transfer to the ANC Archives at Fort Hare: Govan Mbeki, Walter Sisulu, Wilton Mkwayi, Frene Ginwala, Sylvia Neame, and Denis Goldberg. These materials can be found at http://liberation.ufh.ac.za/

TELP GRANT/CAPACITY BUILDING

The third project was multifaceted and again, the leadership for this programme was based in South Africa at the University of Fort Hare. The University was the recipient of a United Negro College Fund TELP grant and selected the University of Connecticut as its partner.

International Partnerships and Leadership Development

In December 2002, three members of the Fort Hare library and archival staff visited the University of Connecticut spending nearly two weeks working with library administrators, liaison staff and archival staff for focused training in outreach activities, information literacy, Encoded Archival Description (EAD) encoding and a discussion of related administrative issues. In 2003 the ANC Archivist visited UConn for two weeks training and in 2004, two UConn librarians and an archivist visited the University of Fort Hare for discussion and training in administration, information and library literacy, academic liaison, and archival facility and organisational issues. On many occasions, participants showed individual initiative by identifying specific next steps in training, developing documentation and other activities which would move the projects forward. For example, librarians used the tools developed for use at the UConn Libraries and modified them to work in their local situation. Independently, librarians took this one step further by developing training materials and tutorials to teach information literacy to the students at Fort Hare.

Developing leaders from within the organisation is an important mechanism in succession planning. Rothwell[2] states that organisations must invest in the talent within their ranks in order to be guaranteed the leaders they will need in the future. By giving staff in the library at Fort Hare exposure to alternative methods of library instruction, faculty outreach, and administration, staff gained confidence and were able to find practical application for the new skills they were learning in the training sessions.

All those involved in the exchanges were committed to utilizing this opportunity to its greatest advantage in their local environments. Jointly, librarians from both universities identified a number of leadership initiatives that would have the greatest impact, and combined their talents to take the lead in the following activities:

1. An open discussion was held with students in the library school at the University of Fort Hare about professional careers in librarianship. Eight students participated in the discussion and talked about their interest in librarianship and how they hoped to use their training to become leaders in their township or village.

2. Training was conducted in team development and leadership with Fort Hare Library staff. Staff were able to use teaming techniques and leadership skills to make an immediate impact on the dynamics of their work groups.

3. A cadre of trainers was developed that could be used to train other staff at the university library and who might become regional consultants.

4. A proactive liaison and outreach programme between library staff, and faculty and students was established.

5. Assistance was provided with the development of information literacy modules for use in the library at Fort Hare.[1][ii]

The experience of the librarians at Fort Hare is similar to the experience described by Wittenborg in *Reflecting on Leadership*.[3][iii] Her observations are that as staff continue to learn new skills, they are exercising leadership because "they generate ideas, they are resourceful even in tough times and they are outwardly focused. Their relationships within the university and elsewhere on campus keep us better informed, more nimble in responding to needs, and more visible to the academic community." The librarians at Fort Hare have been able to take the new skills they have learned and translate that into leadership developing activities.

Examples of the various ways in which this experience has fostered and exhibited leadership by the participants include the following activities of the Fort Hare librarians:

1. Adaptation of the Library Liaison Programme, resulting in two-way communication between the faculty and the library, inclusion of the library in the Faculty Strategic Planning, increased advocacy, visibility of and support for the library, improved training programmes for students, more efficient database training and use of focus groups to evaluate library services;

2. Development of archival skills and adherence to established best practices, including empowerment of a staff archivist, who now works independently, and employment of a project archivist in the Office of the Premier of the Eastern Cape as records manager;

3. Establishment of a budget model that stresses openness and staff buy-in;

4. Staff workshops on how to run an efficient meeting.

The benefits to the UConn staff include further development of the library liaison programme based on this experience, personal skill development of those involved with the projects, and a firm foundation on which to explore other collaborative projects, international and domestic.

ASSESSMENT OF PROJECTS

While all the institutions associated with these projects have reasons to be proud of their accomplishments, we also need to acknowledge some of the obstacles we encountered in the past eight years. At the very least we have had to manoeuvre within and around four large bureaucracies (ANC, Mellon and two universities), each with their own interests, interpretations and concerns associated with the projects and goals. We must also acknowledge that there are cultural differences that needed to be addressed, including expectations, responsibilities and outcomes of the project. Compounding this is the ever-present issue of the need to be aware of the priorities of the home institution, which may or may not remain focused on any specific project once work has commenced, because of the capacity of an organisation to maintain momentum.

A not inconsequential factor involves the logistics of international partnerships. The geographical distance between the participating institutions and the time differences which made real-time conversations difficult to coordinate, was an ongoing concern and had a decided impact on workflow and progress. Difficulties will arise unless expectations, communication and goals are clearly agreed upon in detail at the start of the project and even if these issues have been addressed there will be unexpected difficulties to work through. Most work, and therefore progress, stops while these issues are addressed in mid-project and communication and workflow are adversely affected. While leadership in general was evident from the start of all three projects, when leaders did not pay attention to details of workflow, it often resulted in unforeseen complications. It is vitally important to have detailed structures in place early on in the project. Although it takes time away from the actual work, when everyone involved is excited and ready to move forward, it saves time in the long run and can assist in avoiding confusion and miscommunication once work commences.

Grant funding presents wonderful opportunities to explore avenues that might not otherwise be explored. However, in the area of staffing and project continuity soft money, or grant funding, is not as attractive as full-time, permanent employment when trying to attract the best employees. And last, but most certainly not the very least obstacle to be considered, is the downside of skill building—staff turnover. Once marketable skills are developed, especially when the position is not a permanent one, staff use these new skills as leverage to get positions elsewhere. No retention strategies had been developed to mitigate this scenario and significant staff turnover throughout the course of the projects resulted in staggered progress and the need for regular slowing down to hire and train additional staff.

WHERE DO WE GO FROM HERE?

All the staff participating in the projects, at all the institutions, have had the opportunity to lead some phase or activity associated with the project. Individuals have acquired new skills for managing and organizing archives, personnel supervision and management, compilation of oral history documentation, and similar library service leadership and outreach skills. Given below, for example, is evidence that outcomes of the training provided by the projects described here, have resulted in the following employment opportunities, as the South African staff have moved beyond the project:

- three individuals work in records management, public and private sector;
- one is involved in policy work;
- seven are employed as archivists (National Archives, heritage institution, ANC);
- five are working as outreach officers, researchers or spokespersons for government departments;
- one is employed as a museum outreach officer; and
- one has continued graduate education at the doctoral level.

The librarians and the institutions involved in these projects have become familiar with international collections and have developed a foundation on which to build other partnerships and the benefits to their institutional programmes have been addressed elsewhere in this paper.

For others interested in international partnerships it is advisable to have an agreed-upon structure in place in advance. Procedures, workflow, funds for travel, clarification of interpretation and product(s) should all be agreed upon outcomes decided at the outset. The difficulty of managing long distance partnerships, and varying perceptions and interpretations of processes and goals, affects communication and workflow, and slows productivity. While the final product might not be what you expected when you began, it can be done and what is learned is invaluable.

It has been rewarding to be involved in this worthwhile activity despite the extensive work involved. As the projects progressed, the need for consultation with the more experienced UConn staff decreased proportionate to the increasing experience and development of the South African staff.

REFERENCES

http://www.lib.uconn.edu/online/research/speclib/ASC/findaids/ANC/MSS19990022.html

http://liberation.ufh.ac.za/

[1] Thomas, G. & Fourie, I. Academic Library Consortia in South Africa: Where We Come From and Where We are Heading, Journal of Academic Librarianship, 2006, 32(4), 432–438.

[2] Rothwell, W. Putting Success into Your Succession Planning. The Journal of Business Strategy, 2002, 23(3), 32–37.

[3] Wittenborg, K. Rocking the Boat. In: Wittenborg, K., Ferguson, C., & Keller, M.A. Reflecting on Leadership. Washington, D.C.: Council on Library and Information Resources, 2003: pp1–15

[i] The need for capacity building, and leadership especially, is mentioned specifically as a key issue facing the academic library consortia in Thomas, Gwenda and Ina Fourie, "Academic Library Consortia in South Africa: Where We Come From and Where We are Heading," *The Journal of Academic Libarianship*, v. 32, #4, p. 436–437.

[ii] Companion to state consortial goal. Thomas and Fourie, p. 436.

[iii] Wittenborg, Karin, Chris Ferguson and Michael A. Keller. *Reflecting on Leadership, December 2003.*

LEADING MODERN PUBLIC LIBRARIES: A NATIONAL DEVELOPMENT PROGRAMME FOR ENGLAND

Tom Forrest,
Library Consultant
tom.forrest@btconnect.com

Abstract

Studies carried out for the Museums, Libraries and Archives Council for England (MLA) identified the need to develop leadership capacity in public library services. The government's long-term strategic vision for public libraries, *Framework for the Future: Libraries, Learning and Information in the Next Decade* provided the opportunity to address this need as part of the action plan to deliver the *Framework* vision. The MLA created a development programme, Leading Modern Public Libraries, as a strategic intervention on a national scale to increase leadership capacity in public libraries. This article explains the context, genesis, development and evaluation of the programme. It goes on to look at the transformational leadership behaviours of public library leaders, based on the evidence from the *Transformational Leadership Questionnaire (TLQ)*™. Finally, it looks at the benefits of the programme, the lessons learned and possible ways to build on it in the future.

THE NEED FOR LEADERSHIP DEVELOPMENT IN PUBLIC LIBRARIES

The think tank Demos, in their research report prepared for the Museums, Libraries and Archives Council (MLA), *Towards a Strategy for Workforce Development* (2003)[1] found that *"leadership* was the most frequently cited development need identified in the stakeholder interviews". The report acknowledged that this was not a new concern—the University of Sheffield study, *Retain, Recruit, Lead: the public library workforce study* (2001)[2] had observed: "the general consensus was that there was a lack of leaders in the public library profession, and no identified way in which a new generation of leaders might be fostered. There was also agreement of the need to address not just leadership at the top of the organisation, but leadership 'from the side', and right throughout the organisation." Both the Demos and University of Sheffield reports have extensive bibliographies that track and demonstrate the need for leadership development.

FRAMEWORK FOR THE FUTURE

In February 2003 the Department for Media, Culture and Sport (DCMS) published *Framework for the Future: Libraries, Learning and Information in the Next Decade*[3]. This long term strategic vision for public libraries included objectives to: "equip staff with skills to deliver a clear vision for improving services" and "develop a new generation of library leaders fully trained in business management and marketing skills". One of the strategic objectives of the F4F Action Plan is to: "Build libraries' capacity to improve through better quality of leadership and workforce skills".

To achieve this the DCMS worked with the Museums, Libraries and Archives Council (MLA) and the Society of Chief Librarians (SCL) to create a brief for a leadership development programme that would be:

- A strategic intervention to deliver the vision of Framework for the Future
- National—reaching all library authorities in England
- Contextualised—a programme which draws on a range of leadership theories and practice but is customised to address the specific leadership issues facing public libraries today
- Multi-layered—reaching staff who are already heads of services; senior staff who have experience and responsibility for service-wide developments; and staff who are already showing the potential to be future leaders

A CONTEXTUALISED PROGRAMME SPECIFICALLY FOR LIBRARY STAFF

It was clear that the leadership gap was not a problem only for public libraries. Programmes to improve the quality of leadership in schools, health services, police, fire services, and other areas of public life were being developed at the same time. To ensure that any programme developed for libraries would be in line with current thinking and research in other parts of public service, research was undertaken on the work of numerous agencies, including: the Department for Education and Skills; the Centre for Excellence in Leadership; the

Leadership Development Commission and the Improvement and Development Agency for Local Government (I&DeA).

This research also aimed to address a key question: should there be a leadership programme specifically aimed at library services? In other words, should librarians become participants on the generic leadership programmes for local government; would they have access to such programmes; and was funding a library specific programme justified?

Library services constitute a small part of a local government authority's remit and resources. Although some authorities had nominated library service staff for wider development programmes or included them in their in-house programmes these development opportunity opportunities had been sporadic and usually limited to the head of service level.

The lack of investment in developing library managers as leaders had gone on for many years. The Society of Chief Librarians (SCL) had organised short master classes for aspiring leaders, filling a gap left by other institutions and agencies, but there was little evidence of other development opportunities.

West-Burnham and O'Sullivan[4], looking at leadership development in schools conclude:

> If leadership is to be developed in everyone then they have to be helped to process their personal and professional experiences through a value system and in response to others in order to evolve a growing understanding of what it means to be a leader.

Bush and Glover[5] conducted a review of the literature on leadership development. Among their conclusions, the following recommendations are relevant to the development of a library specific programme:

- Leadership development should be based firmly on participants' leadership contexts;
- Leadership development should also recognise the local and national contexts within which leaders operate;
- Aspiring leaders are in a different position in that they are generally unaware of the context in which they will operate when qualified. Aspiring

leaders need programmes rich in both leadership and management content and skills.

The conclusion was that a contextualised programme of leadership development for library managers could:

- ensure that library managers had access to leadership development opportunities (the evidence to date showed that relying on external opportunities had benefited only a few people);
- provide a learning environment where people who had been given few opportunities for development could feel safe and supported;
- focus the leadership development on the specific challenges of delivering the *Framework for the Future* vision.

The MLA, responsible to DCMS for the Framework Action Plan, concluded that a library-specific programme was justified if the participant cost was no greater than that for similar programmes in the public sector. On this basis, MLA commissioned FPM, a company with experience of contextualised leadership programmes in the public sector, to develop the programme.

DEVELOPMENT OF THE PROGRAMME

A Development Group was created to:

- identify the key areas of development for a public library leaders' programme;
- inform the content of the programme;
- ensure that the structure of the programme was appropriate and workable.

Through further consultation in the sector, a strong consensus emerged that the leadership programme should address the following aspects of leadership:

- Vision, mission and strategy;
- Making sense of the complex environment—internal and external;
- Leading in order to deliver outcomes;
- Creating an adaptive culture;
- Creativity, innovation and risk;

- Positioning the service with key stakeholders;
- Working in strategic partnerships;
- Personal, professional and service integrity.

To meet the key aims that the programme should be national and multi-layered the programme has three levels: Heads of Service; Senior Managers; and Future Leaders, and one place allocated at each of these levels to every public library authority in England. There are 149 library authorities in England, ranging in size from those serving populations of 1.3 million to those serving populations as small as 5,500.

The staffing establishments of the 149 authorities are correspondingly varied and it could be argued that the distribution of places should have reflected the size of the staffing establishment. This ideal position was not achievable with the funding available. It was more important to establish a truly national programme in which every service would have the opportunity to participate.

The Heads of Service and Senior Managers programmes had three residential modules of two days each and the Future Leaders programme had two residential modules of two days each.

Between October 2004 and July 2007, there were 663 participants on the programme:

- Heads of Service: 112 participants;
- Senior Managers: 257 participants;
- Future Leaders: 294 participants.

This is an unprecedented investment in leadership development in the library sector. It has met the objective to be a national programme (every service took part on at least one of the levels). As a strategic intervention, it has created a critical mass of people who have a shared understanding of the leadership challenges involved in delivering the *Framework for the Future* vision

The MLA met the costs of developing the programme. It provides grants of 85% towards the cost of each participant; 15% comes from individual library authority budgets.

TRANSFORMATIONAL LEADERSHIP BEHAVIOURS OF LIBRARY LEADERS

The *Transformational Leadership Questionnaire (TLQ)*™ was chosen as the diagnostic instrument for this programme. This instrument was developed from research conducted at the University of Leeds[6].

The *TLQ* assesses transformational leadership behaviours and qualities in relation to fourteen dimensions grouped into three key areas (Leading and developing others; Personal qualities; and Leading and developing the organisation):

- Leading and Developing others
    o Showing Genuine Concern
    o Enabling
    o Being Accessible
    o Encouraging Change
- Personal Qualities
    o Being Honest & Consistent
    o Acting with Integrity
    o Being Decisive
    o Inspiring Others
    o Resolving Complex Problems
- Leading and Developing the Organisation
    o Networking
    o Focusing Team Effort
    o Building Shared Vision
    o Supporting a Developmental Culture
    o Facilitating Change Sensitively

As a 360-degree instrument, the *TLQ* gathers observation from: self-ratings; ratings by direct reports (subordinates); ratings by boss and peers; ratings by others (some of whom may be external stakeholders). The ratings given are confidential and, apart from the self-rating, the instrument does not identify any individual's score. Participants who completed a TLQ received their personal, confidential report and an individual session with an accredited practitioner of the *TLQ*.

The scores of direct reports are highly significant in the *TLQ*. It was anticipated that participants on the Future Leaders programme would be younger professional librarians and, as such, were unlikely to have subordinates (many library services in England have staffing structures that separate professional responsibilities from operational management and professional librarians assume line management responsibilities at a later point in their career). It was, therefore, inadvisable to use the *TLQ* at this level of leadership; the instrument was only used for Heads of Service and Senior Managers programmes.

MAIN FINDINGS FROM THE TLQ FOR LIBRARY LEADERS

The following data analysis is based on 262 people who completed their *TLQ* between October 2003 and April 2005. Ninety-eight were Heads of Service and 164 were Senior Managers. Of these, 162 were female and 100 were male:

	Male	Female
Heads of Service	47	51
Senior Managers	53	111

Although there were very few differences in leadership behaviour between males and females, and between Heads of Service and Senior Managers, the *TLQ* data showed indications that:

- Heads of Service were more likely than Senior Managers to encourage change
- Females were more likely than males to inspire others

The initial research that led to the creation of the *TLQ*, and its subsequent use in the public sector, provided a large data set. This made it possible to compare library leaders with other leaders in local government, schools and health services.

Direct Report ratings

Rated by their Direct Reports (subordinates), library leaders scored significantly higher than local government staff on nine of the fourteen scales:

- Showing Genuine Concern
- Being Accessible
- Encouraging Change

- Being Honest and Consistent
- Acting with Integrity
- Networking
- Focusing Team Effort
- Building Shared Vision
- Supporting a Developmental Culture.

Boss/manager ratings

Rated by their bosses, library leaders scored lower than local government managers on three of the scales:

- Being Decisive
- Resolving Complex Problems
- Building Shared Vision.

Peer/colleague ratings

There was evidence that the peers of public library managers rated their colleagues more positively than did peers of local government managers on nine of the scales:

- Showing Genuine concern
- Being Accessible
- Encouraging Change
- Being Honest and Consistent
- Inspiring Others
- Networking
- Focusing Team Effort
- Building Shared Vision
- Facilitating Change Sensitively.

Ratings by others

'Others' (people who are internal to or external to the library services but not in the direct management relationships to the Individual) rated library leaders as stronger than their local government counterparts on one scale: Networking

Self ratings

Library leaders consistently under-rated themselves compared to their counterparts in local government, most significantly on three scales:

- Being Decisive
- Resolving Complex Problems
- Building Shared Vision.

The *TLQ* reports indicate that many library managers underestimate their strengths in leading others. This is unusual as "one of the most consistently stated findings from 360 degree feedback studies is that managers' self-ratings are inflated".[7]

It is not clear what lies behind the lower self-ratings in library leaders. This would be an interesting study in itself. The low self-rating may be due to modesty or diffidence and could indicate that library leaders are prone to under-value themselves.

Although modesty can be an attractive character trait it can, as Kets de Vries[8] has observed, create leadership problems. It can be a defensive mechanism against failure, resulting in self-limiting ambition and lack of decisiveness. The low self-value could also relate to the development area identified from Boss ratings: Being Decisive.

Interestingly, one of the most uncomfortable concepts on the programme for participants relates to power. Participants often begin with negative connotations of power, seeing it only in coercive terms and unaware of the varied sources of power available to them. Although they are more comfortable with the idea of power in relation to their library services (rather than themselves), there is an emerging hypothesis that the behaviours connected to low self-rating could affect the status of the library service in the wider organisation.

The *TLQ* offers a rare opportunity for managers to get feedback from the people around them. For some there were wide differences between how they see themselves and how others see them. However, even for those who found this an uncomfortable experience the *TLQ* has enabled them to identify actions to improve their effectiveness as leaders. It is not easy to make such changes; it takes time to practice and embed them in individual behaviours and the organisational culture.

EVALUATION

There are three main sources for the evaluation of the programme:

- FPM, the company responsible for creating and delivering the programme, asked for participant feedback at all stages.
- The Tavistock Institute's report *Evaluation of the Framework for the Future Action Plan 2003–2006* covered all aspects of the Action Plan, not just the leadership development strand.
- Information Management Associates in conjunction with the Centre for the Public Library in Society, University of Sheffield, were commissioned by MLA to conduct the in-depth independent evaluation of Leading Modern Public Libraries

Participant feedback

Participants gave immediate feedback at the end of each module. Over ninety nine percent of participants were satisfied with the experience, with the majority finding the programmes to be 'excellent' or 'very good'—one participant said that 'it's as good as it gets!' An interesting phenomenon occurred in the later stages of the rollout when people came to the first module having heard very positive reports from former participants. The first reactions of the new participants were that the programme was slow and not as 'transforming' as they expected. In most cases, this reaction changed as the programme progressed and later ratings exceeded those by earlier cohorts.

These immediate responses are valuable but the decisive test of success must lie in the longer-term impact of the programme. In many ways, it is too early to apply this test. However, FPM commissioned an external consultant to conduct a series of telephone interviews with a sample of participants from the pilot programmes. This aimed to capture participants' reflections on the programme six months after the end of the course and to explore what, if any, longer term impacts and benefits they perceived.[9]

The main points from this pilot follow-up included:

- Respondents were unanimous in praising the programme. Even those who described themselves as "old cynics" felt the programme overall was of value at the time and in a continuing way both for themselves and for other staff from their service.

- One very experienced Head of Service described the effect on staff from their service who participated on the Senior Manager and Future Leader programmes as "staggering".

- Most participants on the programme referred to working now with greater focus and with a clearer purpose. "Increased motivation" and "confidence" were frequently mentioned.

- Within the Heads of Service group, there was a wide range of experience. Whilst it might be anticipated that new Heads stood most to gain (and there was certainly very enthusiastic feedback from newer heads of service) the more experienced Heads also reported insights from the programme which have impacted on the way in which they now manage their service and communicate with staff.

- Heads of Service are trying to move the service on from a 'dependency' culture by creating opportunities for staff to be more involved in contributing to decision making and taking on greater responsibility for particular projects. The need to create leaders at all levels was a message which has been taken on board and is, by report, being acted upon.

- Where an authority had a participant on each of the three levels of the programme there were clearly added benefits. The combined energy, enthusiasm and learning of more than one participant provided a launch pad for new developments in service planning and delivery. However, this needed a clear lead from Heads of Service to ensure that participants at other levels in their service were able to contribute in a new way to service development and to build on their experience on the programme. Where this did not happen, staff enthusiasm had waned and they struggled, unsupported, to apply new learning—or gave up.

- Many participants from the Senior Managers programme felt more confident about themselves. For some this led to promotion to more senior jobs or even Heads of Service positions, and one took promotion outside libraries. Others saw it as a way to renew their commitment and sense of purpose in their current job and a chance to work in new ways.

- Participants on the Future Leaders pilot programme found that the course gave them the confidence to consider their own personal development. Some went on to higher-level jobs. Others felt invested in by their service and have appreciated that. This has had a positive impact on their morale at work.

- The need to strengthen communications was recognised and has been acted on by many participants.

- Some responders have made conscious efforts to create reflective space for themselves. Others are still struggling with this, whilst recognising its value.

- Many experienced a 'recharging of batteries' which they have been able to maintain six months on.

The picture of longer-term benefits that emerges from this small sample of early participants is encouraging. The residential aspect of the programme provides a rare opportunity for people to have time and space to reflect. When participants take advantage of this, there is an immediate benefit—the 'recharging'—which can easily evaporate on return to the workplace. Some groups have recognised the value of making time for their development and the benefits of doing this with other people who have shared the experience of the programme. These groups have arranged further meetings for themselves—one Heads of Service group has continued to meet every four months.

The need to refresh or top-up is an important message in the programme. A six-day programme cannot meet all the development needs. It can, and does, provide an opportunity to reassess values, purpose and direction.

Evaluation of Framework for the Future

The Tavistock Institute report on the *Evaluation of the Framework for the Future Action Plan 2003–2006*[10] showed that the Leading Modern Public Libraries Programme has been among the most successful initiatives taken in the Framework Action Plan and has had a significant effect on the changes and development needed to deliver the vision of Framework for the Future. The following points in the report support this:

> Framework peer review and leadership training activities have demonstrated both the value of increasing management capacity and how much it is needed. (p.5);
>
> 87% of respondents to a national survey reported that Framework leadership training had made a strong or very strong contribution to developing management in their library service. (p.5);
>
> Almost all survey respondents reported that Framework leadership training had made a very positive contribution to helping develop management in their library. No respondents reported Framework leadership training had not made a contribution to helping develop management in their library service (p.16).

The report states that "the greatest impact of Framework is through the existence of the Framework vision itself, it is this public vision which has given direction, made sense of circumstances, and created a new legitimacy for individual library service change and development" (p.4). There is no doubt that the *Framework* vision gave focus and purpose to the leadership programme.

The Tavistock Institute report concluded that the considerable evidence of the beneficial impact of Leading Modern Public Libraries makes a strong case for maintaining peer review and leadership development as a key element of the action plan. The Tavistock study looked at ways to build on the leadership programme. These are addressed in the section on *Building on the programme* below.

Evaluation of Leading Modern Public Libraries (LMPL)

The *Evaluation of Leading Modern Public Libraries*[11] report by Information Management Associates with the Centre for the Public Library and Information in Society, University of Sheffield identifies many positive aspects of the programme:

> The programme contributed directly to improving the quality of leadership skills of participants and indirectly to enhancing workforce skills; equipped participants with an awareness of how to deliver a

clear vision for improving services, and provided participants with some new business management and marketing skills (depending upon what other recent development opportunities they had experienced).

On the basis of a wide range of feedback from participants, we conclude that anyone who joined the LMPL programme with a readiness to develop their leadership capacity and skills was given ample opportunity, as well as support in doing so.

The LMPL programme was outstandingly successful in providing opportunities for participants to learn and develop alongside colleagues from other authorities who share similar levels of responsibility. Opportunities were provided for participants to formulate action plans for their self-development as leaders.

In terms of what the programme set out to give participants, almost all respondents were able to work on their skills and capacity to deliver transformational change for their library service, although some Future Leaders had little or no chance to put these lessons into practice.

This programme has clearly made a substantial contribution to meeting the aims of the Framework for the Future and we are sure that the future impact can be even stronger if our suggestions for addressing specific limitations in the current programme are addressed.

The evaluation study identifies concerns and recommendations for improvement. Many of these, as the evaluation acknowledges, were addressed by MLA as they emerged. The most significant concerns raised by the evaluation related to the Future Leaders programme. In summary these were:

- The selection of participants by their managers;
- The absence of the TLQ in the Future Leaders programme;
- The lack of opportunities to put the learning into practice.

Even before the evaluation study was complete, MLA commissioned FPM to review and revise the Future Leaders programme. The new version has introduced selection guidance for authorities in choosing their participants. This requires participants to submit an application stating their learning and development aims and how they will use these to benefit their services. At the same time their managers are required to say how they will support the participant through the programme and make opportunities for them to apply the learning in the workplace. A workplace learning element has been added to the programme as inter-module activity.

As stated in the *TLQ* sections above, this instrument would not be suitable for all Future Leader participants. The Myers Briggs Type Indicator™ has been introduced to the new Future Leaders programme. The response from participants to date has been very enthusiastic.

BUILDING ON THE PROGRAMME

Everyone involved in the management and evaluation of the programme is aware of the danger that the benefits could evaporate quickly if there is no strategy for sustainability.

The *Framework for the Future Action Plan 2006–08* includes continuing support from MLA for the programme. The programme itself has achieved its goals and it is likely that any new support from MLA will look at different interventions to address capacity building issues.

There is evidence that individuals and groups are taking action to build on the experience of the programme. There is no documentation of these initiatives and it is difficult to say how much activity there is in these informal developments.

The Tavistock Institute evaluation survey asked whether the impact of leadership training could be enhanced by follow-on activities. Seventy six percent of respondents indicated that the impact of leadership training could be enhanced and indicated their support for these specific follow-on activities:

- 57% supported mentoring;
- 51% supported action learning sets;
- 48% supported involvement in steering groups at regional or national level;
- 44% supported master classes on a specific service;
- 37% supported one-to-one coaching.

The MLA and other agencies concerned with the continuing development of librarians as leaders, such as the Chartered Institute for Library and Information Professionals (CILIP), can apply this useful feedback in planning the next steps.

Two action learning sets, one for Senior Managers and one for Future Leaders, have been funded through the government's new Cultural Leadership Programme (CLP) (www.culturalleadership.org.uk.). The intention is that these, and other learning networks supported by the CLP, will provide evidence of the benefits of action learning and encourage organisations and individuals to set up groups.

CONCLUSIONS

The Leading Modern Public Libraries programme aimed to be a strategic intervention to help deliver the vision of *Framework for the Future*. The independent evaluations of the programme testify that it has been successful in this. Every library authority in England participated in the programme; it has achieved its aim to be a national programme.

Contextualising the programme for public library services has been justified by the participant feedback; numerous quotations point to the benefits of feeling part of a larger movement with a clear vision, refreshing the sense of purpose and importance of library services at a time of great change and the opportunity to explore leadership concepts in a supportive but challenging environment.

Structuring the programme to meet the needs of library managers at different levels has created a critical mass of people with a shared understanding of the leadership challenges facing libraries today. Over 660 key library staff have a foundation on which to build their development. The ongoing development could take the form of action learning and coaching as well as individual reflective practice. The responsibility for that continuing development lies with the individuals and their authorities.

There is little doubt that the success of the programme is due to the vision of *Framework* itself. The vision gave the Leading Modern Public Libraries programme a clear and uniting purpose. The programme has made a major contribution to making the vision a reality.

REFERENCES

[1] Demos Towards a Strategy for Workforce Development, a research and discussion report prepared for Resource. Demos, March 2003, 19. [Online document]. URL www.mla.gov.uk

[2] Usherwood, B., Proctor, R., Bower, G., Coe C., Cooper, J. & Stevens, T. Recruit, Retain and Lead: The Public Library Workforce Study. Resource: the Council for Museums, Libraries and Archives 2001, 91. [nline document]. URL www.mla.gov.uk

[3] Department for Culture, Media and Sport. Framework for the Future: Information, Learning and Information in the Next Decade; Department for Culture, Media and Sport; 2003 [Online document] URL www.mla.gov.uk

[4] West-Burnham, J. & O'Sullivan, F. *Leadership and professional development in schools*, London: Financial Times Prentice Hall, 1998, p24.

[5] Bush, T. & Glover, D. *Leadership development: evidence and beliefs*. National College for School Leadership, 2004.

[6] Alimo-Metcalfe, B. & Alban-Metcalfe, R.J. The development of a new Transformational Leadership Questionnaire. *Journal of Occupational and Organisational Psychology* 2001, **74**, 1–27.

[7] Alimo-Metcalfe, B. 360 degree feedback and leadership development. *International Journal of Selection and Assessment* 1998, 6(1), 35–44.

[8] Kets de Vries, M.F.R. The Dangers of feeling like a fake. *Harvard Business Review*. September, 2005.

[9] Forrest, T. Making a Difference. *Public Library Journal*, 2006. **21**(2).

[10] Kelleher, J., Ramsden, C., Sullivan, F., & Sommerlad, L. Evaluation of the Framework for the Future Action Plan 2003–06. London: Museums, Libraries and Archives Council, 2007 [Online document] URL www.mla.gov.uk

[11] Streatfield, D., Wilson, K., Corrall, S. & Usherwood, B: Evaluation of Leading Modern Public Libraries. London: Museums, Libraries and Archives Council, 2007, p57 [Online document] URL www.mla.gov.uk

EFFORTS IN LEADERSHIP AND SUCCESSION PLANNING, LARGE AND SMALL

Mary L. Chute
Deputy Director for Libraries
Institute of Museum and Library Services
Washington, DC, USA
mchute@imls.gov

Abstract

Recruiting future library leaders and preparing them for leadership positions in the field of librarianship by providing them with the proper education and training has become a critical issue for the profession. This article describes six projects supported by the United States' Institute of Museum and Library Services that address this need. The projects discussed all foster leadership development through efforts in succession planning and mentoring. Key words: development, growth, institutional capacity, transferable competencies.

INTRODUCTION

As the library and information professions look to what is being predicted as a looming shortage of qualified personnel, it is not merely a case of supply and demand and pure numbers. The professional development crisis we are facing is not simply about the quantity of professional and preprofessional or paraprofessional staff who are retiring from our libraries and cultural heritage institutions because of age or alternative opportunities. This predicament is deeply rooted in quality, qualifications, and experience. It is about who is moving on and about recognizing what exactly is the void that is being created.

On closer inspection, it is not difficult to discern that the field is losing individuals with years of experience, tenure, and seniority. We will be losing many members of the group that makes up the community of our current leaders. They possess skill sets, experience, and networks that have taken years to construct. We face a challenge not only to recruit our next generation of library personnel, but to facilitate the development of the new corps of leaders for our institutions in particular, and the field in general.

For those of us engaged in recruitment, education, and capacity building in our institutions, we need to cultivate appropriate means to facilitate the growth and augmentation of the knowledge, skills, and abilities of our future leaders. And we cannot simply rely on existing curricula. We should utilize the rich experience and knowledge base of our contemporary leaders. The field as a whole benefits if we find a way to transfer the legacy knowledge from our current experts to their future successors. Methods that foster that knowledge transfer, such as mentoring and action learning, which entail taking learned skills back to the workplace and applying them to different circumstances, are increasing in popularity. Learning environments that create a forum for cross-organization conversations are being developed.

THE PROBLEM

Today's library directors and administrators face major dilemmas in leadership and succession planning. Controversial topics dealing with collection management, collection development and preservation, electronic access, censorship, and intellectual property, among others, are shifting the field and creating a demand for knowledgeable and experienced library and information science leaders in many specialty areas. Whether prompted by the expanding definition of what it means to be a leader in librarianship in today's knowledge society, by competition from private sector information technology entities for the brightest and the best, or simply by the need to fill the vacancies that will be created by the impending retirements of today's experienced workforce, the need for leadership planning and development is clear. It is essential that we prepare and empower our successors to continue to move the fields of library and information science forward. Discussions on the topic span library and information science schools and professional organizations and associations around the globe.

The creation of this new group is not as straightforward as simply selecting the top tier of middle managers and promoting them. Leadership is recognized as a combination of what may be natural strengths, such as an ability to relate and communicate, and learned skill sets, such as thinking strategically, building consensus, and mobilizing around a vision. But these specific skills and talents also can be seen as an evolving or iterative job description. What was crucial twenty years ago may be less so now. And likewise, some of today's more critical qualifications were not considered necessary then. This is not merely with regard to changing technologies, but with regard to twenty-first-century skills needed for running our libraries as businesses, building collaborations, sharing resources, and placing libraries as central partners in community. Although these timely administrative and management techniques may not have been taught in library school, they have been acquired by current directors, administrators, managers, and trustees through years of creative problem solving and team building.

Building capacity in the nation's libraries and museums is one of the primary purposes of the United States' Institute of Museum and Library Services (IMLS). IMLS recognizes recruiting and educating the next generation as a key element and, since 2003, has offered a major library grant program with that precise focus. IMLS also acknowledges leadership and succession planning for the 'leaders' of this next generation as central to the development of that capacity.

Over the past five years, through its partnership activities as well as its *National Leadership Grant (NLG)* and *Librarians for the 21st Century (L21)* initiatives, IMLS has supported a number of programs and projects designed to educate, equip and recruit the next generation of librarians and leaders. The most successful initiatives contribute to the definition of leadership, clearly delineate effective learning processes, and address sustainability and the ability to be replicated.

To date, no widely accepted single list exists describing what universal traits constitute an ideal leader in the library arena. Noting that libraries and their communities of use come in many shapes and sizes, the components vary. Leadership comprises a skill set and is not merely bestowed with a title; so also do the status and titles of the staff members who may be considered 'leaders', vary. However, many models tend to include certain standard components, such as an understanding of the principles of librarianship; practical experience; demonstrated critical decision-making skills; the ability to creatively envision and innovate; and to communicate effectively and to motivate.

The learning/training processes and tactics designed to equip evolving leaders with this litany of traits include such strategies as providing opportunities for networking; for mentoring; and for engagement in interactive learning scenarios including on-the-job projects, continuing education opportunities, and internships. Ideally, the results tend not to be institution- and role-specific, but fluid, adaptable and transferable.

In the section that follows, six highly successful IMLS-supported projects are described to illustrate some of the core qualities being promoted in current leadership learning opportunities in the United States; they highlight some of the frequently used techniques being employed to foster leadership development. Two of the projects are national-level initiatives in which IMLS is a primary partner. The earliest iterations of two other sample projects described here arose from the NLG program, a highly competitive peer-reviewed grant program that is designed to fund innovative projects that produce national impact by changing the way of doing business, or by providing models that can be replicated elsewhere. Until 2003, one of the elements within the program focused on continuing education and curriculum development. Since 2003 IMLS has implemented a new large-scale initiative focused on recruiting and educating librarians for the twenty-first century, the L21 program. Once this new program was established, continuing education and curriculum development transitioned there. The final two examples cited in this article come from the L21 program.

THE SAMPLE PROJECTS

Urban Libraries Council Executive Leadership Institute (NLG 2001, L21 2005)

IMLS first funded this project in 2001 under the NLG program. The Urban Libraries Council Executive Leadership Institute (ELI) was developed in response to the need to train new leaders in urban public librarianship as a wave of retirements opened new leadership positions, and as institutional reinvention became necessary because of changing community demographics, needs, and technological advances. Each participating library identified a major project that provided a learning lab for applying concepts to complex local situations. The 2005 L21 project continued the success of the 2001 project. Cultural, ethnic, and age diversity became a key element in this project, as did developing a national cohort of new leaders. <http://www.urbanlibraries.org/showcase/eli.html>

Urban Libraries Council Librarians for America's Neighborhoods (L21 2003, 2005)

In 2003, IMLS awarded the Urban Libraries Council (ULC) a grant for its Librarians for America's Neighborhoods (LAN) project. This grant enabled the ULC and its twelve major metropolitan partners from around the United States to recruit eighty students to thirty different schools of library and information science. 'Big picture' seminars were held by partner libraries to introduce students to major facets of librarianship in large metropolitan areas. A national conference was held so that students could meet each other and learn about professional issues of particular concern to urban public librarians. This concept built on the cohort model that had been developed in the original ELI project previously described.

The 2005 project continued the success of the 2003 project, expanding it to twenty-three partner libraries recruiting 115 scholars. Both phases of this initiative placed a strong focus on recruitment from the community in a concerted effort not only to 'grow their own' community librarians, but also to provide diversity. The continuing goal is to have the library staff reflect the communities they serve, promoting stability and responsiveness to community needs. <http://www.urbanlibraries.org/ulcscholars2.html>

Western Council Continuum of Library Education Project (NLG 2003)

The two projects previously described focus on meeting the changing needs of libraries and library users in major urban areas. The Western Council of State Libraries (WESTCO), made up of twenty-one state library agencies in the western United States, addressed the need for trained library professionals in rural and underserved communities by developing a model partnership for a library education continuum involving state libraries, regional library cooperatives, and community colleges and universities including, but not limited to, schools of library and information science.

Goals of the project include collaborating to enhance learning opportunities for library practitioners; formal and informal library education for library practitioners leading to certification or credit; and creating an infrastructure to support multi-state recruitment and retention based on training efforts leading to a regional certification that can be sustained and is transferable to any other partnering state. <http://www.westernco.org/continuum/index.html>

Doctoral Program in Managerial Leadership in the Information Professions (L21 2005)

Simmons College in Boston, Massachusetts, created a flexible, innovative PhD program in managerial leadership that nurtures and strengthens the intellectual and interpersonal assets of students as middle- and senior-level working managers, and that actively involves leading practitioners in shaping the educational experience.

The focus of the degree is on the knowledge, skills, competencies, and personal traits applicable to leadership in libraries and other information intensive enterprises.
<http://www.simmons.edu/gslis/academics/programs/doctoral/phdmanagerial.shtml>

Sustaining State Library Agencies in the 21st Century (IMLS partnership 2006, 2007)

The Chief Officers of State Library Agencies (COSLA) funded and produced this executive leadership institute, with input from IMLS staff in the planning and presentation of the program. The partnership and relationships that exist between IMLS and state library agencies—individually and as a group through COSLA—is the one common bond that exists among the diversified programs found in the fifty state library agencies.

Presenters at this institute included professors of library and information science as well as of political science and public affairs, current and former state librarians, current and former legislators, the director of a state historical society, a public relations professional, a lobbyist, the executive director of a state library association, and the executive director of the American Library Association (ALA).

The Big Read (IMLS partnership 2006, 2007)

The Big Read is an initiative started by the United States' National Endowment for the Arts (NEA), designed to restore reading to the center of American culture. A 2004 study by NEA found that not only is literary reading in America declining rapidly among all groups, but that the rate of decline has accelerated especially among the young. The desired outcomes of this collaboration with NEA include not only the involvement of individuals in literary reading and the expansion of the role of the library in active community engagement, but also the development of partnering and collaborative skills on the part of the librarians themselves.

The Big Read aims to address this crisis squarely and effectively. It provides the opportunity for citizens within a single community to read and discuss a single book collectively. The initiative includes a grant program supporting innovative reading programs in selected cities and towns, extensive resources for discussing classic literature, an ambitious national publicity campaign, and an extensive Web site providing comprehensive information on authors and their works. <http://www.neabigread.org/>

STRATEGIES FOR DEVELOPMENT

Definition of competencies

When engaging in any strategic development effort, it is important to know where one is heading in order to determine the most effective means of attaining the desired end. Two of the projects discussed here make notable achievements in defining that goal by addressing these two questions: How do we define a 'leader'? What are the traits and competencies that we look for in someone who will be fulfilling a leadership position? Although they approach these questions from very different angles—one from academia and the other from the sector of rural librarianship—both the Simmons doctoral program and the WESTCO Continuum of Library Education Project answer the questions. Given the disparity in environments, one might anticipate some significant variations in key factors. Interestingly, the core concepts are strikingly similar, even if on a practical level differences in focus do exist.

The WESTCO initiative refers to a survey that the state data coordinators conducted in 2002, in which it was determined that individuals who lack formal library training manage 66 percent of public libraries in the western states.[1] This is of concern, not only for the libraries themselves, but for the quality of dependable information services available to the general population in those states. Some of the anticipated results/benefits to the library community and their users include:

- identifying existing courses and workshops that can be shared in the WESTCO region to eliminate duplication;
- expanding the educational opportunities for all states;
- systematically improving the core skill sets of library practitioners through an organized and recognized regional certification program; and

- providing a recruitment tool for new professionals.

The WESTCO project identifies nine areas of competency that, when successfully completed, lead to a 'Practitioner Certificate'. These areas of competency include:

foundation skills;

professional philosophy;

public service;

workplace competencies;

library administration;

reader's advisory service;

youth services;

systems and information technology competencies; and

collection management and technical services.

The section on foundations for the Practitioner Certificate highlights 'Leadership' as a major element, listing demonstrable skills such as developing a vision for library services, building effective relationships, managing conflict, communicating effectively, promoting active use of library services by all community members, and making decisions based on professional standards.

Some of the goals of the Simmons College PhD program are: to prepare students for careers as change agents and leaders in managing libraries and other information-related organizations in an environment of globalization and convergence of disciplines; to engender in students an ability to engage in critical thinking and problem solving; to provide students with a conceptual understanding of organizations and behavior within them; and to help students develop competencies in interpersonal and communication skills, leadership, and facilitation. Given the academic setting anticipated for these doctoral students, significant emphasis is placed on the role of research.

The Simmons' 'Information Professions Leadership' model proposes competencies in three arenas: accomplishment, people, and transformation.[2]

Under the heading 'Accomplishment' fall primary competencies such as communication skills, organizational awareness, and knowledge of the library science field, along with secondary competencies like collaboration, initiative, and change leadership. Under the heading 'People', the primary competencies include professionalism and team leadership, with secondary competencies that include relationship building. Achievement orientation, analytical thinking, and problem solving are the primary competencies under the heading 'Transformation', together with the secondary competencies of community and strategic orientation and innovative thinking.

Despite the differing environments in which these lists of competencies evolved, there is a striking number of similarities. Both programs have recognized a need for a number of core traits: knowledge, skills, and abilities—knowledge of the profession or professional philosophy, and understanding of the skills needed to deliver services; innovation or innovative thinking; communication skills; effective relationship building with staff and community, or team leadership and collaboration; and finally, a focus on community-driven service development.

Model programs

For the LAN program, one of the major goals of the project is to bridge the gap between theories of library and information science and the practical realities of urban public librarianship, thus creating real models of practice. The 'big picture' sessions referred to above are conducted as local programming intended to expand and support student understanding of the context of the work of public libraries today. These sessions link the professional principles of librarianship to what it means to actually work in and manage a library on a day-to-day basis. Topics range from creating and managing budgets and strategic planning and efficiency to library design and architecture, services to culturally diverse communities, and intellectual freedom and the library.

Recruiting students from the local communities/neighborhoods generally, and more specifically from the cultural and ethnic populations represented in the geographic community, also is a major thrust of the LAN program. The added benefit is that these new librarians also provide career models for subsequent generations.

Convening nationally brings together all students in the project, from major cities across the United States. Speakers and panels make presentations regarding current issues and trends. Opportunities are provided for these growing professionals to share with each other. Their creativity and inventiveness spark one another, and a new network of emerging professionals is being developed on a national scale.

In the Big Read national partnership, each selected community grant program lasts approximately one month and includes a kick-off event to launch the program locally, ideally attended by the mayor and other local luminaries. Major events—panel discussions, author readings, book discussions—devoted specifically to the book selected, are staged in diverse locations and aimed at a wide range of audiences. Additional events that use the book as a point of departure, such as film screenings and theatrical readings, are often produced.

The individual projects themselves in many cases are replicable models, though ideally each one takes on its own personality reflective of its unique community. In addition, the overall Big Read initiative—with its high-quality teachers' guides, readers' guides, and audio guides, along with outstanding lectures and interviews combined with a national publicity campaign—provide the framework for hundreds of projects well beyond the life of the limited number of community grants, and should have a lasting legacy.

In terms of developing leadership skills in the library workforce, in the course of putting together these community-wide projects, in which the library must be the lead entity or a critical partner, library personnel will be positioned to take on leadership roles in building community collaborations. Not only do both the Simmons and WESTCO definitions cite collaboration as being a key trait in today's library leaders but, from its inception ten years ago IMLS, as a grant maker, has always placed a competitive value on projects that include real partnership and collaboration. The grant monies and high-quality materials of the Big Read help position the local library to add value to these community-wide efforts and to set the stage for future partnering opportunities.

The format developed for the COSLA executive leadership institute is already serving as a model. It has been heralded by ALA and others as a national model for leadership training. State archivists are looking at creating a similar program for their profession.

The COSLA institute was a five-day symposium for thirty participants, ranging from very new employees in leadership roles at state library agencies to state librarians who have held their positions for more than two years. The format was a combination of presentations, case studies, panels, and discussions. The mixture of backgrounds and experiences made the discussion segments at least as rich as the formal presentations.

COSLA plans to repeat this institute in 2007 for another thirty participants. The need for recurrence will be reassessed periodically.

Mentorship

The ELI project goals include creating a national leadership track in public librarianship, providing opportunities for upcoming leaders to acquire new skills and perspectives essential to leadership; and creating an effective model of action learning within the library profession. These goals were accomplished by developing library teams that consisted of a sponsor and a new leader or "fellow" supported by professional coaches. Over the course of fifteen months, each ELI program brought together the entire group of ELI fellows for three multi-day sessions. The middle session was attended only by the fellows and coaches; the first and last sessions also included the sponsors.

In the individual programs, an actual initiative or area of library service was assigned to a fellow to be developed under his or her direction. A critical element for success was for the fellow to have available a support/learning network. This mentorship took two forms: professional in the on-the-job role of the sponsor, and personal in the counseling resource of the executive coaches.

The LAN and COSLA projects, highlighted in more detail in other sections of this article, also include noteworthy mentoring components. Inherent in the LAN project is a structure that provides the students with mentoring resources on the job; mentorship is the whole concept behind the COSLA project, where the more experienced leadership has proactively taken the initiative to foster the development of its successors. An informal mentoring network is also established in addition to the comprehensive curriculum that is designed with many opportunities for learning from the experiences of past and current leaders. This works in all directions as some evolving leaders provide guidance in communicating with and meeting the needs of changing communities and technologies.

Transferability

At the heart of the ELI experience is the concept of 'action-learning', where the learner has the opportunity to internalize the lessons and grow in ways that are memorable and develop behavior in more ways than by lectures or even role play exercises. This action-learning model is intended to help the leader grow, build skill sets, and modify behaviors that will be transferable to other circumstances and situations. Part of the rationale behind the selection of this method is recognition of the dynamic change environment in which the library workforce finds itself. In addition to frequent, daily, adaptations in technology, there are also major shifts in community demographics. Equipping these evolving leaders with the ability to respond flexibly and adapt to change also equips them to be mobile. In this way a transferable learning model was created, and a corps of emerging leaders is being developed in a way that positions them to take their strengths and abilities along as they take advantage of new opportunities.

A further noteworthy element in this highly successful program, and in most of the others, is the strengthening and reinforcement found through simultaneously developing an emerging network of powerful new voices. This cohort augurs well for the future of the information professions with regard to the wave of vacancy and succession that looms ahead in the next decade.

In the WESTCO program, new training opportunities are accessible to library workers in remote rural areas as well as urban centers. Like ELI, this program concentrates on developing current library directors and managers. In the western states, many of these library workers have little or no formal education or training (i.e., MLS degrees) where they live and work. Their demonstrated interest in library work makes them a prime group from which to recruit. Focusing on this pool of current 'local' employees also helps to bring this more diverse group into the education pipeline.

By providing a mutually accepted core set of standards, the WESTCO project fosters an environment that promotes the creation and retention of professionals in locales not served previously by trained librarians. It also provides for a standard of recognized professionalism within the context of mobility from state to state.

The COSLA institute also focuses on fresh talent, in the form of new or prospective leaders in state libraries. Topics covered include leadership in state government; an historical perspective of state libraries; national trends in state government; the legislative process; collaboration and coalition building; and best practices and survival skills. These subjects are universally pertinent despite minor differences in administration from state to state.

Because there is no specific curriculum in library and information schools for this unique type of library, COSLA has taken on the task of creating a core curriculum that meets many of the special needs of these leaders. There is a deliberate effort to shape transferable knowledge and skill sets, recognizing that the representatives sent by each state may well move on to other states.

BUILDING LEADERSHIP CAPACITY

In addition to the planned accomplishments, targets, and objectives of each of the six projects mentioned above, and numerous others, there are several informally observable trends within this overall initiative to develop the next generation of leaders. In some cases we note the power of selection itself: the mere act of designating individuals as potential leaders seems to empower and enhance their self image, prompting them to step forward, be creative, and take action. In some instances there is an additional transference of skills that builds capacity in a particular institution beyond the education and training of a single individual or two. New strategies and techniques are brought back to the home institution through the newly learned behaviors of the trainee(s), and are subsequently demonstrated, practiced, and adopted by others in that institution. As an added bonus, the same faces appear in multiple places. There is enough overlap in a number of these projects not just for individual growth in leadership skills and behaviors to be visible, but for the advancement of a cohort of budding leaders. They are learning from their predecessors and also from each other and, in the expansion and strengthening of their interrelationships, they are reinforcing each others' learning and development.

Recruiting future library leaders and preparing them for leadership positions in the field of librarianship by providing them with the proper education and training has become a critical issue for the profession. Numerous programs and initiatives are addressing the issue from a wide variety of approaches. The six projects described here are just a sampling of the many initiatives supported by one federal agency, the United States' Institute of Museum and Library

Services. In conducting these projects, the successful organizations are investing in their futures. Many libraries are nevertheless small entities, and each organization does not necessarily have the resources to create its own learning program or to recruit a highly qualified leader from outside.

As noted above, IMLS has a strong focus on building institutional capacity. The Institute's desire to effect positive change is not just through the immediate grantees, but also through the national and even international impact of these projects, by providing rich, adaptable resources to the broader field. The six projects discussed all foster leadership development through efforts in succession planning, mentoring, and network development. Several of them help define the necessary traits for a successful library leader in the twenty-first century; several foster these traits as transferable competencies and promote methods of development and learning; and several focus on positioning the evolving leader for success.

The traits and competencies highlighted in this article have been demonstrated to be somewhat universal, adaptable, and transferable from one environment in the United States to the next—urban, rural, and even academic. They are skills and strengths that can support an individual in leading his or her institution forward from any position, be it director, branch or section manager, or simply the creative and motivated staff member.

The question I would pose is whether these same core competencies and strategies are 'universal' enough to also have international value. Have other core values and skills and techniques been developed elsewhere that surpass these in their ability to position emerging leaders to meet the needs of their evolving communities more effectively? And in either case, how do we best share the knowledge to build the capacity of all of our institutions so that each organization, each nation, each section in the field need not invent its own approach from the beginning to best meet the needs of its users?

The views expressed in this article do not necessarily reflect the views of the U.S. Institute of Museum and Library Services or the U.S. Government.

REFERENCES

[1] State Data Coordinators of State Library Agencies, correspondence with Jan Elliott, November 2002.

[2] Hernon, P., Schwartz, C. & Anderson, C. Managerial leadership as an area of doctoral study. In: Hernon, P. & Rossiter, N. (eds.). *Making a difference: Leadership and academic libraries.* Westport: Libraries Unlimited; 2007; 229–250.

THE LEADERSHIP AND MANAGEMENT DEVELOPMENT PROGRAMME IN THE FRENCH NATIONAL LIBRARY

Mr Michel Netzer
Head of the Continuing Professional Development Service
at the French National Library,
Bibliothèque nationale de France.
michel.netzer@bnf.fr

Abstract

The French National Library went through a fundamental change when President François Mitterrand decided to create a library of "an entirely new kind" (a library opened to a wide public, with digitized collections). To face this challenge, it was necessary to reinforce and motivate the management of the library. This paper presents the leadership and management development programme put in place to that end in the French National Library, which consists of training actions, team coaching services, individual coaching and the creation of a "mission for leadership development".

The French National Library, an institution several centuries old, whose principal mission is to preserve, catalogue and communicate to the public all the documents published, printed or distributed in France, went through a fundamental change following the decision of President François Mitterrand to create a library "of an entirely new kind", opened to a wide public and offering digitized collections. With the inauguration of the François-Mitterrand Library, in 1996, staff more than doubled. New missions, new site, new personnel: to take up such a challenge, it was necessary to reinforce management staff skills and to strengthen their cohesion and involvement in the new projects, ensuring the development of the Library.

1. Strategic plan and business intelligence system

The French National Library counts approximately 2.700 employees today (2.475 "Worked Full-time Equivalent"). Placed under the authority of a Chief Executive Officer ("président") assisted by an Executive Director ("directeur général"), the management staff comprises:

- Eight executive managers (each in charge of a "directorate" or a "delegation") assisted by ten assistant executive managers, as well as 32 middle managers (each in charge of a "department"), assisted by 23 assistant departmental directors;
- Eighty-one first-line managers (in charge of a "service");

that is to say altogether 156 managers. To these must be added 100 people constituting the next level of management ("chefs de bureau"—a "bureau" is a unit smaller than a "service"—and team leaders) and the functional management (section leaders and project managers).

The involvement of the managers in the activities and the projects of the Library was facilitated by setting shared and clearly displayed objectives. The BnF developed a strategic action plan which enables it to organize its activities according to priorities that are defined according to its fundamental missions. Renewed every three or four years, the action plan of the Library is prepared with the participation of the management staff. The present plan (2004–2007) is available on the Internet site of the BnF. Meetings at which executive and middle managers participate twice a year make it possible to follow the progress made.

A range of performance indicators was defined in order to help managers to assess the degree of achievement of the objectives laid down (for example, the average time of payment of suppliers, or the average time between the ordering of a book and its delivery to the library user). In order to facilitate the production and the use of these indicators, the Library developed a business intelligence system called Sipil ("Système informatique de pilotage"). It consists of a data warehouse which receives each month the full data resulting from the various information subsystems of the Library (human resources database, financial subsystem, bases related to specific activities such as conservation or cataloguing). Associated reporting software furnishes constantly updated performance indicators. This computerized decision-making system, conceived at first for the directors of departments, is gradually being made available to the first-line managers.

2. The offer of training in the field of management

Since its creation, the BnF has developed an ambitious training plan, conceived mainly in response to the training needs collected each year among the services.

In the field of management, a broad range of training activities is offered, in the form of training courses (one to three days) or workshops (half-day to one day).

a) Training courses for enhancing management skills

These are centred on relationship issues and focus either on communication or team development. They are adapted according to the profile of the management staff, divided into three categories:

- Head of service
- Leader ("foreman") of a library assistants' team
- Functional manager, project leader, assistant director.

The distinction made between heads of service and team leaders ("foremen") reflects the wish to avoid mixing the levels in the training courses in order to encourage the synergy of the groups and the freedom of participation of the trainees. In addition, functional managers, project leaders and assistant directors are treated separately because they are in charge of teams without being in a hierarchical position. Thus, a concept such as the delegation of authority is handled in the training course reserved for the heads of services, not in the course intended for functional managers, which focuses on communication skills. These training courses are supplemented by one day workshops which make it possible to go into more depth on three themes: chairing meetings, speaking in public, and conflict resolution. The three workshops are open to the heads of service as well as to the project leaders and functional managers.

A training course on time management (how to optimize the planning of one's time for more effective management, how to schedule one's activity and that of one's team) supplements training in this area. In addition, a training course on the evaluation interview is offered systematically to managers recently recruited or promoted.

The development and delivery of these courses is entrusted to training companies selected on the basis of schedules of conditions that are established by the Continuing Professional Development Service at the French National Library.

b) Specific training

For specific themes the BnF set up training courses whose programs are specifically adapted to the professional environment of the Library management staff. Some of these courses are conducted by executives of the Library who are experts in the field concerned, others are taught both by internal presenters and by an external person engaged by the Library.

In the field of human resources management, thematic workshops bring together each year small groups of managers in order to give a progress report on regulation, procedures and practices, particularly those regarding "management of absences for health reasons" and "career management" (the development of career of the staff, the role of the manager, the role of the Joint Committees).

In the field of administrative and financial management, short courses one-day courses present an up-to-date synthesis of current knowledge and its application to the French National Library. Various topics are addressed: the budget, the regulation of public procurement, the legal aspects of collection management (intellectual property, regulations regarding the production of documents, legal aspects of digitization).

A particular effort was also made in order to sensitize the management staff to health and safety issues. A training course on the prevention of occupational hazards aims to point out the basic regulations and principal obligations regarding health and safety and to present the system in place at the French National Library (prevention plan, internal role-players). A training course entitled "Alcohol risk: management of difficult situations" makes it possible to specify the part played by managers when they are confronted with this type of situation and how this role should be linked to the intervention of other internal role-players in the Library (social services, psychologist, medical staff responsible for health at the workplace). Lastly, a training course is being elaborated on the theme of workplace illness/injury.

A training programme on the Library's business intelligence system ("Sipil") was also set up in order to teach the managers how to create and run queries and reports. More than just simple training on data-processing software, it also aims to explain how to choose relevant performance indicators and use them knowledgably.

Lastly, a course will be offered for the first time in 2007 on the topic of the manager's responsibility with regard to the documents produced by the Library.

3. The other forms of support to the management staff

a) Coaching a service unit or a team

Unlike the training mentioned above, which gathers managers coming from various horizontal departments of the Library, coaching is a matter of advising a service unit, or the management staff of a department, on the carrying out of a project or implementation of change (reorganization, new orientations etc.) These collective programmes, entrusted to external consultants, are always built to measure according to the particular work situations. The methods are varied, but programmes often consist of a preliminary round of talks by the consultant with the managers, followed by meetings with their colleagues which allow them to build a shared vision of the problems to be dealt with and the objectives to be reached, and to develop solutions together. These are often achieved by developing common tools intended to improve cohesiveness and quality of work and thus of the service rendered to the public.

b) Individual coaching

In addition to these collective forms of accompaniment, individualized coaching is proposed to any manager who is interested. The process consists of a series of talks between the manager and the coach. It is adapted to various situations, in particular: taking up of new duties, difficulties of a situational or a relationship nature, complex work situations, significant development of the sections, organisational changes, crisis situations or strategic situations. More generally, it enables the manager to evolve in his professional behaviour and to improve his personal performance at work. For executive managers, an external coach is employed; for middle managers the BnF has an internal coach. As is required by professional practice, a charter of ethics was established, which guarantees strict confidentiality concerning the contents of the talks.

4. A mission dedicated to the management staff, and a course of training for new managers

The Director of Human Resources of the BnF set up in 2005 a section dedicated to management, which has the role of facilitating the manger's taking up a position and of supporting the development of a managerial culture within the Library. A librarian, former head of the Continuing Professional Development Service of the Library, was appointed for this purpose. Recently recruited or recently promoted managers are systematically invited to meet with the management section leader for a talk about taking up their duties. A workshop entitled "taking up a manager's position" is also offered to them, in the form of three half-days. In this workshop several managers, in particular from the Directorate of Human Resources, approach issues such as staff management; training; health and working conditions; dialogue with staff representatives; financial management; internal communication; and, more generally, the functioning of the Library. The workshop concludes with a meeting with the Library's Executive Director.

This workshop would not be sufficient to meet the training needs of a new manager. A project was therefore launched to set up a actual course of training for managers, with the three half-day long workshop as a first stage. The identification of management skills was already achieved by developing a "skills and employment framework" that describes, for each employment position in the Library, the whole of the activities and related skills. On the basis of the skills defined for management positions (from the department director to the head of service), it will be possible to build a standard course of training which will present, in priority order, the training courses to be followed in order to reach the qualification level expected of a manager at the BnF. This standard course will be modular: it will have to be individualized according to the new manager's profile and former experience.

The actions aiming at developing managerial skills at the French National Library have multiplied during recent years, according to a structured plan. A new managerial culture is making inroads little by little, in spite of the weight of the past and the inertia related to the size of the institution. This evolution is appreciated overall by the management staff, who are often selected according to their scientific rather than to their managerial experience, and who recognize the value of being supported on the questions of management. In conclusion, some of the factors which made possible this evolution should be pointed out:

- a strong commitment by the Library's Executive Director, supported in particular by the Director of Human Resources;
- the granting of significant financial means and adequate staffing;
- the concern for creating overall dynamic action by a systematic effort of training which aims at reaching the whole management staff (on the same hierarchical line or at the same level of responsibility).

LE DEVELOPPEMENT DES COMPETENCES MANAGERIALES A LA BIBLIOTHEQUE NATIONALE DE FRANCE

Michel Netzer
Chef du service des Qualifications et de la Formation/
Head of the Continuing Professional Development Department,
Bibliothèque nationale de France
michel.netzer@bnf.fr

La Bibliothèque nationale de France, institution pluriséculaire qui a pour principale mission de recenser, conserver et communiquer au public l'ensemble des documents édités, imprimés ou diffusés en France, a connu une mutation radicale suite à la décision du président François Mitterrand de créer une bibliothèque "d'un genre entièrement nouveau", ouverte à un large public et offrant des collections numérisées. Avec la construction du site François-Mitterrand, inauguré en 1996, les effectifs ont plus que doublé. Nouvelles missions, nouveau bâtiment, nouveaux personnels: pour relever un tel défi, il était nécessaire de renforcer les compétences managériales de l'encadrement ainsi que sa cohésion et son implication dans les nouveaux projets porteurs du développement de l'Etablissement.

PROJET D'ETABLISSEMENT ET SYSTEME INFORMATIQUE DE PILOTAGE

La Bibliothèque nationale de France compte aujourd'hui environ 2 700 agents (2 475 « équivalent temps plein travaillé »). Placé sous l'autorité d'un président secondé par un directeur général, l'encadrement est constitué de:

- 8 directeurs et délégués, assistés de 10 adjoints, ainsi que 32 directeurs de département, assistés de 23 adjoints, composant l'encadrement supérieur;
- 81 chefs de service.

soit au total 156 encadrants, auxquels il faut ajouter une centaine de personnes constituant l'encadrement de proximité (chefs de bureau et chefs d'équipe) et l'encadrement fonctionnel (chefs de mission et chefs de projet).

L'implication de l'encadrement dans les activités et les projets de l'Etablissement a été favorisée par la fixation d'objectifs partagés et clairement affichés. La BnF s'est dotée d'un programme d'action stratégique qui lui permet d'organiser ses activités autour de priorités clairement définies, en accord avec ses missions fondamentales. Renouvelé tous les 3 ou 4 ans, le programme d'action de l'Etablissement est préparé avec la participation de l'encadrement. Le programme en cours (2004–2007) est consultable sur le site Internet de la BnF. Des revues d'avancement, auxquelles participe l'encadrement supérieur, permettent de suivre deux fois par an les progrès réalisés.

Un certain nombre d'indicateurs d'activité ont été définis afin de permettre à l'encadrement de mesurer le degré d'atteinte des objectifs fixés (par exemple, le délai moyen de paiement des fournisseurs, ou le temps moyen entre la commande d'un ouvrage et sa mise à disposition sur les rayons). Afin de faciliter la production et l'utilisation de ces indicateurs, l'Etablissement a développé un système informatique de pilotage (Sipil). Il s'agit d'un entrepôt de données dans lequel est versé, une fois par mois, un ensemble de données issues des différentes bases de gestion de l'Etablissement (ressources humaines, suivi financier et comptable, bases liées à des activités spécifiques telles la conservation ou le catalogage). Un logiciel de requête associé permet d'obtenir à tout moment des indicateurs de performance à jour. Ce système d'aide à la décision, conçu en priorité pour les directeurs de département, est progressivement mis à la disposition des chefs de service.

L'OFFRE DE FORMATION DANS LE DOMAINE DU MANAGEMENT

Dès sa création, la BnF s'est dotée d'un plan de formation ambitieux, conçu principalement en réponse aux besoins de formation recueillis chaque année auprès des services. Dans le domaine du management, un large éventail de formations est proposé, sous forme de stages (un à trois jours) ou d'ateliers (un demi-jour à un jour).

a) Les stages de formation aux techniques d'encadrement

Ils sont axés sur les aspects relationnels et privilégient tantôt la communication, tantôt l'animation d'équipe. Ils sont déclinés en fonction du profil des encadrants, répartis en 3 catégories:

- Chefs de service;
- Chefs d'équipe de magasinage;
- Encadrants fonctionnels, chefs de projet, adjoints.

La distinction faite entre chefs de service et chefs d'équipe reflète la volonté de ne pas mélanger les niveaux d'encadrement dans les stages afin de favoriser la synergie des groupes et la liberté de parole des stagiaires. Par ailleurs, on a traité séparément les encadrants fonctionnels, chefs de projet et adjoints car ils encadrent des équipes sans être en position hiérarchique. Ainsi, une notion comme la délégation d'autorité est abordée dans le stage réservé aux chefs de service, elle ne l'est pas dans celui destiné aux encadrants fonctionnels, qui est centré sur la maîtrise des techniques de communication. Ces stages sont complétés par une offre d'ateliers d'une journée qui permettent d'approfondir trois thématiques : la conduite de réunion, la prise de parole en public, la gestion de conflit. Les trois ateliers sont ouverts aussi bien aux chefs de service qu'aux chefs de projet et encadrants fonctionnels.

Un stage sur la gestion du temps (comment optimiser la gestion de son temps en vue d'un management plus efficace, comment planifier son activité et celle de son équipe) complète le dispositif.

Par ailleurs, une formation à la conduite de l'entretien d'évaluation est proposée systématiquement aux encadrants nouvellement recrutés ou nouvellement promus.

L'animation de ces stages est confiée à des organismes de formation extérieurs sélectionnés à partir de cahiers des charges établis par le service Formation de la BnF.

b) Les formations spécifiques

Sur des thématiques particulières, la BnF a mis en place des formations dont le programme est spécifiquement adapté à l'environnement professionnel des encadrants. Certaines de ces formations sont animées par des cadres de l'Etablissement, experts du domaine considéré, d'autres sont coanimées par des intervenants internes et un prestataire extérieur.

Dans le domaine de la gestion des ressources humaines, des ateliers thématiques réunissent chaque année des petits groupes d'encadrants afin de faire le point sur la réglementation, les procédures et les pratiques, notamment en matière de « gestion des absences pour raison de santé » et de « gestion des carrières » (le déroulement de carrière des agents, le rôle de l'encadrant, le rôle des commissions paritaires).

Dans le domaine de la gestion administrative et financière, des formations de courte durée (une journée) présentent une synthèse des connaissances les plus actuelles et leur application à la Bibliothèque nationale de France. Les thèmes abordés sont divers : le budget, la réglementation de l'achat public, le droit appliqué à la gestion des collections (droit d'auteur, droit de la communication des documents, aspects juridiques de la numérisation).

Par ailleurs, un effort particulier a été fait afin de sensibiliser les encadrants aux questions d'hygiène et de sécurité. Un stage sur la prévention des risques professionnels a pour objectif de doter les encadrants de bases réglementaires, de rappeler les principales obligations en matière d'hygiène et de sécurité et de présenter le dispositif en place à la BnF (plan de prévention, acteurs internes). Un stage intitulé « Risque alcool : gestion des situations difficiles » permet de préciser le rôle que peut jouer l'encadrant lorsqu'il est confronté à ce type de situation et la façon dont ce rôle s'articule avec l'intervention des autres acteurs internes de l'Etablissement (service social, psychologue, médecin de prévention). Enfin, un stage est en cours de construction sur la problématique de la souffrance au travail.

Un programme de formation à l'outil informatique de pilotage (Sipil) a également été mis en place afin d'apprendre aux encadrants à construire des requêtes pour interroger le système. Plus qu'une simple formation à un logiciel informatique, il s'agit aussi d'expliquer comment choisir des indicateurs de performance pertinents et les utiliser à bon escient.

Enfin, une formation sera proposée pour la première fois en 2007 sur le thème de la responsabilité de l'encadrement dans la gestion et l'archivage des documents produits par la Bibliothèque.

LES AUTRES FORMES D'APPUI A L'ENCADREMENT

c) L'accompagnement d'une unité de travail

A la différence des formations évoquées plus haut, qui regroupent transversalement des encadrants provenant de différents départements de la Bibliothèque, il s'agit là d'accompagner les équipes d'une même unité de travail, ou l'encadrement d'un département, dans la réalisation d'un projet ou dans une démarche de changement (restructuration, nouvelles orientations...). Ces actions d'accompagnement collectif, confiées à des consultants extérieurs, sont toujours construites sur mesure en fonction des situations de travail rencontrées. Les modalités en sont variées, mais elles consistent souvent en une phase préalable d'entretiens du consultant avec les encadrants, suivie de réunions avec leurs collaborateurs qui permettent de construire une vision partagée des problèmes à traiter et des objectifs à atteindre, et d'inventer ensemble des solutions. Celles-ci s'appuient souvent sur l'élaboration d'outils communs destinés à améliorer la cohérence et la qualité du travail, et donc du service rendu.

d) L'accompagnement individualise

En complément de ces formes collectives d'appui à l'encadrement, un accompagnement individualisé est proposé à tout encadrant qui le souhaite. La démarche s'organise autour d'une série d'entretiens entre le cadre et le coach. Elle est adaptée à des situations diverses, notamment : prise de nouvelles fonctions, difficultés de positionnement ou d'ordre relationnel, situations de travail complexes, évolution significative des missions, changements organisationnels, situation de crise ou à fort enjeu. Plus généralement, elle permet au cadre d'évoluer dans ses comportements professionnels et d'améliorer sa performance personnelle au travail. Pour l'encadrement supérieur, il est fait appel à un coach extérieur, pour l'encadrement intermédiaire, la BnF dispose d'un coach interne. Comme l'exige cette pratique professionnelle, une charte déontologique a été établie, qui garantit une stricte confidentialité concernant le contenu des entretiens.

UNE MISSION POUR L'ENCADREMENT, UN PARCOURS DE FORMATION POUR LE NOUVEL ENCADRANT

La direction déléguée aux Ressources humaines de la BnF a mis en place en 2005 une mission d'appui à l'encadrement qui a pour vocation de faciliter la prise de fonctions des encadrants et de favoriser le développement d'une culture managériale au sein de l'Etablissement. Une chargée de mission pour l'encadrement, qui exerçait auparavant les fonctions de chef du service des Qualifications et de la Formation, a été désignée à cet effet. Elle reçoit systématiquement en entretien les cadres nouvellement recrutés ou nouvellement promus, afin de leur apporter informations et conseils lors de leur prise de fonctions. Un atelier de « prise de poste d'encadrement » leur est par ailleurs proposé, sous forme de trois demi-journées. Cet atelier, où interviennent à titre d'experts plusieurs cadres de l'Etablissement, notamment de la direction déléguée aux Ressources humaines, aborde des sujets tels que la gestion du personnel, la formation, la santé et les conditions de travail, la mise en œuvre du dialogue avec les partenaires syndicaux, la gestion financière, la communication interne et plus globalement le fonctionnement de l'Etablissement. L'atelier se conclut par une rencontre avec la direction générale de la Bibliothèque.

Cet atelier ne suffirait pas à lui seul à couvrir les besoins de formation d'un nouvel encadrant. Une réflexion a donc été engagée en vue de mettre en place un véritable parcours de formation de l'encadrant, dont l'atelier de 3 demi-journées sera la première étape. L'identification des compétences nécessaires à l'exercice de l'encadrement a déjà été faite dans le cadre d'un « référentiel des emplois et des compétences », qui décrit, pour chaque emploi exercé à la Bibliothèque, l'ensemble des activités et des compétences associées. Sur la base des fiches de ce référentiel consacrées aux emplois de l'encadrement (du directeur de département au chef de service), il sera possible de construire un parcours de formation type qui présentera, par ordre de priorité, les formations à suivre pour atteindre le niveau de compétence attendu d'un encadrant de la BnF. Ce parcours type sera modulaire : il devra être individualisé en fonction du profil et de l'expérience antérieure du nouvel encadrant.

Les actions visant à développer les compétences de l'encadrement de la Bibliothèque nationale de France se sont multipliées au cours de ces dernières années, selon une démarche volontariste et cohérente. Une nouvelle culture managériale fait peu à peu son chemin, malgré les pesanteurs héritées du passé et la force d'inertie liée à la taille de l'établissement. Cette démarche est globalement appréciée par l'encadrement, souvent choisi à partir de ses compétences scientifiques plutôt que managériales, et qui reconnaît l'utilité d'un appui sur les questions de management. Il convient de dégager, en conclusion, quelques-uns des facteurs qui ont rendu possible cette évolution:

- une volonté forte et durable de la direction générale de l'Etablissement, portée en particulier par le directeur délégué aux Ressources humaines;
- l'octroi de moyens financiers et humains à la hauteur de l'enjeu;
- le souci de créer une dynamique d'ensemble par un effort de formation systématique et qui vise à atteindre l'ensemble des encadrants (d'une même ligne hiérarchique ou d'un même niveau de responsabilités).

E-LEARNING:
ONE PATH TO LEADERSHIP DEVELOPMENT

Marilyn Gell Mason
Executive Director WebJunction
marilyngmason@earthlink.net

Rachel Van Noord
Special Projects Coordinator WebJunction,
Dublin, Ohio, USA
http://webjunction.org
vannoorr@oclc.org

Abstract

This article discusses the value of e-learning for providing staff training, particularly around leadership development. Findings from WebJunction's 2005 North American survey *Trends in E-Learning for Library Staff: A Summary of Research Findings* and phone interviews are presented. This survey showed that over 70% of respondents have plans to pursue e-learning in the next 3 years, either by developing their own e-learning or purchasing online courses. Benefits of e-learning cited by survey respondents include convenience for learners, greater reach, cost effectiveness and the freedom for learners to direct their own learning. Barriers cited include staff time, lack of funding and trainer expertise. International library organizations face added challenges, including digital readiness and empowering learners. An in-depth discussion of course development and the importance of providing trainers with expertise in instructional design follows. Software features for online course developers are also examined, as is the potential for collaboration between library organizations developing e-learning modules. The paper concludes with a discussion of how a library organization may begin using e-learning effectively and WebJunction's next steps.

Leadership has never been more important for today's libraries and other information providers. Most of us would agree that for a leader to be effective he/she needs to have up-to-date skills and contacts with others in the field who are on the forefront of innovation. Continuing education has always been one way that information professionals have bridged the gap between where they are and where they want to be.

As technology becomes a more dominant force worldwide we are faced with an increasing struggle to keep pace. One of the answers to the question of how to keep pace with information technology may be found in the technology itself. E-learning is fast emerging as an efficient, low cost way to keep up.

Libraries in the United States are at a pivotal moment in their use of e-learning. An independent survey commissioned by WebJunction in 2005 found that 70% of responding library organizations plan to use e-learning within the next three years. The survey also identified benefits, barriers, and strategies necessary for successful implementation of e-learning among libraries.

WebJunction has been offering online courses to the library community since 2003. In 2006, with funding from the Bill & Melinda Gates Foundation, we began working more intensively with our partners, members, and others in the field to develop strategies for the effective and productive use of online learning. The survey referenced above was conducted to provide baseline data for the field and the full report, *Trends in E-Learning for Library Staff: A Summary of Research Findings*, is available on the WebJunction website[1]. This paper summarizes key findings of the survey and examines implications for e-learning usage worldwide.

WHAT IS E-LEARNING?

E-learning describes electronically delivered learning, using tools like web conferencing, web-based tutorials, message boards, online assessments, and more. The term e-learning includes self-paced learning, asynchronous facilitator-led learning, where the students and instructors interact at different times, and synchronous facilitator-led learning, where the students and instructors interact at a set time. The current trend among e-learning developers is to blend self-paced and facilitator-led modules to create a single, interactive training experience.

BENEFITS OF E-LEARNING

Survey respondents indicated that e-learning benefits both individual learners and library organizations. The most commonly cited benefits were:

- Convenience for learners;
- The ability to reach more learners;
- Cost effectiveness of e-learning;
- Freedom e-learning provides for learners to direct their own learning.

Briefly, when fully realized, e-learning programs can provide convenient, high-quality training opportunities for a broad array of staff at substantial savings over conventional face-to-face training. This is especially true when we consider indirect costs of travel and missed time at the library. It is easy to see how emerging leaders in library organizations can benefit from online training. Staff in small or isolated libraries also experience huge benefits as access to a broad range of training opportunities is increased through e-learning. See Table 1 for a detailed list of benefits.

Table 1: Benefits of E-learning

Developers (n=143, respondents selected multiple answers)	**Purchasers** (n=108, respondents selected multiple answers)	**Potential adopters**
- Convenience for learner (54%) - Ability to reach more learners (54%) - Cost-effective vs. other modes of training or education (47%) - Provides learners the opportunity to direct their own learning (31%) - Instructional effectiveness vs. other modes of training or education (26%)	- Convenience for learners (58%) - Provides learners the opportunity to direct their own learning (41%) - Cost-effectiveness (38%) - Ability to reach more learners (32%) - Instructional effectiveness vs. other modes of training and education (10%) - Other (7%)	- Geographic reach - Cost-effectiveness - Convenience for learner - Meets a need - Keeps the organization competitive, helps the organization keep up

BARRIERS TO E-LEARNING

Respondents identified the major barriers to using e-learning to be:

- Staff time constraints;
- Lack of funding;
- Lack of expertise.

As with any new program, getting started can be a challenge. Setting up an e-learning program requires time, money and expertise. Many libraries find that in spite of the promise of a long-term benefit, funding for start-up can be hard to come by.

But barriers to starting an e-learning program can vary significantly depending on whether an institution plans to create its own courses or buy courses already developed by another institution. Most of those taking part in our survey were engaged in developing online courses and their responses reflected the high cost of development. Small libraries and others that choose to offer courses developed by others will find that barriers to entry are dramatically reduced by purchasing e-learning modules, rather than developing them independently. Organizations will need to overcome these challenges before e-learning will be an effective method for leadership development, but our research shows that the stage has been set for using e-learning to train leaders. See Table 2 for full list of barriers.

Table 2: Barriers to E-learning

Developers (n=141, respondents selected multiple answers)	**Purchasers** (n=108, respondents selected multiple answers)	**Potential adopters** (n=297, respondents selected multiple answers)
• Lack of funding (76%) • Staff time (56%) • Expertise (42%) • Fear that it will not be used (26%)	• Staff time (82%) • Expertise (45%) • Lack of Funding (67%) • Concern for effectiveness (19%)	• Lack of funding (73%) • Staff time (71%) • Expertise 41%) • Fear that it will not be used (33%)

• Concern about end users' technology (25%)	• Fear that it will not be used (13%)	• Concern for effectiveness (18%)
• Concern for effectiveness (21%)	• Concern about end users' technology (11%)	• Concern about end users' technology (16%)
• NNeed for management buy-in (11%)	• Other (6%)	• Need for management buy-in (11%)
• Resistance from trainers or current training program (8%)	• Need for management buy-in (2%)	• Other (8%)
	• Resistance from trainers or current training program (0%)	• Resistance from trainers or current training program (3%)

BENEFITS AND BARRIERS FOR DEVELOPING COUNTRIES

Not surprisingly, the top benefits of e-learning for library staff in developing countries are similar to those cited by our North American survey respondents. The potential to improve quality and lower the cost of training while increasing accessibility is attractive worldwide.

However, there are additional barriers to overcome before these benefits can be fully realized. In addition to lack of funding, time, and staff expertise those in developing countries also face issues of digital readiness. Nidhal Guessoum, of the American University of Sharjah, United Arab Emirates, wrote in a 2006 article for eLearn Magazine that, while there is much interest in online learning in the Arabic world, digital readiness is lacking[2]. Low bandwidth and slow transmission rates, and even lack of readily available telephone service in some areas, impede the ability of many around the world to take full advantage of e-learning opportunities. These challenges are seen in many other parts of the world, including some rural areas in highly developed countries.

As countries work to establish an infrastructure to overcome the challenge of digital readiness, e-learning modules that get around this hurdle are being developed. Some of these are described below.

ALTERNATIVE APPROACHES TO DISTRIBUTION

In another *eLearn Magazine* article, Richard Larson, Director of MIT Learning Interactive Networks Consortium, predicted that in 2007, e-learning in many parts of the world will consist of a combination of stored local content and low-bandwidth interactive modules in an effort to overcome connectivity limitations[3]. This blended approach to developing e-learning modules may offer library organizations without high-speed internet connections an alternative way to pursue e-learning now, without having to wait.

Another prediction in the same article noted that innovations in mobile learning have the potential to shift the way e-learning is produced and distributed[3]. Mobile learning takes the ideas of e-learning one step farther. While e-learning allows a student to learn outside a classroom, but still in a fixed place of home or work, mobile technologies allow students to learn anywhere they can use their mobile device, whether that device is a phone, PDA, digital audio player, voice recorder, or digital camera.

While the development of highly effective mobile e-learning modules may be further away than modules developed using the blended approach described by Larson, countries that still have some way to go in building their technology infrastructure may move directly to mobile learning, skipping over the e-learning formats being used today.

EMPOWERING LEARNERS, DEVELOPING LEADERS

It is most likely that technological barriers are only a temporary hurdle to pursuing e-learning for staff training. Perhaps more important was Guessoum's comment that another barrier to e-learning in Arab countries is empowering learners to take ownership for their own learning, rather than follow the traditional, passive model of learning through face-to-face lectures[2]. We heard similar comments in our pre-survey interviews and, as organizations overcome the issues of technology, funding, expertise and time, it is likely that this will become more of a concern for trainers and administrators in library organizations. Not only that, but as learners empower themselves to take control of their own learning, they will establish critical leadership skills that will serve them well into the future.

Fortunately, library trainers using e-learning are already working to overcome this issue. From January through October 2006, WebJunction conducted a small pilot program that provided library organizations with the tools, training, and support to develop their own synchronous and asynchronous e-learning activities.

As part of this program, we gave participants training on instructional design and facilitation for the online environment. One module developed through this pilot program by Lori Reed is entitled "7 ½ Habits of Highly Successful Lifelong Learners" <http://www.plcmc.org/public/learning/player.html>. This module was incorporated into the larger Learning 2.0 < http://plcmclearning.blogspot.com/> staff training program designed by Reed and her colleague Helene Blowers at the Public Library of Charlotte and Mecklenberg County. Reed and Blowers told us that they felt that empowering learners to take charge of their learning was so important that this module was incorporated into the first exercise, and they cite it as one of the reasons Learning 2.0 succeeded.

As learners become empowered, e-learning techniques can be woven into a formal leadership training program, providing leader-learners with a way to pursue training in a more timely, cost-effective way. The American Library Association's Emerging Leaders program is an example of an informal training opportunity that has combined in-person meetings with virtual communication via blogs and wikis. The State Library of Iowa has established a more formal certification program for public library staff that blends in-person and online training elements, including in-person meetings, web-conferencing, and discussion boards into an opportunity for library staff to increase their skills and enhance the image of public library staff in the state. The blended elements in both examples highlight the importance of face-to-face networking for leadership development as well as the value in offering library leaders opportunities to learn and communicate virtually.

COURSE DEVELOPMENT—THE BIGGEST BARRIER

Even with empowered learners, course development is critical to a successful e-learning experience. In our pre-survey interviews, organizations repeatedly noted that when an individual has a bad experience in a conventional course she is likely to blame the instructor. When she has a bad experience in an online course she is likely to blame the format and will be unlikely to pursue additional e-learning experiences.

Mary Ross, of Seattle Public Library, who has been developing online courses since 2001, discussed this tension with us recently. She noted that there is no question in her mind that developing online courses takes more time than face-to-face courses because online courses have to be good enough to stand alone when there is no instructor to compensate for weak course design.

WebJunction's 2005 survey, as well as a 2003 Outsell report commissioned by OCLC[4], indicate that the library field is interested in having access to e-learning modules that provide leadership training. As such modules are developed, excellent course design must be employed. When done well, online training events will make a large number of professional and leadership development courses available to library staff with limited travel budgets and time, lowering costs to end users, even though the initial costs of course creation are likely to be high.

Ross believes that the cost and time to develop e-learning can be reduced if the online learning is designed to be scalable and generic enough to be easily customizable for many different libraries. She recently developed a course on intellectual freedom which has been used by the Seattle Public Library, Illinois State Library, Montana, and other states—reusing the course in each of these situations was possible because she planned for customization early on in the design phase.

Ross' experience speaks to the importance of trainer expertise, which, in WebJunction's experience is just beginning to rise on the field's radar. We have found that the library field currently lacks widespread training programs for library trainers to develop skills and experience in e-learning design, development and delivery, though this is changing. In the WebJunction pilot program described above we found that participants were initially skeptical of the need for training in instructional design, preferring instead to spend time learning about new technologies. However, as the participants developed their own courses they all recognized the value and importance of the instructional design and facilitation training they received.

Ross also emphasizes the importance of "purposeful instructional design" in the online environment. When asked about developing online courses, Ross did have this word of warning: in her experience, it is easier to build a completely new online course than to modify an existing face-to-face training, since the modifications required for a successful conversion of in-person training are so extensive.

Given the cost and experience needed, it is no surprise survey results showed that library organizations in North America most likely to develop e-learning have at least one of the following characteristics:

- Budgets over $10 million;
- More than 200 staff;
- More than 300 member organizations.

Library organizations with smaller budgets are more likely to purchase e-learning developed by another organization or have not yet pursued e-learning in any form.

COURSE DEVELOPMENT—SOFTWARE

In the survey, after course developers identified themselves, they were asked specific questions about what they consider when choosing software. Not surprisingly, 'cost' was at the top of the list but 'features offered' ranked almost as high (see Table 3).

Table 3: Software considerations

Synchronous (n=66, respondents selected a single answer)	**Facilitator-led asynchronous** (n=68, respondents selected a single answer)	**Self-paced** (n=68, respondents selected a single answer)
• Cost (41%) • Features offered (41%) • Support services (18%)	• Cost (38%) • Features offered (37%) • Support services (25%)	• Cost (45%) • Features offered (40%) • Support services (15%)

Asked to identify features required, respondents overwhelmingly ranked *ease of use* for learners and instructors as their top software requirement. Other requirements may be found in Appendix 1.

Recent technology has expanded the possibilities of online learning and course developers want as much of that functionality as possible to create high quality and interactive courses. Budget limitations make it necessary for organizations to make trade-offs. While some functions, such as screen capture software, can be relatively inexpensive others, like web conferencing software and learning management systems (LMS), are often beyond the reach of a single library organization.

When software costs are added to the amount of staff time to create courses, the number of organizations that can afford to develop and deliver e-learning drops sharply. While many library organizations debate the benefit of high quality technology, libraries reporting budgets of under $1 million indicated that cost is always their primary consideration as they consider developing e-learning.

COLLABORATION—THE KEY TO SUCCESS

At WebJunction, we have seen the tremendous potential of e-learning as a way to expand training and education opportunities for the library field. By collaborating, library organizations can ensure easy access to high quality e-learning on a range of library topics.

During our pre-survey interviews, we heard a strong desire among e-learning developers to reduce duplication of effort in developing e-learning across all types of library organizations. One participant said, "Why not share? This would be a great opportunity for e-learning providers to further develop and share their expertise more widely."

Julie Erickson, of the South Dakota State Library, noted that there was no easy way to find out what other library organizations are doing. More than once, after she put time into creating something 'new', she found out that another organization had created something similar that she had not known about before beginning her efforts. She finds this frustrating, especially since librarians are so willing to share information with each other when asked.

Erickson and her colleague Colleen Kirby prefer sharing materials, emphatically stating "we are not going to reinvent the wheel." Currently, South Dakota utilizes training materials from both Idaho and Wyoming, noting that it is much easier to tweak something that already exists than to create it yourself. This reinforces Ross's comments about the importance of developing online courses that can be easily customized to meet the needs of many library organizations.

The inefficiency of the current system is something that the field must work together to overcome. It also highlights a new issue: can many organizations afford to develop the same online course content? Traditionally, library training providers have had to cover the entire spectrum of training content to effectively meet the needs of their learners. Given the possibility of customization and the importance of scalability to reduce development costs, it's unlikely this pattern will continue, especially if the field works together to collaborate.

Pre-survey interviews indicated that there is a lot of interest in establishing a course development pipeline in North America that would allow e-learning developers to see who is planning to develop what courses in the future. One example of this type of collaboration is the development of a web portal for LIS Education in Asia (LISEA) as a repository of learning objects[5]. With this information, organizations could focus on producing other content that expands the breadth of e-learning opportunities for the field.

GETTING STARTED

Most libraries will choose to purchase courses rather than to develop them themselves. This is especially true for small libraries. Respondents who indicated that they are e-learning purchasers rather than developers gave the following reasons for using their resources this way:

- It's more cost and time-effective to buy;
- We have no in-house experience with e-learning;
- We are too small to develop our own.

Essentially, these organizations consider purchasing e-learning as a way to make the format available while overcoming some of the barriers. For example, the South Dakota State Library works with database vendors and e-learning providers in North America to provide online learning opportunities for the library staff in their state. However, they are also investigating turning a 2-week long in-person training event that is held each summer, into a blended learning experience, where participants would come together face-to-face for a shorter period of time and use the state's satellite down-link and web-based training tools to complete their training.

Some states have statewide organizations that develop online courses that may be used by library staff throughout the state. These include LibraryU in Illinois and InfoPeople in California. Regional networks like Amigos and Solinet (among others) are also course producers that make their e-learning available to libraries within and beyond their regions.

But simply purchasing courses is not enough for e-learning to be successful. Surprisingly, when ranking barriers to e-learning, survey respondents listed "resistance from trainers or current training programs" and "management buy-in" at the bottom of their list of concerns. In interview after interview experienced individuals have told us that these two elements, along with empowering learners, are critical to the success of an e-learning program.

E-learning is most effective when:

- It is part of an ongoing in-service training program that is actively supported by management;

- Staff members are given the uninterrupted time needed to participate, just as they would be given release time to attend a face-to-face training session;

- Staff members receive credit for their efforts. This can range from a certificate of participation to credit toward advancement; and

- Staff are provided access to a quiet location with a computer and phone or VOIP headset with microphone.

NEXT STEPS

With funding from the Bill & Melinda Gates Foundation, WebJunction is exploring ways to work with libraries to improve quality and reduce costs of e-learning through collaboration.

We expect to release a survey in 2007 that looks more broadly at staff training and development in library organizations, with an emphasis on e-learning, in an effort to obtain base-line data and set benchmarks for the field. This survey will be international in scope and we look forward to sharing the findings when the research is complete.

Additional initiatives include:

- *Course development.* Improve the quality and lower the cost of online courses by training trainers nationally and pooling purchasing power for needed software;
- *Course consumption.* Lower the cost of courses already developed through bulk discounts and improve the effectiveness of e-learning through organizational coaching and implementation guides;
- *Course distribution.* Create a national distribution partnership to enable course developers to reach a wider audience and give course consumers choice and easy user tracking among a variety of offerings;
- *Grow the community of library trainers* by providing a space for them to share materials and best practices and obtain professional development;
- *Create a course development pipeline* that will enable course developers to communicate about courses in progress and avoid duplication of effort;

Working together, the library community can realize the benefits and overcome the barriers to the effective use of e-learning.

REFERENCES

[1] Chesemore S, Van Noord R, Salm J, Saletrik, C (2006). Trends in e-learning for library staff: a summary of research findings [WWW document]. URL <http://webjunction.org/do/DisplayContent?id=14077>

[2] Guessoum, N (2006). Online learning in the arab world. eLearn Magazine [Online serial]. URL <http://www.elearnmag.org/subpage.cfm?section=articles&article=40-1> Accessed February 9, 2007.

[3] Neal, L (2007). Predictions for 2007. eLearn Magazine [Online serial]. URL <http://www.elearnmag.org/subpage.cfm?section=articles&article=42-1> Accessed January 29, 2007.

[4] Wilkie, K., & Strouse, R. (2003). OCLC library training & education market needs assessment study [WWW document]. URL <http://www.oclc.org/index/needsassessment/>

[5] Chaudhry A (2006). Collaboration in LIS education in Southeast Asia [WWW document]. URL <http://mg.csufresno.edu/papers/forum_2/Chaudhry.pdf>

Appendix 1: Software Requirements

E-learning developers responding to the WebJunction survey ranked *ease of use* for learners and instructors as their top software requirements. Below are the five software requirements for synchronous and asynchronous e-learning that were ranked just behind ease of use:

Synchronous software requirements:
- Show Web pages   75%
- Ability to archive and replay presentations   70%
- Screen casting   66%
- Show PowerPoint slides   58%
- Application sharing   52%

Facilitator-led asynchronous software requirements:
- Orientation help   67%
- Discussion forums   58%
- File exchange   54%
- Online grading tools   52%
- Automated testing and scoring   48%

WHICH LEADER ARE YOU? OR: THREE FUNCTIONS FOR LEADERSHIP, LINKING WITH STRATEGIC GOALS

Dr Marielle de Miribel
Mediadix, Université Paris 10, France
miribel@u-paris10.fr

INTRODUCTION

What proves that I am the actual person in charge in my department?

Let me introduce myself briefly and tell you what I am and on what grounds I present this paper before I explain the way I view things, as far as the notion of leadership in libraries is concerned. I am a chief librarian, "on the admission list" of associate professors in information sciences, and a transactional analyst qualified in the field of organizations. I used to manage several kinds of libraries and used to be in charge of library networks. As such, I coach department executives, especially in the field of organizational change, and I devise, organize and manage continuing education for library staff in the field of management and human relationships in libraries.

A large part of the concepts that I will use in my demonstration come from transactional analysis, especially from a book by Eric Berne entitled *Structure and dynamics of organizations and groups*.

THE THREE HATS OF LEADERSHIP

There are three dimensions in leadership, corresponding to three ways of representing the organization of a library: the functional organization chart (the roles), the staff organization chart *("who is where?")* and the view each member of the staff has of his/her place in the library and how s/he is regarded by the leader (*"Where do I position myself?"*). Here is a brief summary of these three aspects. I will expound later in full detail:

- **The responsible leader** is the person who has the position of leader in the organizational chart
- **The effective leader** is the person who makes the real decisions, whatever his/her position in the organizational chart. He/she can sit somewhere in a

remote study in spite of his/her being the most influential person as far as managing is concerned.

- **The psychological leader** is the most influential person as far as personal representations of each member of the team is concerned. He or she is the person in whom others confide.

These three kinds of leadership can be taken care of by the same person but every combination is possible and can cause many malfunctions in the way the library is managed. It is not always easy to distinguish between these three types of leadership except when there is a crisis. In any case, whatever the size of the library or unit taken into consideration these three dimensions still exist.

THE RESPONSIBLE LEADER

- S/he is the person who has to report to the boss.

S/he was appointed by his/her hierarchy and s/he has report to his/her superiors, especially in a crisis situation

- It is the hat of legitimacy.

His/her appointment gives rise to public communication, is published in a newspaper, with photos, welcoming ceremony and official establishment. S/he takes on responsibility for the library.

- S/he gives a sense of direction

His/her role is to give a direction, a meaning to the operations of the library. S/he says: *"This is where we have to go and this is how we must go there"*. For instance, s/he makes decisions in the fields of acquisition policy, circulation, rules and regulations, etc. S/he validates priorities and future projects aiming at some segments of the public: young adults or people in wheelchairs, college students or researchers, etc. Each type of library must make choices depending on its space, budget, external and internal resources, partners, qualifications of its staff, etc.

S/he plays an important role in the field of reflection

His/her prerogatives are to reflect, think, diagnose, anticipate. S/he is an actor in the field of reflection.

His/her three criteria of personal power

Here are three criteria to assess his/her power in this role:

- S/he can modify the organization chart without having to require a preliminary authorization;
- S/he can give rewards and impose sanctions irrevocably;
- S/he can modify objectives, priorities, rules and professional culture depending on circumstances.

S/he vouches for internal consistency

In other words, the responsible leader is the person who vouches for the coherence of the library s/he manages, coping with various types of pressure that people or other units of the environment exert on it. A few examples of this:

- Parent organizations exert pressures: they require high productivity and substantial results, efficient actions with low staff and equipment costs;
- Partners want the plans worked out with the library to increase their own efficiency;
- Readers and users require a fast, efficient and free service, with extensive opening hours, an unlimited loan period, a warm and convivial welcome, opportunities to meet people, etc.

In relation to the existence and legitimacy of the library

It is a fact that the responsible leader remains focused on the role played by the library in its environment, on its added value. The role of the elements of the environment of the library consists in exerting pressure on its external boundary, in requiring services which meet their needs. In fact, if the library ceases to meet the requirements and needs expressed through pressures exerted on it—demanding that the library acts and meets these expectations—it may collapse or disappear, due to its perceived uselessness. Indeed, the library needs pressures to live and to adapt to them. In order to do this, the library must develop and act consistently for its own sake and for its environment.

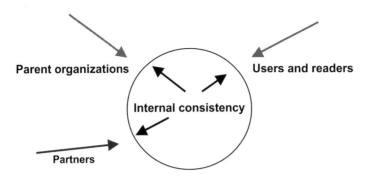

Consequently, the role of the library, represented by its 'responsible leader', consists in meeting these pressures and opposing them with consistency in its aims and objectives.

Otherwise, if the priorities of the library are not clearly defined and consistent, made explicit and comprehensible to everyone, the multiplicity of the assumed aims may plunge the library into disarray.

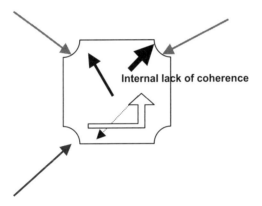

For instance, imagine that the young adult service of a library spends months of mediation work outside its premises in order to bring in uncertain sections of the public: teenagers, young people from working-class housing-estates, illiterate parents, etc. If, after constant efforts to establish long term ties, the mediator brings young people to the library, for example, and if one such person is soon rejected because s/he does not abide by the rules and regulations of the library and by the norms of polite behaviour, is the work of the mediators consistent with the functioning and the rules of the library?

THE EFFECTIVE LEADER

The hat of the expert

S/he is the repository of the expertise of the unit. S/he is the person you consult in case of a professional problem and whose advice you follow. S/he is the person whose suggestions tend to be the most accepted and followed in a stressful situation.

The expert in strategic scanning

In his/her role as a proficient expert, s/he knows the strategic elements of the surroundings: for example the opportunities and threats of the current situation (in reference to the SWOT marketing audit): s/he knows how to use those ensuring the durability of his/her unit. S/he knows and controls the key elements within the framework of the library and can plan ahead of time the main changes which will compel the library to adapt to these new data.

For example, a merger of communities as it occurs in Quebec or a community of communes as it occurs in France, profoundly modifies the nature of the services which must be offered.

Similarly a legal modification in purchasing procedures, especially for electronic documents, entails important changes in the acquisition policy.

Or, as a further example, curricula and syllabi of exams and competitive exams for M.Ds and attorneys require very particular vigilance and a specific procedure for the collections concerned, so as to maintain equality for all and prevent some students from keeping all the prescribed books throughout the whole year.

S/he prescribes a method

S/he is the referent as far as professional activity is concerned. S/he is the one who is consulted in case of difficulties in the operational field *"What do you do for...."* or *"I don't know how to catalog, index, weed, sort out, do this or that operation"*.

S/he plays an important part in the field of technical tasks and hand-turns

S/he shows, explains, comments, assists and instructs his/her collaborators.

S/he is co-opted

Contrary to the function of the leader in charge, a duty discharged by the "boss", the real dimension of leadership is a co-opted role. It is the others, colleagues and co-workers, who, without officially saying so, choose the person that, in their opinion, will inform and help them in the most efficient way.

S/he is in touch with the strategic objective of the library

In terms of the various types of expertise required, several different people can be considered as experts in their field. But the effective leader, perceiving strategic changes in the environment, can identify the strategic objectives of the library, those that ensure its survival or (in other words), the most strategic pressure that is exerted on the library: *" If the library were set on fire tonight, who would suffer the most from this fire? Who would be in big trouble or in danger?"*

Five criteria of personal power

- Expertise, as a special or rare competence, or, at least, a scarcely shared one;
- The power to tap in, sort out, keep or control information;
- The ability to create or modify working rules;
- The authority to allocate to others financial and material resources;
- Access to an external network of relations, relationships with the media, with international organizations such as IFLA, with professional associations and unions;

For s/he is considered by his/her co-workers as the person who really "knows the job".

THE PSYCHOLOGICAL LEADERSHIP

The hat of influence

S/he is the most influential person in the minds of his/her co-workers. His/her voice and opinion have a special weight and greatly influence the opinion of others.

His/her co-workers demand special qualities from him/her

The psychological leader of a group holds a privileged position in terms of his/her image, regardless of whether or not s/he is at the same time an actual leader in charge. Co-workers demand from him/her special qualities: s/he is expected to be: omnipotent, omniscient, immortal, invulnerable, never sick, incorruptible, not easily influenced, indefatigable and fearless. These are the same qualities as those attributed to emperors in times past, such as: The "Unequalled", the "All-powerful", the "Invincible".

If, in daily life, s/he is short of one of these qualities, there will always be someone to reproach him/her about it.

Everyone unconsciously projects on to this person his/her child's expectations and disappointments with his/her parents.

A role of counsellor

S/he takes on the role of counsellor, in a private capacity, for questions of a personal nature or about a career profile. People ask for his/her opinion to choose a course, validate a post profile, answer an offer, etc.

S/he provides good and secure relationships

S/he is the person who consolidates the relationships between the members of a team. S/he often initiates the rites of conviviality: farewell and welcome drinks parties, cakes etc. S/he may also propose sporting activities or organize cultural activities outside the library, during which time the co-workers have a chance to meet each other in a more personal way.

S/he plays an important role in the way people express themselves

In his/her office, many colleagues come and speak about all kinds of matters. If some crisis occurs, everybody comes to see him/her, and reports to him/her about the most recent developments and tries to be acquainted with the rumours which circulate. It is an office where everyone can express his/her feelings freely. It is sometimes the place where people complain.

His/her 4 criteria of personal power

- S/he listens well;
- S/he is endowed with charisma;
- His/her colleagues like him/her;
- He is discreet and maintains privacy.

S/he is co-opted

S/he too, is co-opted by his colleagues in matters of atmosphere, relationships, counselling. She/he cannot proclaim him- or herself as psychological leader of his group.

SPECIFIC QUALITIES FOR EACH DIMENSION OF LEADERSHIP

To come to a conclusion about the qualities of each dimension of the leadership, I can say in broad outline that:

The **responsible leader contributes and** responds **to a need of his/her co-workers** for a structure, **a sense and a framework**:

S/he gives a sense of direction, sets objectives, priorities, limits;

S/he defines precise aims, makes decisions, clarifies the stakes;

S/he has clear conceptions and favours openness;

S/he can say no, and take responsibility;

S/he takes into account the general interest before vested interests;

S/he organizes work and arranges meetings;

S/he is in good health.

The effective leader contributes to meet his/her co-workers' need for stimulation:

S/he shows directorial skills, can manage a team and be a model for his/her colleagues;

S/he is able to adapt, to take a course and develop her/himself;

S/he can ask questions about himself/herself, can remain open-minded.

The psychological leader contributes to meet his/her co-workers' need for tokens of appreciation

S/he shows respect, consideration, ability to listen to his/her colleagues;

S/he is fair and equitable: s/he does not show personal preferences and does not have a "pet" or a "punch-bag";

S/he is insightful and gives everyone the feeling of being important.

WHAT HAPPENS WHEN THERE ARE DYSFUNCTIONS?

Problems for the responsible leader

A lack of legitimacy

This happens when the person in charge is not really appointed. S/he is a chief, but only ad interim, for a short period of time, for want of anything better. S/he was not officially announced and appointed. As a result, his/her colleagues do not know whether they should put a lot of energy into adapting to the way s/he works. This causes anxiety, a wait-and-see attitude and opposition to change. People wait…

This also happens when people know that the present chief is on the verge of leaving, without knowing who will replace him/her. People wait…

A lack of guidelines

In this situation, the chief doesn't know where s/he is going. S/he may receive contradictory instructions from his/her boss, and may themselves not agree with one another. This is often seen during the construction of a building: orders and counter-orders. People wait...

A lack of limits

It sometimes happens that the person in charge of a team tries to be liked by his/her co-workers rather than to command respect. This frequently occurs when the leader is a former member of the team, who became a person in charge (responsible leader), due to his/her operational qualities. S/he often has not let go of the good social interaction there was within the team, s/he feels lonely, isolated and looks for intimacy with his/her former co-workers. S/he finds it difficult to set the limits of his/her new role, and not to grant privileges and favours in order to make himself/herself accepted, which is harmful to the well-being of the team.

This also happens when the leader maintains personal and private relationships with one of his/her co-workers. Other people feel it as unfair preference.

Problems for the effective leader

The need to look ahead

This happens when the leader does not update his/her skills, which tend to deteriorate. Even though s/he used to be an expert some time ago, if s/he doesn't keep up his/her knowledge permanently, the environment and the strategic elements may change without his/her realizing it. Then s/he may make decisions which are harmful for the aims of the library.

This can occur, for instance, when members of the team continue to spend a lot of time cataloguing materials already treated in other libraries, *"because we have always done it like that"*.

It occurs, too, when librarians do not realize that the library rules and regulations are so strict that they impose inappropriate constraints on the public and cause readers to gradually leave.

The withholding of information critical for the smooth running of the library

An expert with advantaged status might "rest on his/her laurels" and "lord it over everyone". Consequently s/he can appropriate for personal objectives information belonging to the library: s/he makes his/her career at the expense of the library and its members.

It might be so the case, for example, that a person in charge would use some data related to his/her library, not to aim at a better management but so as to sell himself/herself better elsewhere.

A lack of humility

A responsible leader, knowing that his/her department or the information s/he handles, deals with strategic elements in his/her library, may feel above other people and disparage or despise their work, which s/he considers as less important than his/her own. This could happen, for instance, with the person in charge of a "local community" department, who, in a strong position because of the Mayor's support, would look down on his/her colleagues, regarded as less important. This behaviour harms the good quality of the atmosphere.

Separation of responsible leader and effective leader

It is the most serious malfunction: when the responsible leader (person in charge) is not the effective leader and does not control the strategic elements in the environment: s/he is unable to see the changes in the environment which could jeopardize the survival and the smooth running of the library. In that case s/he is not the person who manages the library. Another person is the effective leader.

Problems for the psychological leader

Both leaders have incompatible conceptions

When the psychological leader does not perceive or does not approve of the views and objectives of the responsible leader, nothing new is done, for everyone expects a counter-order. If, for instance, the responsible leader wants to launch reforms and the psychological leader is against them, the changes will not occur, for nobody will carry them out.

It is in the own interests of the responsible leader to identify the psychological leaders, to recognize their role and their influence and to establish a bond with them.

Very often, executive secretaries or assistant directors are psychological leaders.

A failure to acknowledge the psychological leader

If the psychological leader is not acknowledged in his/her role, s/he may suffer from it and try to compensate for the failure by "acting important" at the expense of the library and his/her colleagues. For instance, s/he may set people against each other by hawking malicious gossip: *"You know, yesterday I heard Janet say that you didn't work well and that you were never on time".*

A failure to maintain privacy

If the psychological leader spreads confidential information, acquired through his/her role, s/he endangers the safety of colleagues who may feel betrayed.

This also happens when the psychological leader, sometimes the previous one, has left the library and continues to play his/her role as a leader from a distance, without a bond with the new responsible leader. This situation contributes to poisoning the atmosphere and keeps back unavoidable changes.

WHAT CAN BE DONE TO MAKE THE SITUATION BETTER?

Make the responsible leader the effective leader

In order to have a wholesome situation in a library, the responsible leader must also be the effective leader of the library. S/he must keep on paying attention to the environment so as to make sure that the activities and services offered by the library are still in line with the needs of the environment, needs that are constantly altering.

If s/he has to discharge some duties, s/he must maintain control on the strategic objectives of the library, which may change unexpectedly according to the changes and developments in the environment.

For instance, a library often has to take a stand with regard to online services, such as Google, which develops rapidly.

Enable the responsible leader to identify and form a bond with the other leaders

Each type of leader plays a specific role in the management of the library and acts, as we have seen, along different lines of thought. It matters a great deal that the energy resulting from each person's activity should be channelled in the same direction and not in opposite directions. The duty of the responsible leader is to establish a bond with the psychological leader/s.

One or several leader/s?

The responsible leader may be both the effective leader and the psychological leader in his/her library: in this case, s/he has considerable influence on his/her team, and can lead them wherever s/he wants, preferably toward brilliant actions. But when s/he leaves the library, all the mainstays of activity go with him/her and it is long and arduous to close the chapter. This creates a difficult situation for the leader who comes after him/her.

Balancing the energy coming from the leadership with the energy coming from the team

If all the decisions are made by the leadership, the members of the team only have to enforce these decisions. This way of functioning is conducive to passivity in colleagues who have the feeling that they do not have their say in decision making. They may feel that their skills and judgment are not taken into consideration.

Balancing the energies avoids tiring out one or the other. This means asking the opinion of professionals who practise their job every day and see the public.

How is it possible, for instance, to work out an efficient and realistic library users' charter without consulting widely with those who work with the public, who know their demands, and asking these people for their thoughts about this plan?

QUEL RESPONSIBLE ETES-VOUS?

OU: LES TROIS FONCTIONS DU LEADERSHIP, EN LIEN AVEC LES OBJECTIFS STRATEGIQUES DE VOTRE BIBLIOTHEQUE

Dr Marielle de Miribel
Mediadix, Université Paris 10, France
miribel@u-paris10.fr

Qu'est-ce qui prouve que je suis véritablement le responsable de mon service?

Quelques mots pour vous dire qui je suis et à quel titre j'interviens, avant de vous présenter ma façon d'aborder les choses, en ce qui concerne la notion de leadership en bibliothèque : Je suis conservateur en chef de bibliothèque, sur liste d'aptitude des maîtres de conférence en information communication et Analyste transactionnelle certifiée dans le champ des Organisations. J'ai dirigé plusieurs établissements et animé des réseaux de bibliothèque. À ce titre, j'accompagne des responsables de service, particulièrement dans le changement organisationnel et je conçois, organise et anime des formations pour les personnels en poste en bibliothèque concernant le management, la dimension et la relation humaine dans les bibliothèques.

Une grande partie des concepts sur lesquels je vais m'appuyer sont issus de l'Analyse Transactionnelle, et tout particulièrement d'un ouvrage d'Éric Berne qui a pour titre: Structure et Dynamique des organisations et des groupes.

Les 3 casquettes du leadership

Il y a trois dimensions dans le leadership, qui correspondent aux trois manières de représenter l'organisation d'une bibliothèque: l'organigramme fonctionnel (les rôles), l'organigramme personnel *(« qui est où ? »)* et la représentation que chacun a de sa place dans la bibliothèque et dans l'estime du leader *(« où je me situe ? »)*. Voici brièvement ces trois aspects sur lesquels nous reviendrons en détail.

- **le leader responsable** est celui qui occupe la position de leader dans l'organigramme.

- **le leader effectif** est celui qui prend véritablement les décisions, quelle que soit sa place dans l'organigramme. Il peut être installé dans le bureau du fond, mais être la personne qui a le plus d'influence sur l'activité et les décisions à prendre
- **le leader psychologique** est la personne la plus influente dans les représentations personnelles de chacun des membres du groupe, et celle à qui ils viennent se confier.

Ces trois sortes de leadership peuvent être assurées par une même personne mais toutes les combinaisons existent, et peuvent générer de nombreux dysfonctionnements dans la gestion de la bibliothèque. La distinction entre ces trois types de leadership n'est pas toujours aisée à faire, et se repère plus facilement en cas de crise. En tout état de cause, quelle que soit la taille de la bibliothèque ou structure considérée, ces trois dimensions existent toujours.

LE LEADER RESPONSABLE

- **C'est lui qui rend des comptes à N+1**

Il a été nommé par son ou ses supérieurs hiérarchiques et c'est lui qui rend des comptes à ses supérieurs, particulièrement en situation de crise.

- **C'est la casquette de la légitimité**

Sa nomination fait l'objet d'une communication publique, parution au journal, photo, cérémonie d'accueil et d'intronisation. Il porte la responsabilité de la bibliothèque.

- **Il donne le sens**

Il a pour rôle de donner une direction, un sens aux activités de la bibliothèque. Il dit : « *c'est là qu'on va, et on y va de cette manière* ». Par exemple, c'est lui qui prend les décisions en termes de politique d'acquisition, de prêt, de charte d'accueil, etc. C'est lui qui valide les priorités et les projets à mener sur certaines cibles de publics : les jeunes adultes, ou les personnes à mobilité réduite, les étudiants de premier cycle ou les chercheurs, etc. Chaque type de bibliothèque doit faire des choix en fonction de son espace, ses budgets, ses ressources externes et internes, ses partenaires, les compétences de son personnel, etc.

- **Il joue un rôle important au niveau de la pensée**

Réfléchir, penser, diagnostiquer, anticiper sont ses prérogatives. Il est acteur dans le domaine de la pensée.

- **Ses trois critères de puissance personnelle**

Voici trois critères pour évaluer sa puissance dans son rôle :
- Il peut modifier l'organigramme sans avoir à demander une autorisation au préalable
- Il peut donner des récompenses et des sanctions irrévocablement
- Il peut modifier ses objectifs, ses priorités, le règlement interne et la culture professionnelle en fonction des opportunités.

- **Le garant de la cohérence interne**

Pour dire les choses d'une autre manière, le leader responsable est le garant de la cohérence de la bibliothèque qu'il dirige, face aux différents types de pressions que les personnes ou autres structures de l'environnement exercent sur elle. À titre d'exemple :

- **Les autorités de tutelle** exercent des pressions telles que : l'exigence de rendement et de résultats significatifs, des actions efficaces avec des moyens peu coûteux en personnel et en matériel ;
- **Les partenaires** veulent que les projets menés conjointement par la bibliothèque augmentent leur propre efficacité ;
- **Les lecteurs et usagers** aspirent à un service gratuit, rapide, efficace, ouvert le plus largement possible, une durée de prêt illimitée, un accueil chaleureux et convivial, des occasions de rencontre, etc.

- **En lien avec l'existence et la légitimité de la bibliothèque**

De fait, le leader responsable reste centré sur le rôle que remplit la bibliothèque dans l'environnement, sur sa valeur ajoutée. Le rôle des éléments de l'environnement de la bibliothèque est d'exercer des pressions sur sa frontière externe, d'exiger d'elle des services qui répondent à leurs besoins. En effet, si la bibliothèque cesse de répondre aux attentes, aux besoins qui se manifestent sous forme de pressions exercées sur elle, – lui demandant d'agir et de répondre à ces demandes –, elle risque de péricliter ou de disparaître, en raison de son inutilité perçue. En fait, la bibliothèque a besoin de pressions pour vivre, et s'y adapter. Pour s'y adapter, elle doit se construire et agir dans la cohérence, vis-à-vis d'elle-même et vis-à-vis de son environnement.

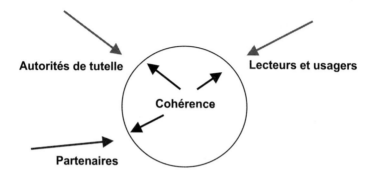

De ce fait, le rôle de la bibliothèque, représentée par son leader responsable, est de faire face à ces pressions et de leur opposer de la cohérence dans ses missions et objectifs.

Dans le cas contraire, si les priorités de la bibliothèque ne sont pas clairement définies, cohérentes entre elles, explicites et compréhensibles à tous, la pluralité des missions assumées risque de plonger la bibliothèque dans l'incohérence interne et la fragilité.

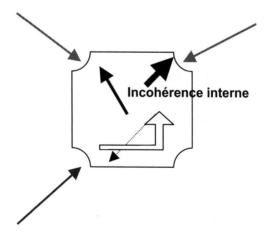

Par exemple, imaginons que la section jeunesse d'une bibliothèque consacre des mois de travail de médiation hors les murs pour amener à la lecture des publics fragilisés, adolescents, jeunes de cités, parents illettrés, etc. Si au bout de constants efforts et de liens tissés dans la durée, le médiateur attire le jeune à la bibliothèque, par exemple, et que celui-ci se fait rejeter rapidement pour ne pas appliquer les règles implicites de la civilité ou du règlement intérieur, le travail des médiateurs hors les murs est-il en cohérence avec le fonctionnement et le règlement de la bibliothèque ?

LE LEADER EFFECTIF

- **C'est la casquette de l'expertise**

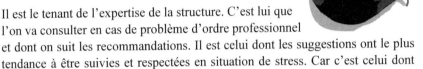

Il est le tenant de l'expertise de la structure. C'est lui que l'on va consulter en cas de problème d'ordre professionnel et dont on suit les recommandations. Il est celui dont les suggestions ont le plus tendance à être suivies et respectées en situation de stress. Car c'est celui dont les collègues considèrent qu'il est celui qui connaît vraiment « le boulot ».

- **Le spécialiste de la veille stratégique**

Dans son rôle et ses compétences d'expert, il connaît les éléments stratégiques de l'environnement: les opportunités et menaces, par exemple, de la situation en cours, (en référence à l'audit marketing SWOT) ; il sait utiliser ceux qui garantissent la pérennité de sa structure. Il connaît et maîtrise les éléments clés dans le contexte de la bibliothèque, et peut prévoir les changements décisifs qui vont obliger la bibliothèque à s'adapter à ces nouvelles données.

Par exemple, une fusion des mairies comme au Québec ou une communauté de communes comme en France modifie profondément la nature des services à proposer;

Ou bien une modification légale des procédures d'achat des collections, notamment sur les documents électroniques entraîne des modifications importantes dans la politique d'acquisition;

Ou encore, les programmes de concours ou d'examens pour les médecins ou les avocats nécessitent une vigilance toute spéciale et un traitement particulier sur les collections concernées, pour maintenir l'égalité des chances pour tous et éviter que quelques étudiants ne s'approprient à l'année les ouvrages nécessaires aux études.

- **Il donne la méthode**

C'est la personne référant en termes d'activité professionnelle. Il est celui que l'on va consulter en cas de difficulté d'ordre opérationnel : *« comment fais-tu pour... »* ou *« je ne sais pas comment cataloguer, indexer, référencer, désherber, sauvegarder, trier, effectuer telle ou telle opération »*.

- **Il joue un rôle important au niveau de la tâche et du geste**

Il montre, il explique, il commente, il assiste, il forme ses collaborateurs

- **Il est coopté**

Contrairement à la fonction du leader responsable qui est une charge déléguée par N+1, la dimension effective du leadership est un rôle coopté. Ce sont les autres, les collègues, les collaborateurs, qui, sans le dire officiellement, choisissent la personne qui, à leur avis, va les renseigner et les aider le plus efficacement.

- **Il est en lien avec l'objectif stratégique de la bibliothèque**

Selon les différents modes d'expertise nécessaires, il peut y avoir plusieurs personnes différentes considérées comme experts dans leur domaine. Simplement, le leader effectif, en raison de sa perception des changements stratégiques dans l'environnement, sait repérer les objectifs stratégiques de la bibliothèque, ceux qui garantissent sa survie : ou (pour dire les choses autrement), la pression la plus stratégique exercée sur la bibliothèque: « Si la bibliothèque brûlait cette nuit ? qui serait le plus incommodé par cet incendie ? Qui serait lui-même en grande difficulté ou en danger ? »

- **Cinq critères de puissance personnelle**

  - L'expertise, comme une compétence particulière ou rare, en tout cas peu partagée
  - La possibilité de capter, filtrer, retenir ou contrôler l'information
  - La capacité de créer ou modifier les règles de fonctionnement
  - L'avantage d'attribuer aux autres des moyens financiers et matériels

- L'accès à un réseau relationnel externe, comme les liens avec la presse, avec des institutions internationales comme l'IFLA, avec les associations professionnelles et les syndicats

LE LEADERSHIP PSYCHOLOGIQUE

- **C'est la casquette de l'influence**

Il est le personnage le plus influent dans les représentations personnelles de ses collègues. Sa parole et son opinion ont un poids particulier et influencent largement l'opinion des autres.

- **Ses collaborateurs exigent de lui des qualités particulières**

Le leader psychologique d'un groupe occupe une place privilégiée dans les représentations, qu'il soit ou non en même temps leader responsable et effectif. Ses collaborateurs exigent de lui des qualités particulières; on attend de lui qu'il soit : omnipotent, omniscient, immortel, invulnérable, jamais malade, incorruptible, non influençable, infatigable et sans peur. Ce sont les mêmes qualités que celles attribuées jadis aux Empereurs, comme: 'l'Inégalé', 'le Tout-Puissant', 'l'Invincible'.

Si, dans la vie quotidienne, il manque à l'une de ces qualités, il y aura toujours quelqu'un pour le lui reprocher.

En effet, chacun projette sur lui, de manière inconsciente, ses attentes, espoirs et déceptions d'enfant vis-à-vis de ses parents.

- **Une fonction de conseiller**

Il assume la fonction de conseiller, à titre privé, pour des interrogations d'ordre personnel ou concernant le profil de carrière. On demande son avis pour choisir une formation, valider un profil de poste, répondre à une offre, etc.

- **Il donne du lien, de la sécurité relationnelle**

C'est lui qui cimente les relations entre les membres d'une équipe. Il est souvent à l'origine des rituels de convivialité: les pots de départ, d'arrivée, les gâteaux ... Il peut proposer aussi des activités culturelles ou sportives hors bibliothèque, au cours desquelles les collègues ont l'occasion de se connaître sous un jour plus personnel.

- **Il joue un rôle important au niveau de la parole, et du ressenti**

Dans son bureau, il y a souvent du monde, et on y parle beaucoup, sur les sujets les plus divers. En cas de crise, tout le monde vient le voir, lui raconter les derniers développements et y connaître les rumeurs en cours. C'est un bureau où chacun se sent libre de laisser libre cours à ses émotions. C'est parfois le « bureau des pleurs ».

- **Ses quatre critères de puissance personnelle**
- Il sait écouter
- Il fait preuve de charisme
- Ses collègues ont de l'affection pour lui
- Il respecte la discrétion et la confidentialité
- Il est coopté

Lui aussi est coopté par ses collègues pour les questions d'ambiances, de relations, de conseils. Il ne peut s'autoproclamer leader psychologique de son groupe.

DES QUALITES SPECIFIQUES POUR CHAQUE DIMENSION DU LEADERSHIP

Pour conclure sur les qualités de chaque dimension du leadership, on peut dire pour schématiser que:

- **Le leader responsable répond au besoin de structure, de sens et de cadre de ses collaborateurs:**

    il donne du sens, des objectifs, des priorités, des limites

    il donne des missions définies, prendre des décisions, clarifier les enjeux

    il a les idées claires, il joue la transparence,

    il sait dire non, être responsable et assumer,

il considère l'intérêt général avant les intérêts particuliers,

il organise le travail, il organise et anime des réunions,

il est en bonne santé

- **Le leader effectif répond au besoin de stimulation de ses collaborateurs:**

Il montre une compétence managériale, il sait gérer une équipe, être un modèle pour ses collaborateurs,

Il sait s'adapter, aller en formation, évoluer,

Il sait se remettre en question, garder l'esprit ouvert

- **Le leader psychologique répond au besoin de reconnaissance de ses collaborateurs:**

Il montre du respect, de la considération, de l'écoute pour ses collaborateurs

Il pratique la justice, l'équité: en ne manifestant pas de préférence et en ne choisissant ni « chouchou » ni « tête de turc »

Il sait être psychologue, il donne à chacun le sentiment d'exister et d'être important

QUAND ÇA DYSFONCTIONNE, QUE SE PASSE-T-IL?

Les problèmes au niveau du leader responsable

- **Manque de légitimité**

C'est le cas quand le responsable n'est pas nommé vraiment. Il est chef, mais par intérim, pour un temps, en attendant mieux ... Il n'a pas été officiellement annoncé et intronisé. De ce fait, ses collaborateurs ne savent pas s'ils doivent ou non investir de l'énergie pour s'adapter à son fonctionnement, ce qui génère de l'angoisse, de l'attentisme et de l'immobilisme. On attend...

C'est également le cas quand on sait que le chef actuel va partir, sans savoir qui va le remplacer. On attend...

- **Manque de directives**

Dans ce cas de figure, le chef ne sait pas où il va. Il peut recevoir lui-même des consignes contradictoires de son ou ses N+1, qui peuvent eux-mêmes ne pas être d'accord entre eux. On voit ça souvent lors de la construction ou la rénovation d'un bâtiment : chacun s'épuise et se décourage entre les ordres et contre-ordres.

- **Manque de limites**

Il arrive parfois que le responsable d'une équipe cherche à se faire aimer de ses collaborateurs plutôt que de se faire respecter. Ce phénomène est fréquent quand le leader est un ancien membre du groupe, qui est devenu responsable en raison de ses qualités opérationnelles. Il n'a souvent pas fait le deuil de la convivialité qui existait au sein de l'équipe, il se sent seul, isolé, et cherche la complicité avec ses anciens collègues. Il a de la difficulté à fixer les limites de son nouveau rôle, et risque, pour tenter de se faire accepter, d'octroyer des passe-droits et des faveurs, dommageables à la santé de l'équipe.

C'est également le cas quand le leader entretient des relations intimes ou privées avec l'un de ses collaborateurs. Les autres le ressentent comme du favoritisme et une injustice : *« pourquoi lui et pas moi ? Ah ouais, d'accord... »*.

Les problèmes au niveau du leader effectif

- **Manque de perspective**

C'est le cas quand le leader ne remet pas à jour ses compétences, qui s'usent avec le temps. S'il a été expert à un moment donné, mais s'il ne se remet pas en question en permanence, l'environnement et les éléments stratégiques risquent de changer sans qu'il s'en aperçoive. Et alors, il risque d'entraîner la bibliothèque dans des décisions dommageables à ses missions.

C'est le cas par exemple, quand les équipes continuent à passer un temps considérable à cataloguer des ouvrages traités ailleurs, *« parce qu'on a toujours fait comme ça »*

C'est également le cas quand la bibliothèque ne se rend pas compte que la rigueur de son règlement, devenu inadapté, par rapport aux contraintes vécues par son public, fait fuir peu à peu ses lecteurs.

- **Rétention d'informations vitales pour le bon fonctionnement de la bibliothèque**

Un expert, bien installé dans son statut, risque de se « reposer sur ses lauriers » et de se considérer « en pays conquis ». De ce fait, il peut s'approprier pour des objectifs personnels des informations qui appartiennent à la bibliothèque : il poursuit une carrière personnelle au détriment de la bibliothèque et de ses collègues.

C'est le cas par exemple d'un responsable qui utiliserait les données de sa bibliothèque, non pas en vue d'un meilleur fonctionnement, mais pour aller se vendre, mieux, ailleurs.

- **Manque d'humilité**

Un responsable, sachant que son secteur ou les informations qu'il traite sont les éléments stratégiques de la bibliothèque risque de se sentir au dessus des autres, et de dénigrer ou mépriser le travail des autres, jugé comme moins important que le sien. Ce pourrait être le cas, par exemple, du responsable du département « vie locale » d'une bibliothèque municipale, qui, fort de l'appui du maire, regarderait de haut ses collègues jugés moins importants. Ce comportement nuit extrêmement à la qualité de l'ambiance.

- **Séparation du leader responsable et du leader effectif**

C'est le dysfonctionnement le plus grave : quand le leader responsable n'est pas leader effectif, et donc ne maîtrise pas les éléments stratégiques dans l'environnement : il ne sait pas voir les changements dans l'environnement qui pourraient mettre en cause la survie et le fonctionnement de la bibliothèque : si c'est le cas, ce n'est pas lui qui dirige la bibliothèque, c'est un autre, le véritable leader effectif.

Les problèmes au niveau du leader psychologique

- **Incompatibilité de vues avec le leader responsable**

Quand le leader psychologique ne comprend pas ou n'approuve pas les vues ou les objectifs du leader responsable, rien ne se fait, car chacun attend le contre-ordre. Si par exemple, le leader responsable veut initier des réformes et que le leader psychologique n'est pas d'accord, les réformes ne se feront pas car personne ne va les mettre en œuvre.

Le leader responsable a donc tout intérêt à identifier le ou les leaders psychologiques, à reconnaître leur rôle et leur influence et à faire alliance avec eux.

Bien souvent, les secrétaires de direction ou les adjoints au directeur sont des leaders psychologiques.

- **Manque de reconnaissance du leader psychologique**

Si le leader psychologique n'est pas reconnu dans son rôle, il risque de souffrir d'un manque de reconnaissance et de rechercher à compenser ce manque en se donnant de l'importance au détriment de la bibliothèque et des collègues : par exemple, il va monter les gens les uns contre les autres, en colportant des ragots : *« tu sais, j'ai entendu hier Janine dire que tu ne faisais pas bien ton travail, et que tu n'étais jamais à l'heure »*

- **Manque de confidentialité**

Si le leader psychologique diffuse des informations confidentielles, que son rôle lui permet de connaître, il met en danger la sécurité des collègues qui risquent de se sentir trahis.

C'est également le cas quand le leader psychologique, parfois le responsable précédent, a quitté la bibliothèque et continue d'exercer son rôle de leader à distance, sans alliance avec le nouveau leader responsable. Cette situation contribue à empoisonner l'atmosphère et à freiner les changements inévitables.

Comment faire pour améliorer les choses ?

- **Permettre au leader responsable d'être leader effectif**

Pour qu'une bibliothèque soit saine, il est nécessaire que le leader responsable soit aussi le leader effectif de la bibliothèque. Il veille à observer l'environnement pour vérifier que les activités et services proposées par la bibliothèque sont toujours en phase avec les besoins de l'environnement, besoins sans cesse en évolution.

S'il doit déléguer certaines des responsabilités de son rôle, il est impératif qu'il conserve le contrôle des objectifs stratégiques de la bibliothèque, qui peuvent changer de manière subite, en fonction des évolutions ou révolutions dans l'environnement.

Par exemple, une bibliothèque doit bien souvent se positionner par rapport aux services en ligne, comme Google, qui lui, évolue très rapidement.

- **Permettre au leader responsable de reconnaître et faire alliance avec les autres leaders**

Chaque type de leader joue un rôle spécifique dans le fonctionnement de la bibliothèque, et obéit, comme on l'a vu, à des logiques différentes. Il est important que l'énergie produite par l'activité de chacun aille dans le même sens, et pas en sens contraire. La responsabilité du leader responsable est donc de faire alliance avec le ou les leaders psychologiques

- **Un ou plusieurs leaders ?**

Il arrive que le leader responsable soit aussi leader effectif et leader psychologique de sa bibliothèque : dans ce cas de figure, il a beaucoup d'influence sur son équipe et peut les mener où il veut, de préférence vers des actions d'éclat. Mais quand il quitte la bibliothèque, tous les soutiens de l'activité s'en vont avec lui et le deuil à faire est très grand et très long. C'est difficile pour le leader qui arrive après lui.

- **Équilibrer l'énergie qui vient du leadership avec celle qui vient du groupe**

Si toutes les décisions viennent du leadership, les membres du groupe n'ont qu'à appliquer ces décisions. Un tel fonctionnement invite à la passivité chez les collègues qui ont le sentiment de n'avoir pas leur mot à dire dans la prise de décision. Ils peuvent avoir le sentiment que leurs compétences et leur jugement ne sont pas pris en compte.

Équilibrer les énergies permet de ne pas épuiser l'un par rapport aux autres. Cela signifie demander l'avis des professionnels qui pratiquent tous les jours leur métier et voient tous les jours les publics.

Comment, par exemple, élaborer une charte d'accueil efficace et réaliste sans consulter très largement et faire réfléchir à ce projet les personnels placés en présence du public et qui connaissent leurs demandes ?

RESEARCH LIBRARY LEADERSHIP DEVELOPMENT: CREATING A BEST PRACTICE

James Neal
Columbia University, Vice President for Information Services
& University Librarian,
New York, USA
jneal@columbia.edu

Victoria Owen
Head Librarian, University of Toronto,
Ontario, Canada
owen@utsc.utoronto.ca

William Garrison
Syracuse University Library,
Deputy University Librarian & Associate Dean of Libraries
New York, USA
Wagarris@syr.edu

Abstract

The Association of Research Libraries (ARL) created a Research Library Leadership Fellows (RLLF) program to develop the skills of prospective research library leaders. The program curriculum was designed to build on self-assessment in a group-learning setting and to explore strategic issues that are most pressing for future leaders of large research libraries. These topics shaped the design of three, week-long Strategic Issues Institutes that each featured leaders active in the ARL community. The RLLF curriculum was enhanced through site visits to participating ARL libraries and attendance at ARL Membership Meetings. Specific components of the RLLF program are described from the instructional design, to Fellow selection and participation, program roll-out, and evaluation. The RLLF program models a best practice in the area of continuing leadership development and succession planning.

RESEARCH LIBRARY LEADERSHIP FELLOWS: THE CONTEXT

The Association of Research Libraries (ARL) launched the Research Library Leadership Fellows (RLLF) Program in the fall of 2004 in response to the documented and widely discussed need for future leaders to assume senior-level administrative positions in ARL libraries. It was recognized that a variety of library management and leadership development programs was available, but they did not address the specific organizational realities of very large academic and research libraries. In order to cultivate the essential skills in aspiring directors, a tailored experience was crafted in the form of a customized curriculum, a rich group learning process, and individual development goals.

The directors of five ARL member libraries served as sponsors of the RLLF Program: University of California at Los Angeles, Columbia University, University of Illinois at Urbana-Champaign, University of Texas at Austin, and University of Washington. Each designated two staff members to participate, and selected in a competitive process, additional Fellows from other ARL libraries. A total of 21 individuals (20 actually completed) joined the extensive two-year program. This paper describes the goals and context of the RLLF Program, outlines the content of the program, and summarizes the results of the assessment and outcomes of the program.

The RLLF Program sought to provide each fellow the opportunity to:

- prepare to shape libraries and librarianship at the national and international levels;
- develop a global perspective on libraries and their role in society;
- learn to create a strategic vision for their library;
- research and discuss critical current academic issues;
- explore major themes within the academic and research communities;
- develop an entrepreneurial mind-set and skill-set appropriate to the university leadership environment;
- clarify what advancements and innovations in information technology mean for research library leadership;
- expand understanding on the dynamics and politics of campus life.

The RLLF Program recognized the new and extraordinary demands that challenge leaders of North American research libraries. The key success criteria for those positions have been transformed by a number of factors: the increasing political and competitive complexity of the academy, accelerating economic pressures, growing opportunities for information technology, new models of scholarly publishing, new roles in teaching and learning, and expanded resource development and fundraising expectations. Concurrent with a growing demand for multitalented individuals to tackle these issues, the desire to take on leadership challenges seems to wane as potential leaders encounter the turbulence, stress, demands and difficulties of succeeding in these roles. Demographics demonstrate the ageing of the research librarian population, particularly directors, and document that retirements will cause an increased number of openings over the next decade, but without a generation of leaders eager and ready to assume these assignments in ARL institutions.

The RLLF Program has been designed to respond to a series of research library imperatives:

- a succession imperative, the challenge of responding to the realities of workforce replacement and leadership turnover;
- a strategic imperative, new kinds of professional challenges that demand new kinds of library leaders;
- a performance imperative, defining new capacities, capabilities and competencies and ways for developing and delivering these attributes and skills;
- a business imperative, linking leadership development to organizational relevance and impact;
- a personal imperative, promoting leadership as a challenging and rewarding individual aspiration;
- an accountability imperative, both the need to integrate leadership development into organizational and individual responsibility, but also a mandate for assessment and measuring progress.

RESEARCH LIBRARY LEADERSHIP FELLOWS: THE PROGRAM

The two-year program was ambitious and rigorous. Three Strategic Issues Institutes and a one-week site visit hosted by the sponsoring libraries formed the cornerstone of the program. Fellows attended two ARL Membership Meetings and an ARL Forum. A closing capstone event drew on the two-year experience and rounded off the RLLF program.

The Director of Organizational Learning Services at ARL framed the RLLF program and guided the Fellows throughout the program. Community norms were established and embraced. Fellows agreed to a culture of participation and group learning, the need to lean into areas of discomfort, to focus, to offer timely feedback, and to respect confidentiality. The RLLF program was predicated on participation and while the Institute sessions were led by experts, a high level of participation was expected of the Fellows.

Strategic Issues Institutes

The first Strategic Issues Institute set the tone of the RLLF program. It was held at the University of Illinois at Urbana-Champaign in February 2005. The RLLF program achieved excellence through thorough planning, expertise of the ARL staff, the detailed communication plan, binders replete with readings, case studies, learning plan, instructional design and other essential information.

On day one the Fellows plunged in at the deep end. The instructional design framework for the RLLF program set out a four-tiered approach that identified strategic domains, topical issues in each domain, learning outcomes, and key questions that enlarge or focus the issues, compel the exploration of the topic and attempt to answer the key questions.[1]

Strategic Issues Institute I began with the strategic domain of *Challenges and opportunities*. The issue of environmental analysis was developed. A scenario-planning exercise followed as the learning outcome. Fellows were expected to have an in-depth understanding of the issue, articulate a strategy regarding the issue and implement a plan to advance the research library with one or two initiatives. The Learning Insight Sheets from the binder allowed the Fellows to describe in writing a) what was learned from the session, b) what would be useful in the current work environment, and c) what would be pursued further.

The same pattern was followed for the strategic domains *New Roles in Teaching and Learning; New Models of Scholarly Communication; The Work of the Organization; The University's and the Library's International Strategy;* and *The Leadership Challenge*. Presentations by experts in each area launched the discussions with the Fellows, challenging and deepening the understanding of the topic. Fellows then used the Learning Insight Sheets to capture in writing the learning outcomes described above.²

The Fellows provided helpful feedback to the organizers when the program deviated from high caliber programming. The Fellows found that *The Leadership Challenge* unit was not a good fit with the rest of the program in presentation technique and in some of the content.

The first Institute introduced the Fellows to each other. Most of the Fellows' time was scheduled with program activities and Fellows formed spontaneous, informal groups as interests and experiences became apparent. Overall, the group bond remained strong and harmonious throughout and since the conclusion of the program, with some smaller units cohering, but without negative impact to the whole group dynamic.

Strategic Issues Institute II was held at the University of Washington in July/August 2005. The strategic domain covered organizational culture. Experts explored the topical issues of assessment, and intentional leadership in a complex environment and in conjunction with other academic leaders. The Fellows examined a variety of learning spaces and discussed the way each library responded to the community's needs, built its community, and demonstrated new roles for teaching, learning and research. An impressive and gracious panel of library donors met with the Fellows to discuss how they became donors and their perspective on the cultivation of donor relationships with the academy. Another stellar panel with the provost, dean, chair and other academic leaders engaged the Fellows with a discussion of the research enterprise. Binders were again filled with readings, case studies, worksheets for developing a personal vision, biographies of presenters, and worksheets to describe the evidence for learning in different spaces.³

The third and final Strategic Issues Institute was hosted by Columbia University in the City of New York in February 2006. Fellows were invited to facilitate the week long program, by contacting the speakers and introducing them and their topic to the group. Fellows met with academic leaders from New York and environs: Columbia University, New York University, Brown University, New York Public Library, Princeton University, and The Andrew W. Mellon Foundation. This final institute tailored its program to provide the Fellows with an understanding of the spiraling complexity of large research libraries in the academic milieu of their own institution and also in their relationship with other research libraries in their environment. Columbia University Library illustrated this to the highest degree through its membership in many groups by virtue of its location, size, budget, special collections, reputation, stature as a private institution, and leadership on specific public policy issues.[4]

Site Visit

The site visit was the second Fellows event. Each Fellow selected a location for a site visit from the five sponsoring Libraries in March and April 2005. Each Library hosted Fellows for one week, providing them with an in-depth look at their institution.

For example, the site visit to Columbia University, offered a 'no holds barred' look at its libraries and academic community. Fellows were given access to the highest levels of academic leadership in order to understand the central role of the library in the academic enterprise and to get a sense of the University Librarian's leadership responsibility in a large research institution. Department Heads engaged the Fellows with candid discussions about the issues they managed—such as budget problems, divergent opinions, personnel issues, and structure. Fellows were introduced to unique programs in new media, the entrepreneurial perspective in IT and academic computing, and the drive for distinction and excellence through the acquisition of special collections. The site visit provided a rare opportunity to discover the unvarnished internal workings of a large research library. Throughout the week, the Director was unstinting with his time and advice. Enhancing the effectiveness of the site visit was the personalization of many events. Special tours and meetings were arranged upon request. Fellows were invited to lunch with the Provost and entertained in the Director's home and at a top-tier museum. For the duration of the site visit, fellows were made to feel part of a privileged group in the academic milieu.

ARL Membership Meetings

The Fellows were formally invited to attend the ARL Membership Meeting in Washington DC in October 2005. The program presented an exhilarating look at the University Librarian's executive level of activity. Briefing sessions on ARL's strategic directions acquainted Fellows with the newest and most current thinking on critical issues in academic libraries. Specialists conversed on digital repositories and public policies affecting research libraries. There were programs on preservation of licensed content and on the research library's role in teaching and learning. A special day long forum on "Managing Digital Assets" concluded the event. For many Fellows this was their first opportunity to attend an ARL Membership Meeting. The first-rate programming and high level of discourse that occurred made membership in this community of library leaders very compelling.

Similar to the earlier ARL meeting, the May 2006 joint ARL and Canadian Association of Research Libraries (CARL) program featured high profile, expert speakers from many institutions including the British Library, the Library of Congress, Canadian and American universities and academic organizations. Through the speakers and panels the membership examined "The International Dimensions of Digital Science and Scholarship". The Fellows capstone event was held during this joint meeting of ARL and CARL. The Fellows presented a program session to the membership. A team of three or four Fellows led discussions on "The Politics of Research Library Leadership: Mission, Identity, Constituency". Library directors attended and contributed to one of four concurrent sessions discussing a particular aspect of Research Library Leadership.

The ARL Membership meeting in May 2006 concluded the formal part of the RLLF program.

BEST PRACTICES FOR A LIBRARY LEADERSHIP PROGRAM

The RLLF program was developed to create a pool of talent that would be poised to succeed current library leaders. The dearth of potential leaders is recognized in many constituencies and the literature on leadership development supports this finding. While the literature on leadership development for research libraries generally focuses on early and mid-career development and not on programs at the more advanced levels, components of a leadership program that are referred to include identification of potential leaders[5]; opportunities for professional education[6]; experiences for growth and achievement[7]; connection to organization purpose[8]; and a mentor relationship[9]. The RLLF program features all of the components advocated in the literature as well as others that enhanced the experience. ARL created a best practice in professional development based on the literature and early indications of desired results. The program can be used as a model for leadership development programs elsewhere.

Critical to the success of the RLLF program were the following:

1. Commitment from the highest level:
   - Involvement of five top level ARL Directors who consulted with the ARL Director of Organizational Learning Services to create the instructional design and plan the Institutes and events;
   - ARL Director level support from home institutions.

2. High caliber programming with explicit learning outcomes:
   - Fellows met with experts in each of the four strategic domains;
   - Fellows had immediate and frequent immersion at the expert level;
   - Program schedule built in time for reflection between events;
   - A variety of programs (site visits, interviews, focused discussion, lectures, panels, etc.) were tailored to different aspects of the learning plan.

3. Judicious selection of Fellows:
   - High level of interest among Fellows in assuming leadership roles;
   - Harmonious group dynamic based on common goals.

4. Access to ARL Directors and academic leaders:
   - Frequent individual and group access to sponsoring Directors;
   - Two sponsoring Directors attended each Institute and were available throughout the week for discussion and meeting;
   - At each institute the University President met with the Fellows as did other academic leaders, provosts, chairs, etc.

5. Mentor Program:
   - Two Fellows developed valuable mentor relationships with an ARL Director from the mentor pool;
   - This component of the program languished in the inaugural run but could be developed as a more robust element.

6. Ongoing contact with Fellows and Directors:

- The myriad of opportunities to learn throughout the program and the promise of ongoing connection with ARL;

- Valuable post-program contact with Directors and Fellows for ongoing advice and collegial exchange;

- Continuing dialogue with ARL Directors at home institutions regarding new opportunities for growth and development.

RESEARCH LIBRARY LEADERSHIP FELLOWS: PROGRAM EVALUATION

Background

At the August 2005 Strategic Issues Institute at the University of Washington, the Fellows discussed the need to evaluate the program and to measure the success of the program. The initial evaluative issues identified included:

1. Assessing the program's influence on increasing the participants' capabilities, capacities and confidence in being promoted to positions of increased responsibility;

2. Assessing the program's costs and benefits to participating and sponsoring institutions;

3. Assessing the program's design and sustainability for addressing succession planning for executive leadership in large research libraries.

A subgroup of the Fellows formed to develop a program evaluation that would focus on the Association of Research Libraries RLLF program's impact on the participants, the institutions and the profession. A multipart survey was developed that included separate survey questions for the Fellows, the Fellows' directors, the sponsoring directors, the mentors, and the ARL staff.

The survey was conducted on the ARL website and was completed in June 2006. Although only some of the program's impact could be realized so shortly after the completion of the program, the Fellows agreed that it was important to document the elements of the program and its perceived impact on the first group of Fellows and sponsoring institutions in order to inform future iterations of the program.

The Survey

The complete survey questions and evaluation cannot be printed in this paper. The survey questions covered the following areas:

1. The application process for the program;
2. The 2004–2006 Fellows (including the Fellows' backgrounds, positions, professional experience and expected outcomes from the program);
3. The assessment and rating of the program design;
4. The evaluation of the program's institutes and events;
5. The assessment and rating of the program content;
6. The evaluation of the role of directors at institutions with Fellows in the program;
7. The evaluation of the role of the sponsoring institutions;
8. The evaluation of the role of mentors;
9. The evaluation of the ARL program coordinator;
10. Overall written comments;
11. A set of appendices with estimates from the sponsoring directors on costs and time spent on the program.

The Fellows

The group of Fellows came from fifteen public and six private university libraries. There were four Fellows each from New York and Texas, three each from California and North Carolina, two each from Illinois and Washington, one each from Indiana, Massachusetts and Ontario, Canada. There were eleven females and ten males.

The Fellows were motivated to apply for the program to gain exposure to a broader range of library issues; to other types of university environments; to a broader range of higher education issues; to other management styles and to a broader range of campus dynamics; to participate with other library leaders; to develop a strategic vision for libraries; and to gain a global perspective of libraries.

The areas of specialization in libraries for the Fellows were five in administrative roles, four in technical services, three in health sciences or medical libraries, three in special collections, two each in information technology, public services, and social sciences or humanities areas.

Highlights of the Survey

The initial expected outcomes of the program from the Fellows were reported in ranked order as a) seeking increased responsibilities with a broader impact in the library or on campus; b) participating in administrative groups in the library or on campus in new ways; c) moving to a higher level position at a different institution; d) moving to a higher level position at the current institution, e) increasing effectiveness in the current position; and f) gaining a richer perspective from which to perform any job. At the conclusion of the program, the Fellows almost unanimously reported that they had gained much more from the program than reflected in the initial expected outcomes. The exposure that the Fellows gained from the institutes and site visits with campus leaders and administration proved to be invaluable. The Fellows focused on broader campus and higher education enterprise issues rather than exclusively on library issues. Overall, the program was viewed as extremely successful, with several participants commenting that this program was the best professional experience of their careers.

The Fellows also ranked their satisfaction with the issues and content of the program. The highest ranked areas for the Fellows were the opportunities to interact with campus leadership at the sponsoring institutions; the importance and process for environmental scanning; the discussions about fund raising for libraries; the role of the library on the campus and as a campus unit; and the discussions on information policy and scholarly communication. The lowest ranked content areas for the Fellows were the assessment and redesign of work processes; the assessment of personal leadership skills; and the role of information technology on the campus and in the library.

One immediate outcome of the program was evidenced during the course of the program, as the Fellows reported the following changes in their current positions: a) twelve Fellows indicated that they had begun to participate in groups in their libraries or on their campuses in expanded or new roles; b) eleven accepted responsibilities for a library-wide or campus-wide project or initiative; c) four moved to higher level positions at their current institutions; d) four served as interim library director or dean of libraries; e) three indicated no significant changes in their responsibilities; and f) two moved to higher level positions at different institutions.

Overall evaluative comments from the sponsoring directors were very positive. One director wrote:

> There were numerable and powerful benefits: 1) heightened visibility for the library at the institution; 2) opportunity to bring together opinion makers and influencers at the institution to interact with the Fellows and with each other; 3) provided me with an opportunity to reflect, examine and synthesize my own leadership values and goals; 4) opportunity to expose twenty Fellows to my institution and library which should have future impact on recruitment; 5) opportunity to expose library staff at my institution to emerging leaders from other institutions and exchange ideas and best practices; 6) opportunity to work closely with four other ARL directors; 7) opportunity to get to know twenty very fine Fellows and help them with their careers (and thus contribute to succession planning for ARL libraries).

Another director commented that "My assessment is that the university benefited from this experience at a level equal to the benefits the participants derived from it."

In the area of program design, the sponsoring directors indicated high satisfaction with the size of the Fellows group, the length of the program, the personal contact with the Fellows, the informal discussions with the Fellows at the various events, and the opportunities that the Fellows had to participate. They indicated the least satisfaction with the capstone event, the learning management system that was to have been used, and the e-mail discussion list that was put in place. The Fellows' level of satisfaction with the program design mirrored that of the sponsoring directors very closely.

There were portions of the program that were less successful than others. Only two of the Fellows formed meaningful relationships with the library directors selected as mentors. There was some lack of clarity about the mentoring relationship that was desired, and there was little organization for the mentoring process.

The capstone project that the Fellows presented at the ARL Directors Meeting in May 2006 was also viewed as somewhat less than successful. The capstone project's purpose seemed to shift during the course of the program, and the Fellows were divided into three groups that ultimately led facilitated discussion sessions at the May 2006 meeting. While the discussion sessions were lively and beneficial, these sessions were not what were envisioned at the beginning of the program.

The Fellows program was costly to conduct. The institutions that had Fellows participating in the program paid an annual fee for their participating fellow(s) and had to bear the cost of the expenses and release time of the Fellows to participate in the institutes, site visits, and the ARL Directors meetings. The sponsoring directors' institutions also had costs to absorb in time for preparation, administrative details, meals and other activities. The relatively high costs, however, seem to be overcome by the benefits gained. Nevertheless, there is a significant cost factor to conducting the program.

The amount of time that the library directors spent with the Fellows was extraordinary. Each of the directors whose institutions hosted an institute or a site visit spent almost one full week of his/her time with the Fellows. While the onus may have been on the director to schedule this, it was beyond all expectations held by the Fellows. This concentrated exposure to the directors was invaluable for the Fellows. It not only allowed the Fellows to know the directors better, but it also provided the directors with exposure to the Fellows who did not work at their institutions and to observe firsthand the leaders that were being groomed.

During the ARL Directors Meeting in Ottawa, Canada, May 2006, members of the ARL Leadership Development group held an informal luncheon to talk with the Fellows about the program to learn about the Fellows' perceptions of its effectiveness and success.

Although no survey has been completed since the end of the RLLF program, one outcome that has been reported is that many of the Fellows are being recruited for library director or dean of libraries positions at ARL institutions and other institutions of higher education in the United States and Canada.

CONCLUSION

This was the first Association of Research Libraries, RLLF program. Both the sponsoring directors and the Fellows benefited greatly from the program. While some aspects of the program need to be reviewed and reworked, the program was judged to be a great success. As a result of the evaluation and feedback received from the Fellows and the sponsoring directors, ARL is in the process of forming and planning the second ARL RLLF program.

REFERENCES

[1] Association of Research Libraries. Research Library Leadership Fellows Program, Instructional Design. 2005: 1–7.

[2] Association of Research Libraries. Research Library Leadership Fellows Program 2004–2006, Strategic Issues Institute I, University of Illinois at Urbana-Champaign. 2005: 1–6.

[3] Association of Research Libraries. Research Library Leadership Fellows Program 2004–2006, Strategic Issues Institute II, Complexity, Community, and Collaboration, University of Washington Libraries. 2005: 1–6.

[4] Association of Research Libraries. Research Library Leadership Fellows Program 2004–2006, Strategic Issues Institute III, Columbia University. 2006: 1–6.

[5] Whitmell, V. *The Future of Human Resources in Canadian Libraries, 'the 8RsStudy: Considerations for the Canadian Association of Research Libraries*. CARL/ABRC, 2006, 22

[6] The 8RsResearch Team. The Future of Human Resources in Canadian Libraries.2005 8Rs Research Team. 2005: 181–186

[7] Raschke, G. T., Hiring and Recruitment Practices in Academic Libraries: Problems and Solutions. Portal: *Libraries and the Academy* Vol. 3, No. 1. 2003: 63

[8] Kaufman, P. T., Where Do the Next "We" Come From? Recruiting, Retaining and Developing Our Successors. *ARL Bimonthly Report* 221 (April 2002): 3

[9] Best Practices in Leadership Development and Organizational Change. Wiley. 2005: xxiii

A QUESTION OF CONFIDENCE?: DEVELOPING FUTURE LEADERS AND MANAGERS FOR LIBRARY AND INFORMATION SERVICES—A CASE STUDY OF A TAILORED APPROACH TO PERSONAL AND PROFESSIONAL DEVELOPMENT

Sue Roberts,
University Librarian, Victoria University of Wellington, New Zealand

Coral Black,
Head of Public Services, Senate House Library, University of London (UK)*

(Both formerly of Edge Hill University, UK)

Abstract

This paper focuses upon several interlocking key themes relevant to the IFLA CPD conference: it considers what are the skills needed by emerging leaders in the library and information world and then explores one model of leadership development and the impact it has had on a range of individuals. This critically evaluative paper is grounded in the literature but also provides a very real and relevant case study of a tailored leadership development programme. Qualitative data from the participants provides us with multiple insights into how library and information staff at different levels view leadership, their own skills and abilities, and the effect that such leadership development approaches have on them. It concludes with generic reflections on how organisations can develop self-confidence and leadership potential.

---

* *Contact: Coral Black, Head of Public Services, Senate House Library, University of London Research Library Services, Malet Street, London WC1E 7HU. Tel: 020 7862 8441; Email: Coral.Black@London.ac.uk*

INTRODUCTION

In recent years there have been a number of papers, reports and other documents that have expressed concern about succession planning for leadership in the information management profession. There is an evident concern both within the literature and within professional practice for future leadership. Corrall[1] identifies that "There is a serious shortage of candidates for senior positions", whilst the Public Library workforce study[2] paints a worrying picture of a sector in a state of crisis. Moreover, demands on leaders within the information services context are greater than ever before with the pace of change, the demands of stakeholders and rising expectations of staff all impacting on leadership requirements and skills. Corrall[3] "has lost count of the number of articles, reports and papers expressing concern about the quality of leadership in library and information services" and comments that the sector is not alone in worrying about this problem.

In light of the above context, and the need to proactively develop leaders at all levels and to consider the skills they require, this paper critically explores an experiential and practical approach to succession planning within a higher education library and information context. Edge Hill University's 'Leaders and Managers' programme was introduced in 2005 and took a bespoke approach to leadership development, beginning with the individual and using mentoring and coaching as key tools. This paper, in addition to providing an overview and assessment of the programme and the implications for other services and contexts, includes a qualitative evaluation that examines the impact that the programme has had on the first cohort—in relation to careers, self-confidence, self-perception and service development.

CONTEXT—TRENDS IN LEADERSHIP THEORY

It is important to briefly contextualise approaches to leadership development within current theory and thinking on leadership and management, particularly as this has influenced the case study illustrated here. The study of leadership is a relatively recent discipline and writers have discussed and argued extensively over the distinction between leadership and management. Most agree that there is a distinction, summarised as:

Managers—internally focused, will complete the task, an operator, problem-solver;

Leaders—externally focused, has vision, a strategists, catalyst, looking to the future;

Management—concerned with what people with responsibility for others actually *do*;

Leadership—ability of people to *influence* others towards achievement of goals.[4]

Such distinctions are felt by some people to be unhelpful, as they portray leadership as positive and management as negative. In addition, some authors view the two concepts and roles as mutually exclusive—one person cannot be both as they have incompatible values. However, Yukl[5] argues convincingly that, whilst they are distinct processes, and that people can lead without being a manager and can manage without being a leader, they are interlinked as leadership is an essential management role that pervades other roles. Writers also stress the value of effective management and feel strongly that it should not be denigrated as a function.

So, how do we conceive of 21st century leadership? There remain tensions in modern concepts of leadership with the 'new leader' still seen as a visionary, charismatic individual, seemingly at odds with the concept of the 'superleader' who aims to develop leadership at all levels of the organisation. Authors are certainly now more critical of the 'larger than life' leader who leads from the front, seeing effective leadership as a process created by an individual (the 'learning leader') rather than dependent on their personal qualities.[6] There is a definite de-emphasis of control in new leadership models, revealing a shift towards participative management and distributed leadership where staff at all levels are empowered in their roles.

LEADERSHIP IN LIBRARY AND INFORMATION SERVICES

As highlighted in the introduction to this paper, both public and academic library sectors are concerned with leadership, and particularly succession planning for the future. In the public library sector, research undertaken by Mullins[7] into the perceptions of senior managers, indicates an apparent lack of distinction between management and leadership. Moreover, he concludes that leadership qualities are scarce with the focus too much on 'library' skills and not enough on leadership. Both Mullins[8] and O-Connor[9] suggest that the library and information profession have been too 'narrow,' too focused on "the ordinary and the mundane" and that staff need to consider the intelligences that they require to pursue their work and lives. If there is to be significant change in perceptions on library leadership and the attributes and behaviours needed for the future, we will require a "mental shift".

A project undertaken in UK higher education institutions, led by Birmingham University, explored recruitment, training and succession planning issues for heads of information services.[10] Challenges included obstacles to recruitment, skills gaps, training and development needs, the increased pace of change for managers and the increase in hybrid roles that encompassed diverse services, not simply libraries. The key management skills found to be lacking were:

- Strategic management and leadership
- Ability to manage change
- Customer focus-orientation

It should also be stressed that leadership is a concern right across library organisations, required in all levels and functions, as "the development of leadership throughout the organisation is the only way to succeed."[11] Eastell[12] also highlights this non-hierarchical approach, "It's much less about finding the next head of library service and far more about finding ways of offering library staff at all levels the opportunity to demonstrate and develop their leadership skills."

This brief review of the literature would appear to indicate that the nurturing of leadership potential within the library and information profession is a key priority globally, nationally and locally. What tools and approaches are available to harness and develop this potential?

STAFF DEVELOPMENT APPROACHES

People learn in different ways, often by being formally taught or by experience with the workplace as an ideal environment for experiential learning. Experiential learning has been defined as the insight that is gained through the internalisation of our own or observed experiences.[13] This learning theory builds on the influential work of Kolb[14] who described learning as the process whereby knowledge is created through the transformation of experience.

Kolb's model has four distinct phases:

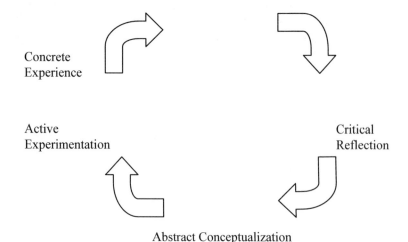

Table I: Kolb's Learning Cycle

This sequence of do, think, plan and act can be applied with particular relevance to experiential learning. Experiential learning can be extremely powerful. As a process of reflection and learning which is supported by colleagues, individuals can learn with, and from, each other. Rather than learning by telling, as is the case in a talk or a lecture, the learner learns by doing, thinking and internalising the situation before applying relevant aspects to themselves, influencing their future actions and thoughts. Coaching and mentorship are also viewed as key tools within experiential learning, enabling reflection, personal one-to-one discussion and action planning, and aiming for tailored and contextualised learning experiences.

Recent theories on leadership development have also highlighted the centrality of self-knowledge linked to authenticity and congruence. Authors argue that to be really effective as a leader, individuals must have a high degree of self-awareness and must strive for congruence between their actions and their personal values and beliefs.[15]

In the UK there has been a new-found focus on formal leadership development programmes, for example the SCONUL/UCISA Future Leaders and the CLORE Leadership programmes. However, there is less evidence of what is happening at a local level. Neither should such programmes be just be for aspiring directors, the current focus of the majority of national programmes and research.

Leadership and management development methods for library professionals have included:

- Formal education (MBA, DMS,IPM);
- Training e.g. Emotional Intelligence programmes;
- Experiential learning (often seen as the most effective), incorporating secondments, job rotation, coaching;
- Mentoring.

However, management and leadership development should not simply be viewed as competency and skills based. It must aim to challenge all staff to self-develop through increased self-knowledge, personal reflection and personal challenges. The development of effective leadership is thus a complex process, summarised by Adair as encompassing a blend of:

Leadership quality—what you are;

Leadership situational—what you know;

Leadership functional—what you do;

Leadership values—what you believe.[16]

THE CASE STUDY

Edge Hill University: the imperative to develop leaders and managers for tomorrow

One of the country's newest Universities, Edge Hill is located in the North West of England, with 9,000 students on a range of degree and diploma courses and a further 6,000 on continuing professional development courses, particularly in education and health-related areas. The University has strong centralised academic support structures enhanced by the formation of Learning Services in 2002. The service is both large and diverse, incorporating learning resource centres and information provision, learning support, ICT user support for learning and teaching, e-learning development and support, media services, study skills and dyslexia support.

Many staff both at senior and middle manager level are fully engaged in service development activities with the need to manage staff resources in order to support the strategic direction of the institution and to enhance the student experience. While the University has a central programme for leadership development with a formal Leadership College programme, this is currently aimed at head of service level. Within Learning Services, however, leadership and management development is not viewed as simply being a requirement of the Senior Management team, but almost a necessity for all staff in middle manager and supervisory positions. The service has a strong commitment to staff development and training across all staff teams with a strategic focus on service delivery/development with a need to continually develop and prepare staff to take on new and changing roles.

Succession planning was a topic that the service started to discuss as early as 2003, but at that time it was not felt to be a priority for the service. During the period that followed, however, a number of factors culminated in growing concerns around middle and senior management roles that would, in effect, impact on the delivery and development of the service in the future. Following further discussion, programme planning started in 2004 with a start date of January 2005. Priority was given to succession planning both in terms of time and resources, as a result of concerns in relation to the following areas:

- A high staff turnover had resulted in the appointment of a number of new managers and supervisors across the service. New appointees often needed substantial support to ensure they developed to the necessary level;

- A need to reduce the perceived gap between the work of our Senior Management Team and the staff at the level directly below;

- Difficulties in recruiting to senior posts staff who have the right mix of skills, knowledge and experience. Posts often had to be re-advertised;

- A need to tap into the potential of our existing staff and develop their self-confidence. We knew they were good but we just needed them to realise it too!

Interestingly we also felt that we needed to almost 'demystify' staff perceptions in relation to what they saw as 'management roles'. While management roles are often difficult and certainly challenging they are not 'rocket science', and staff should not feel they are beyond reach in terms of their own career progression.

DEVELOPING MANAGERS AND LEADERS—OUR APPROACH

Participation on the programme was open to all staff but there would be a selection process. Those who applied had to submit an application, which explained why they wanted to take part in the programme and what personal, team and service benefits they felt they would receive. A total of 15 applications was received and a cohort of ten selected, comprising a range of backgrounds and experience from new managers, supervisors and staff wanting to refresh existing skills. Staff also came from all areas of the service, from the Learning Technology Development Manager to the Lending Services Manager.

The key aims of the programme were as follows:

- Develop management skills and knowledge through training and practical activities;
- Raise awareness of leadership behaviours allowing members to reflect and develop their own capabilities while understanding their impact on others;
- Provide a range of development opportunities and support mechanisms to enable members at different stages of their personal development and understanding to gain some benefit;
- Enable and promote positive cross-service relationships and networking through cohort members actively engaging in group development activities.

Both management and leadership were viewed as crucial and were seen as interconnecting. To ensure success the programme needed to include a range of activities, which were both theoretical and practical and, in addition, looked outside of the service, either within the institution or externally at other Library and Information Services. The main areas of focus included Skills audit and Personal Development Plans; a Programme of training and development; Mentoring; and Putting theory into practice through group activities. These will now be explored in more detail.

SKILLS AUDIT AND PERSONAL DEVELOPMENT PLANS

At the start of the programme, all staff completed a skills analysis questionnaire. The aim of this was to audit the skills that were part of their current role and look to identify skills and/or areas of knowledge they felt they needed to develop for future progression. The questionnaire formed the basis of their Personal Development Plan (PDP) and this was discussed in depth at their first mentor meeting and with their line manager. The PDP provided a framework for the year's activities and identified priorities for development along with details on how this was to be achieved. Early feedback from staff indicated that they found this a useful exercise, as it enabled them to both reflect on skills that they already had and identified skills that needed further development. In some ways it provided immediate positive feedback as many staff underestimated the point they were starting at and often took for granted skills and experience already attained.

The PDPs helped inform the training and development activities on which we needed to focus and provided the building blocks for the programme. Some examples of areas that staff felt needed further work and development included:

- Managing performance of individuals and the team;
- Communication skills for managers;
- Time management and delegation skills;
- Chairing meetings effectively;
- Leading a team and establishing respect;
- Influencing and negotiating skills;
- Managing and delivering change.

PROGRAMME OF TRAINING AND DEVELOPMENT ACTIVITIES

The programme of events was varied and diverse—with some sessions being delivered by external trainers and some in-house. Full day sessions included Managing Performance; Communicating Effectively; Service Development—Problem Solving and Decision Making; Emotional Intelligence; and Politics and Influencing. Staff also attended shorter sessions on absence management, giving feedback and chairing meetings. We also felt it was important to engage staff in thinking outside the service and looking at how other managers approach aspects of their work. As part of the programme we included presentations, talks and case studies from professionals from higher education, public and private sectors. These sessions included Managing Change, Customer Relations and Project Management and were useful because they gave the group perspectives from different sectors and organisations. This was particularly effective when, for example, the group looked at how customer relations are managed in the private sector and how we could learn from a sector where best practice is already well developed.

MENTORING

A key element of the programme was the need to provide staff with support, advice and guidance both in terms of the programme but also in relation to their role and things they where trying to achieve. Mentors also acted as confidante and sounding board while posing questions to get staff to reflect and evaluate, to look at things differently, often at a more strategic level, with a need to look at the 'bigger picture'.

Each participant was allocated a mentor for the duration of the programme—this mentor was a member of the Senior Management Team and therefore an experienced member of Learning Services in terms of managing staff, teams, projects and dealing with challenging situations.

PUTTING THEORY INTO PRACTICE—GROUP ACTIVITIES

Throughout the programme staff were encouraged to put into practice what they had learned through the training and development activities. In order to strengthen this, one of the final elements of the programme involved the formation of small projects groups. These had to look at a specific scenario within leadership, and then feed back to the main group how they would approach dealing with the issues it raised. Examples of topics included staff morale, communication and developing externality. The groups had to approach each topic as they would do in a real life situation with other pressures and commitments competing for their time. It resulted in their having to deal with staff in a more negative situation, respond to feedback and develop strategies for future change.

This element of the programme proved to be a real challenge for everyone but certainly gave them an insight into what it can be like to manage difficult staffing situations and influence cultural change across a team.

EVALUATION OF THE PROGRAMME—IMPACT ON INDIVIDUALS

In order to assess the impact of the programme on each individual, a detailed reflective activity was undertaken. Individuals were asked to consider several 'headlines' but also to include any aspect or outcome relevant to them. The headlines included:

- What have you learnt about yourself?
- What do you feel has been the impact on your colleagues and team?
- What practical developments arose that you implemented as a result of the programme?
- Your assessment of the different elements of the programme contents and ideas for the future;
- Benefits to you of the programme.

The reflective pieces received far surpassed expectations, and revealed a sophisticated level of self-analysis and an openness to exploring self-doubts, revelations, career aspirations and assessment of personal strengths and areas for development. A key message from all the reflections was that participants saw this programme as a major step on their journey of development as leaders and managers and that it was part of an ongoing continuum.

An analysis of the reflections raises several common themes; these are summarised below with qualitative data from the evaluations.

Confidence building and self-perception—the most resounding theme throughout every analysis was that of self-confidence and self-actualisation, with individuals at the end of the programme seeing themselves as managers and leaders: "it made me re-evaluate my perception of myself as a manager." The approach and programme appeared to enable personal and professional transitions that were unique to each individual and that led to deeper self-awareness and self-understanding, for example, "This process and the critical reflection ... have acted as a catalyst for development and change in my role, working relationships and confidence." Individuals talked about the importance to them of positive feedback and reinforcement from their mentors and from their peers: "My mentor ... provided positive and constructive feedback." Some truly saw the experience as transformational: "I wouldn't be where I am now so it has literally changed my life" and, "I feel that I have grown tremendously." It was also viewed as a great confidence boost, as "one of the biggest benefits has been the increase in my own confidence and the development of this confidence in a number of situations."

Self-analysis and critical reflection: Many of the personal reflections commented upon both the difficulty of critical reflection and also its value: "To reflect on one's own performance and identify your own strengths and weaknesses can be quite difficult", but it also "improved my own self esteem and encouraged me to progress with a more positive attitude." It should also be noted that several individuals found the process "incredibly challenging" and it "prompted me to ask hard questions of myself."

Personalised and contextualised learning: Many of the programme members commented on how they had valued the ability to tailor their own learning and that they had found different elements of the programme rewarding depending on their own learning styles: "I think the strength lies in the fact that this is in-house, tailored and developmental in structure." There was an evident link between their learning and 'real life,' with several participants appreciating the ways that they could directly apply the lessons learnt, particularly through their own roles as well as through the group project. Individuals felt that the flexibility of the programme enabled them to both build on prior experience and recognise what strengths they already possessed, highlighting that there is no definitive 'right' way as "The programme has enabled me to look at a variety of management styles and helped me to develop my own style which I can [sic] comfortable with."

Internal and external networking and relationship building: Several participants commented on how the programme had empowered them to develop networks, with the other participants and with the Senior Management Team who acted as mentors, and also with external colleagues whom they met via job-shadowing and professional development courses. There is a strong sense of peer learning and support from their reflections, and mutual understanding between all participants: "I know my understanding of the challenges other managers face has developed and [sic] in turn feel they also have a greater understanding of my teams concerns", and "I felt I learnt a lot from the others ... and benefited from building relationships in this way with colleagues from other teams." Individuals' relationships with their mentors were also singled out for specific praise: "My mentor was on hand to help guide me through the process, to be a confidante and sounding board—but was also someone who could get me to think, develop, reflect and evaluate," and "the role of the mentor in this is of paramount importance."

Link between the programme, individuals' skills and enhancing the service: Service enhancement was one aim and this was realised in every individual case. For example, one team manager focused upon developing her presentation skills and used these in team building events and in staff development; another was working in a project management role and used skills learnt to delegate to staff and be more confident in decision making. Yet another manager felt that the skills and awareness she developed improved her relationships with her team because "I had more effective tools such as negotiation, persuasion and listening skills." One individual felt that the programme had clarified what was expected of managers and that "excellence is what I feel we all strive for after this programme."

Other noticeable themes included how the programme had raised aspirations; how it had interlinked with individuals who each had their own motivations; and how participants saw continued and ongoing development as essential: "At the end of the programme it was (and still is!) clear to me that there are areas that still need further work and development i.e. time management and delegation." There is also a palpable sense of raised aspirations: "I would like to continue with this and if possible take this to a higher level. I would like to raise my profile both within Edge Hill and externally."

The personal reflective paragraph below gives a more holistic sense of the impact of the programme on one individual:

> "I started the Leaders and Managers programme as a supervisor in Learning Services. However, the enormous range of skills and experience that I gained throughout the programme gave me the confidence to apply for a secondment to a manager's position within the service. I am now four months into this new position, and am so glad that I was chosen to be part of the programme. It has given me a lot more confidence, a wide range of new skills, a belief in my own

ability and an insight into what managing staff, teams and projects is really all about. Since starting my new role I have already been involved in a wide variety of projects and new developments, where I have been able to draw on the skills that have I developed throughout the programme. Learning Services is presently in the process of developing various service areas including self issue and other self service developments—and I have gained the confidence to become involved in the development of these projects and take on a leadership role."

EVALUATION OF THE PROGRAMME—IMPACT ON THE SERVICE

From a service perspective the Leaders and Managers programme has been a great success. We have not only received very positive feedback from the staff involved, but also from colleagues across the service. We have seen staff take on additional responsibilities, lead project groups and generally have a more positive approach to their roles. Three members of the group have now been promoted internally, and other members have moved on to new roles outside the service. The programme has certainly given them real opportunities to put management and leadership theory into practice; they also feel they have developed the necessary tools to do this with confidence.

CRITICAL ASSESSMENT

As highlighted above, a great deal of the programme and the approach taken can be seen as having 'worked'. What we would do differently, following a critical review from both the mentors and the participants, can be summarised as:

- Further training is required for the mentor role, given the complexity and demands;
- Consider the timing of the programme and build in further time for reflection;
- Include more group activities and feedback in the early stages;
- Include more time to spend as a group: "I feel I got an awful lot out of networking with the group and would have appreciated more time, with a focus, to do that."
- Consider in more detail how the different elements relate to each other and build on each other.

Considering the evaluation of the programme, we can identify and propose several lessons for considering leadership development and succession planning in a library and information context. Certainly, the model of experiential learning used as the framework of the programme could be applied to other organisations; using tools such as a self-audit and a PDP gave a firm foundation as well as enabling individual tailoring and adaptation. In addition, the duration of the programme over a 12-month period provided 'room' for growth and multiple opportunities for learning, rather than a 'quick fix' solution that may not recognise individuals' learning styles. The opportunities for group work and group networking were fundamental to the success of the programme and should be encouraged in local leadership programmes. Moreover, including the Senior Management Team as mentors can build bridges across organisations—as one participant commented: "By Senior Management being involved it de-mystified the whole structure of Learning Services"—and may also prompt personal reflection and provide learning opportunities for the mentors themselves. The most important lesson to emerge from this approach, however, must be the importance of building self-confidence and self-belief, inspiring staff to believe that they either are or can become effective and valued managers and leaders.

CONCLUSIONS

Concepts of management and leadership have evolved throughout the 20th century and will continue to do so in the 21st. What is evident is that information services need effective management and inspirational leadership. As this programme has highlighted, individual beliefs, values and behaviours of both managers and leaders are in many ways more important than their competencies. This approach to leadership development can be viewed as an example of 'learning leadership' where senior managers showed genuine commitment to their staff and their personal development. For "Managers need to genuinely listen to people, seek to understand them and mentor them. They need to demonstrate respect, and communicate people's worth and potential so clearly that they come to see it themselves—which is the true essence of leadership"[17] Effective leadership therefore fosters leadership in others. Perhaps it is as simple as that.

REFERENCES

[1] Corrall, S. How can our leaders thrive? *Library and Information Appointments* 2003, **6** (1),1–2.

[2] Usherwood, B., Bower, G., Coe, C., Coope, J. and Stevens, T. *Recruit, Retain and Lead: the Public Library workforce study* Library and Information Commission Research Report 106. Sheffield: Centre for the Public Library and Information in Society, Department of Information Studies, University of Sheffield and Resource: the Council for Museums, Archives and Libraries, 2001.

[3] Corrall, S. How can our Leaders Thrive? *Library and Information Appointments* 2003, **6 (1)**,1–2.

[4] Roberts, S. & Rowley, J. *Managing Information Services*. London: Facet Publishing, 2003.

[5] Yukl, G. *Leadership in Organizations*. 5th edition. New Jersey: Prentice Hall, 2002.

[6] Hooper, A. & Potter, J. *Intelligent Leadership: creating a passion for change*. London: Random House Business Books, 2001.

[7] Mullins, J. Are public libraries led or managed? *Library Review* 2006, **55** (4), 237–248.

[8] Mullins, J. Are public libraries led or managed? *Library Review* 2006, **55** (4), 237–248.

[9] O'Connor, S. The heretical library manager for the future. *Library Management 2007,* **28** (1/2), 62–71.

[10] Parsons, F. (ed) *Recruitment, Training and Succession Planning in the HE Sector: findings from the HIMSS project*. Birmingham: The University of Birmingham, 2004.

[11] Gent, R. & Kempster, G. Leadership and Management. In: Melling, M. & Little, J. (eds) *Building a Successful Customer-service Culture: a guide for library and information managers*. London: Facet Publishing, 2002, 53–73.

[12] Eastell, C. The key to Ciara and the next generation of public library leaders. *Library + Information Update* April 2003, 40–41.

[13] Beard, C. & Wilson, J. P. *The power of experiential learning*. London: Kogan Page, 2004.

[14] Kolb, D. *Experiential learning; experience as the source of learning and development.* New Jersey: Prentice Hall, 1984.

[15] Gardner, W.L., Avolio, B. J., Luthans, F., May, D. R. & Walumbra, F. Can you see the real me? A self based model of authentic leader and follower development. *The Leadership Quarterly* 2005, **16**, 343–372.

[16] Adair, J. *The Inspirational Leader: how to motivate, encourage and achieve success.* London: Kogan Page, 17.

[17] Gent, R. & Kempster, G. Leadership and Management. In: Melling, M. & Little, J. (eds) *Building a Successful Customer-service Culture: a guide for library and information managers.* London: Facet Publishing, 2002, 53–73, 57.

THE NEW JERSEY ACADEMY OF LIBRARY LEADERSHIP: WHAT IMPACT HAS IT HAD?

Dr Jana Varlejs
Associate Professor
Rutgers, the State University of New Jersey, U.S.A.
varlejs@scils.rutgers.edu

Abstract

Ninety librarians who participated in one of four leadership institutes held in New Jersey between 2002 and 2006 were asked about the effect it has had on their professional lives. Sixty responded (66%), and 53 of those (88%) reported that they had used skills and insights gained as a result of attending. The majority felt that the institute had a positive impact on their work, career, or both. Although there were individuals who did not perceive much value, or could not attribute aspects of their professional development to institute participation, many respondents testified to increased confidence and willingness to foster change and take risks. Comparing the objectives of the Academy, which is modeled on the Snowbird Leadership Institute, with the comments made by the respondents, it can be said that the benefits gained warrant continuation of the annual Academy.

BACKGROUND

Leadership institutes for librarians have proliferated recently in the United States, yet there has been little evaluation to show whether they are effective in producing leaders.[1-3] In New Jersey, where the fourth Academy of Library Leadership was held in October 2006, it was time to inquire what impact the Academy has had. Evaluation is especially important because the New Jersey State Library has subsidized the institutes with federal funds from the U.S. Library Services and Technology Act. The Academy has been administered by the Central Jersey Regional Library Cooperative, and it is this organization that is accountable to the State Library and was therefore anxious to have an evaluation conducted.

While the investigation is limited to New Jersey, it is more widely useful because the design of the Academy closely follows that of similar leadership institutes regularly offered in other states, and is led in many cases by the same facilitator.[4] The survey instrument developed for New Jersey is available for others to use elsewhere, so that over time it might be possible to develop a rich data set on the impact of library leadership institutes.

The most recent New Jersey Academy of Library Leadership (NJALL) was a five-day residential program, limited to 25 participants from all types of libraries. The 'ideal applicant' was described as "a mid-career librarian who is ready for increased involvement in the New Jersey library community. Selection will be based on personal qualifications, and also to ensure that Academy participants represent as many types of librarianship and areas of the state as possible." The program content included the following topics:

- Leadership in libraries today: challenges and opportunities
- Leadership self-assessment
- Principles and practices of effective leadership
- Power and influence; influencing others
- Resonant leadership: building effective relationships with followers
- Presentation skills
- Risk taking
- Reinventing your library for the 21st century: a new 12 step approach
- Leading change
- Managing differences
- Conversations with library leaders
- Working with groups and teams
- My leadership story
- Working with community groups
- Working with others: creating a culture of commitment
- Your leadership practice: ethical leadership
- Personal planning.

NJALL'S CONCEPTION OF LEADERSHIP

Judging by the above list, NJALL reflects current understandings of the difference between management and leadership.[5] As John Kotter explains in a frequently quoted article in *Harvard Business Review*, "Good management controls complexity; effective leadership produces useful change."[6] The Academy addresses leadership within one's institution, community, and profession. Implicit within the array of topics is the idea that one does not have to be a top administrator or elected officer in order to be a leader, but that one can exercise leadership wherever one is situated.

While it is not clear to what degree the Academy has focused on advocacy, which has been a major theme recently for library associations at state, national, and international levels, this is a subject that can hardly be avoided. In fact, the burgeoning interest in leadership training can be seen as closely tied to the priority given to advocacy by presidents of the American Library Association, the International Federation of Library Associations and Institutions, and the American Association of Law Librarians; see, for example, http://aallnet.org/AALL_2005_SD.pdf. This evaluation therefore looks for evidence of involvement in advocacy as well as other leadership activities.

EVALUATION OF LEADERSHIP INSTITUTES

As leadership institutes have proliferated, articles and reports about them have also increased in number. Few of these, however, can serve as models for examining the impact of institutes on participants over a period of years. Evaluations of the Snowbird Leadership Institute by Teresa Neely and Mark Winston;[7] of the Urban Libraries Council's Executive Leadership Institute by Maureen Sullivan;[8] and of the Aurora Leadership Institute by Kay Barney, are among the exceptions.[1] Between them, they provide examples of attempts to assess both long-term and short-term impact on attendees' professional lives, together with participants' perceptions of the usefulness of the experience, what they learned, and the effect on their career goals.

Generally speaking, positive results were reported. Barney's e-mailed questionnaire received 27 out of a possible 32 responses, while Neely and Winston surveyed 215 participants from 1990 to 1998 by mail, garnering a 71% return. Sullivan selected 20 out of 35 participants to interview by telephone, and used more open-ended questions than the others. As with any evaluation, the questions to ask depend on the purpose to which the results will be put. Sullivan's study was solicited by the Urban Libraries Council, and was therefore concerned not only with the impact on the fellows, but on lessons learned about designing and running a program like the Executive Leadership Institute. Neely and Winston's article was addressed to academic librarians, and their questions were shaped by their definition of leadership in academic librarianship. Consequently, they asked about publications and conference presentations, in addition to seeking measures of career progression. Barney, as the coordinator of the particular Aurora institute that she evaluated, was more generally interested in participants' perceptions of its value to their work and careers. Barney provides a discussion of the difficulty of evaluating impact of leadership training, and accepts the conclusion of others who have addressed the issue:

> This involves asking leadership program attendees whether they think their skills/knowledge/behaviour have improved in certain areas, and using the perceived change as the criterion for determining the impact of the program. This approach is given validity by the concentration of leadership training programs on developing participants' self-perception of leadership behaviour.[1]

It is true that Snowbird and other institutes modeled on it, including NJALL, put a great deal of emphasis on self-analysis, and there is a major focus on instilling confidence and a positive stance toward change and risk taking.[9] One can say, therefore, that reliance on participants' attributions of changes in their careers to the institute experience is a legitimate way to measure impact.

However, impact at the level of the individual's skills, knowledge, attitudes, and behavior is not the final effect that training aims to achieve. Donald Kirkpatrick's classic *Evaluating Training Programs: The Four Levels*[10] calls the final level "evaluating results", by which he means determining the benefit to the organization. Thus the ultimate evaluation of a leadership training program should be an attempt to answer the question, how have participants affected their institutions? Are libraries providing better service to the public? One could take it even a step further and ask whether leadership training has improved the profession in any way. Clearly, evaluation at these levels is extremely complex, difficult, and expensive, and therefore one must settle for the third level—evaluating behavior.

METHODOLOGY

The question is, what effect has the New Jersey Academy of Library Leadership had on its alumni? What have the Academy graduates done differently and what has happened that they can attribute to their participation? It is not possible to demonstrate direct links between Academy attendance and change in behavior and performance, let alone the impact on the individuals' libraries, library users, communities, and the profession. On the other hand, it *is* possible to ask what changes have occurred in the professional practice and careers of alumni, and to what degree they attribute these changes to their Academy experience. The extent to which the participants can remember specific actions that they took as a result of their participation can serve as an indicator of training impact.

The Central Jersey Regional Library Cooperative (CJRLC) office, which administered the four Academies, supplied the registration lists and contact information for 92 participants in the years 2002, 2003, 2004, and 2006 (the Academy was not held in 2005). Two individuals who were listed turned out not to have attended, and one could not complete the program. Two librarians had left New Jersey and contact information could not be obtained. E-mails to an unknown number of others did not reach addressees, due partly to filtering and partly to obsolete e-mail addresses. Nevertheless, the base number of 90 is used for determining the response rate, which might be higher, given the uncertainty about how many potential respondents there actually were. Appendix I shows the questionnaire, which drew on the Neely/Winston, Sullivan, and Barney studies for its design. Most questions were open-ended in order to capture respondents' perceptions without imposing pre-established answers.

RESULTS

Table 1 summarizes the returns by cohort, with a total response rate of 66%. It should be noted that less than three months had elapsed after the 2006 Academy, even when sending out the questionnaire was delayed until the last possible moment. There was not much time for this last cohort to apply what they had learned, nor was there enough time to send second and third requests for participation in the study. If one excludes the 2006 group, the response rate for the 65 attendees in the first three cohorts is 72%.

Table 1 Survey response by cohort

Institute Year	No. Attending	No. Responding
2002	25	19 (76%)
2003	24	17 (70%)
2004	16	11 (68%)
2006	25	13 (52%)
Total	90	60 (66%)

Tables 2 and 3 show the distribution by age and number of years worked in library organizations at the time of attendance. In a number of cases it was clear that respondents counted pre-professional as well as post-master's experience. All but two of the respondents hold the MLS degree, and one of them is enrolled in a degree program. All but nine are women.

Comparing Tables 2 and 3, one sees that, while most Academy participants were over 40 years old, their years of experience tended to be in the lower end of the range. Although the description of the "ideal applicant" calls for mid-career librarians, it is difficult to say how many of the participants actually fall in that category. The criterion seems to have been applied quite flexibly.

Table 2 Respondents' age at time of attendance (n=52)

Age	No. of respondents
25–29	3
30–34	11
35–39	7
40–44	5
45–49	19
50–54	9
55–59	4

Table 3 Years worked in library organizations at time of attendance (n= 53)

Years worked	No. of respondents
0–4	6
5–9	17
10–14	17
15–19	8
20–24	6
25–29	3
30–34	2

Table 4 shows that by far the greatest number of participants were public librarians, and that few moved to a different institution after their Academy attendance. Even fewer are now working in a different type of institution. There were six individuals in this category; two moved from academic to public, one went from public to special and another from public to 'other'; one went from special to academic, and one from 'other' to public. In all but one case, these moves were seen as advantageous.

Table 4 Respondents' employers

Type of Library	In Year of Attendance	Now (2007)	Same Institution	Different Institution
Academic	10	9	8	1
Public	37	37	29	8
School	6	7	6	1
Special	3	3	1	2
Other	4	4	3	1
Total	60	60	47	13

As shown in Table 5, the most extreme change in employment post-Academy was in directorships, where eight individuals rose in rank or moved to a larger library. If one compares the number of pre-Academy department head and higher jobs with those post-Academy, there is an increase of five. Across the board, however, 21 had achieved a position of greater responsibility by 2007. Omitting the 13 respondents from the 2006 cohort, none of whom changed jobs since attending, the 21 who rose in rank constitute 44% of the 2002–2004 cohorts who returned the questionnaire.

Table 5 Respondents' positions

Type of Position	In Year of Attendance	Now (2007)	Same position	Different position	Higher position
Director/ acting director	8	15	7	8	8
Assistant director/ deputy director./ associate dean	5	6	2	4	4
Branch head	2	4	2	2	2
Department head	15	10	8	2	1
School librarian	6	7	6	1	0
Consultant/coordinator	6	7	3	4	4
Librarian	18	11	6	5	2
Total	60	60	34	26	21

When asked whether they had used any of the skills or insights gained as a result of participating in NJALL, 53 of the 60 respondents (88%) were able to name one or more, or said that the Academy reinforced skills they already had. Frequently mentioned were:

- gaining self confidence
- listening
- better understanding of self and others
- appreciating different learning and work styles
- networking and collaboration
- communication
- risk taking

- change management
- conflict resolution
- advocacy
- involving the community
- personality types
- public speaking
- interpersonal/people skills
- involvement in library issues
- exposure to different career paths
- better understanding of self and others
- team building/leadership
- decision making
- management style
- collaboration
- organizational structure
- working with boards, politicians
- delegating
- seeing the big picture
- group process techniques
- leading by example and empowerment
- a way to look at planning and development.

Some of the comments that capture the general tone of beneficial impact are quoted below:

> "…changed my life by encouraging me to visualize my perfect job and to go after it and make it happen. I would never have applied for my current position … had I not attended the Academy. I continue to believe that I am capable of making positive things happen in my life and I am convinced that change is good."

"I have always embraced change and been excited by it; I finally learned/accepted how fearful change is for many people. Better yet, I learned to seek out and to use effective ways to diffuse this fear and help people participate in change."

"I have learned to 'lean against my discomforts' and strive to continually think outside the box"

"Taking time to think and read. This is a critical component of being a professional and shouldn't be considered a luxury. I still struggle to do this though. Considering I gave an entire day a month to the NJALL I strive to continue allowing myself that much reflection/planning time per month. It is not easy."

"Another way in which I am changed is that I am now constantly seeking out new books or articles to read on leadership. I want to know about the different theories of leadership and discover a way to find what will work best for me. As well, I find that I more closely observe those around me who I consider to be leaders and that I am trying to learn from what they do—or don't do, as the case may be. I feel as if doors are opening and I am going to find a way to make a difference."

In addition to asking about the skills and insights gained and applied, the questionnaire looked for evidence of changes in leadership activities and overall effect. As shown in Tables 6 and 7, most respondents reported positive outcomes. No attempt was made to define leadership. The question did, however, suggest that there were various contexts for exercising leadership: "Since attending the Academy, what activities have you undertaken where you have been able to exercise leadership—at work, in the community, in professional groups and associations." A follow-up question asked which of these could be attributed to the Academy experience. It is important to note that almost every person reported some activities that they defined as leadership, and that more were *not* due to NJALL than those that were. As one librarian put it, "I undertook these activities through my desire to grow professionally." Most respondents were careful to differentiate those activities that they would most likely not have engaged in, had they not been influenced by the Academy experience.

Table 6 Changes in behavior and goals

Impact	Yes	No
Used skills/insights acquired/reinforced at NJALL	53	7
Undertook leadership activity due to NJALL	32	28
Goals differed after NJALL	39	20
NJALL made a difference to goal achievement	48	11

Of the participants who reported leadership activities that they attributed to NJALL, 17 (54%) gave examples that were related to their workplace position. Fourteen (45%) became involved in statewide or regional professional activities, but only three named national professional associations. The New Jersey Library Association appears to have been a primary beneficiary of newly motivated members.

Several questions were asked about career goals, on the assumption that motivation to participate in a leadership institute was most likely to reflect a desire for personal achievement that goes beyond the current state of one's career. As shown in Table 6, goals changed for more than half the participants, and an even greater number felt that the Academy had made a difference in achieving their goals.

Table 7 Value of NJALL to work and career

Value	Great	Moderate	Little	No value
To work	32	18	9	0
To career	28	25	6	0

The final questions replicate Barney's value-to-work and value-to-career questions. Following her example of comparing number of years in the profession to the perceived value of the leadership institute, the results are displayed in Table 8.

Table 8 Value by years worked in library institutions

Years worked	Great value to work &/or career	Not of great value to work &/or career
10 years or less (n=27)	16 (59%)	11 (40%)
11 years or more (n=32)	17 (53%)	15 (46%)

Whereas Barney found that those with fewer years of experience felt Aurora to be of greater value than did those with more years in the profession, Table 8 shows that the results for the NJALL participants do not show much difference. In other ways, however, Barney's respondents and New Jersey librarians had very similar reactions to the leadership training, volunteering many comments that are almost interchangeable.

DISCUSSION

Even if the 30 Academy participants who did not respond to the survey had replied with negative responses, the evaluation of NJALL would still be positive. It is disappointing, however, that there is not more evidence of professional association activity at the national level. On the other hand, when one looks at the current roster of officers of the New Jersey Library Association, one sees many names of NJALL alumni. A number of those individuals would be there even without the Academy influence, and one always has to remember that those who are selected to attend leadership institutes are already identified as having potential.

Nevertheless, this study has found ample indication that there are very specific actions and goals that institute participants firmly associate with the NJALL experience. A number of them have declared that they owe their current jobs to the Academy, and several others have formulated specific plans for obtaining further education to help them achieve higher goals. A few who previously did not aspire to directorships are now thinking about it. The overall impression created by the responses is that the personal, career, orientation seems dominant, but that may be because of the nature of the survey questions. For example, there was no specific query about advocacy, yet a strong commitment to advocating for libraries and librarianship is certainly something one hopes to see as a result of leadership training. Several people mentioned that they would work to improve salaries, a number stated that they were already reaching out more to their communities and increasing library visibility, and a few reported that they were campaigning for more resources. A fair number said that they now felt they had found their voice and could imagine being a change agent and making a difference.

In some cases, where little impact or value was assigned to participation, individuals noted that family issues had intervened. Others attributed modest impact to the fact that they had already had similar training, or are working in an environment that is not conducive to exercising leadership. In a number of cases, respondents checked "moderate" value to work and career, but added a comment that suggests a greater value. For example:

> "NJALL was the single most important career development activity that I have done since attending graduate school. Discovering my leadership style and learning to appreciate the need for a variety of styles within an organization was key in changing my work strategies. The opportunity to network with others and the time to do it properly has had a lasting effect on me."

This kind of discrepancy underlines the methodological problem inherent in research which depends on written replies to questions which not everyone will interpret the same way. On the other hand, using open-ended questions and inviting comments does allow for nuances and cavils to be introduced.

One of the difficulties with evaluating leadership institutes is that, despite sponsor and facilitator care in distinguishing between management and leadership, there are bound to be some participants who have more of a management mind set and a local rather than cosmopolitan orientation. This conclusion rests more on the kinds of comments that were rare, rather than typical. While there were frequent positive remarks about developing more self confidence, networking, and resolving to learn more, such comments do not herald the same ambition and vision as remarks such as these:

> "I seriously think that even if I don't change course I will be looking to change libraries in the future. I need challenges and whether it is bringing out the best in a small library or eventually managing a larger more urban one, change is the one thing that will keep my passion alive."

This comment came from a young director of a small library who could not attend after the first day, and reinforces the suspicion that leadership is more likely to emerge when the motivation and passion are already there. At the same time, the fact that this individual took the time to respond to the survey beyond just sending it back with a note saying she had to drop out is a strong indication in the value of mounting a leadership institute that energizes people and gets them to reflect on their own and their profession's development.

REFERENCES

[1] Barney, K. Evaluation of the impact of the 2003 Aurora Leadership Institute—'the gift that keeps on giving'. *Australian Library Journal* 2004, *53* (4), 337–348;

[2] Nichols, C.A. Leaders: Born or bred? *Library Journal* 2002, 127(13), 38–40;

[3] Maurer, M.B. & Coccaro, C. Creating a more flexible workforce for libraries—Are leadership institutes the answer? *Technical Services Quarterly* 2003, 20 (3), 1–17.

[4] Paul, C. Just do it! Leadership training builds strong networks. *American Libraries* 2004, 35 (9), 44–45.

[5] Lynch, B.P. Theory and practice. *Library Administration & Management* 2004, 18 (1), 30–34

[6] Kotter, J.P. What leaders really do. *Harvard Business Review* [reprint of May-June 1990 article] 2002, 79 (11), 85–96.

[7] Neely, T.Y. & Winston, M.D. Snowbird Leadership Institute: Leadership development in the profession. *College & Research Libraries* 1999, 60 (5), 412–425.

[8] Sullivan, M. Evaluation of the Executive Leadership Institute, Annapolis, MD: Maureen Sullivan Associates for Urban Library Council, 2004 [unpublished manuscript, 11 pp.]

[9] Bonnici, L.J. Creating the library leadership institute at Snowbird: An exercise in leadership. *Library Administration & Management* 2001,15 (2), 98–102.

[10] Kirkpatrick, D.L. *Evaluating training programs: The four levels.* San Francisco: Berrett-Koeheler, 1996.

The New Jersey Academy of Library Leadership: What Impact Has It Had?

Appendix I: Questionnaire

Dear New Jersey Academy of Library Leadership Graduate:

The Central Jersey Regional Library Cooperative and the New Jersey State Library are interested in what has been the effect of the Academy on its alumni. In addition, they are responsible for reporting to the funding source, the U.S. Institute on Museum and Library Services. Please help them meet their obligation for accountability by returning the survey. Only I will be able to connect your name with the information you provide, and I guarantee that no one else will see your reply. The data will be reported in the aggregate, and individuals' names and employing libraries will not be identified. Please sign the attached consent form, keep a copy for your records, and fax or mail one copy to me.

Your name

What year did you attend the Academy?

How many years had you worked in libraries at that time?

Did you have an MLIS degree?   If yes, when did you earn it?

How old were you at the time you attended the Academy?

Where do you work now? Name of library/ branch; address

Is this the same library as the one you worked in when you attended the Academy?

What position do you hold now?

Briefly describe your major responsibilities

What position did you hold at the time you attended the Academy?

What were your major responsibilities?

Since attending the Academy, what activities have you undertaken where you have been able to exercise leadership—at work, in the community, in professional groups and associations. Please list each one and give a brief description of your contribution:

Of the activities you have listed, were there any that you undertook specifically because of the Academy? If yes, which?

In general, can you identify any skills that you learned or insights that you gained at the Academy that you have been applying since attending?

Have you kept in touch with colleagues you met while participating in the Academy? If yes, please give some examples.

What are your career goals now?

Are they different from what they were before attending the Academy? If yes, how?

Overall, do you feel that the Academy experience has made any difference to the achievement of your goals?

Please rate the value of the Academy to your work? __great __moderate __little __no value

Please rate the value of the Academy to your career? __great __moderate __little __no value

LEADERSHIP NEEDS OF ASIAN LIBRARIANS: AN ACCOUNT OF AN ASIAN LIBRARY LEADERSHIP INSTITUTE

Peter Edward Sidorko
Deputy Librarian, The University of Hong Kong
peters@hku.hk

Abstract

What qualities are required for effective organizational leadership? What qualities are required for effective library leadership? Can these qualities be acquired or are leaders born? Evidence suggests that leadership skills can be learnt but that learning these skills must be based in not merely theory, but experiential and sustained learning. In 2003, the University of Hong Kong Libraries launched its inaugural Library Leadership Institute. This residential leadership and management training experience is aimed at providing library directors and senior librarians from the East Asia region with the unique opportunity to develop new skills in the volatile area of innovative management and leadership in the information sector. Following four consecutive successful Institutes, this paper draws on the experience gained in delivering such an Institute. The author, who is also the principal organizer for the Institute and a regular facilitator, briefly outlines the purpose behind developing such an Institute for Asian librarians, with participants hailing from mainland China, Hong Kong, Taiwan, Macau, Singapore, Malaysia, Thailand, the Philippines and several other countries in the region, as well as providing an overview of the operations of the Institute.

The paper also discusses changing leadership needs of Asian librarians, as identified by participants of the Institute, and the degree to which such an Institute can realistically meet these needs. For example, many participants of the Institute identify a need for some form of change within their organizations and many attend the Institute to develop leadership abilities to progress organizational change. Yet the ability to initiate and lead successful organizational change may not be possible after a 4–5 day leadership Institute. The paper concludes with a review of the degree of success of the Institute as identified by participants.

INTRODUCTION

The range and depth of challenges facing libraries in this digital age are unprecedented. Countless articles, books and conferences have been dedicated not only to these challenges, but to the need for strong management and leadership, shifting skills sets and an underlying commitment to change. While strong leadership in libraries is essential during times of crisis and significant societal change, leadership is also, it can be argued, just as important during day to day operations of the library where changes may be singularly less dramatic but where the incremental effect, over time, leads to a transformed organization.

In terms of understanding and defining leadership, there is a wealth of literature upon which one may draw. In terms of understanding and defining *library* leadership there is less to draw upon. But are the desired qualities of a library leader any different from those of a leader in any other type of organization? Can leadership skills be taught anyway? Does training enhance leadership abilities?

CHANGE AND LIBRARIES

Crises focus leaders to perform and achieve. Winston and Quinn argue that there is "limited focus on leadership in the library and information science literature" yet there is a "need for leadership in ensuring the organizational performance and success of libraries".[1] They further argue that there is even less literature on library leadership during times of crises. They cite crises such as war and terrorism, civil and natural disasters, social movements, medical and other healthcare dilemmas, and large-scale economic and technological shifts, as periods requiring strong library leadership roles. Indeed, as the world moves through what appear to be increasingly turbulent times, libraries do not find themselves exempt from the effects of such events. The need for strong leadership in libraries is obvious during such periods.

But what of the everyday changes facing libraries. Certainly *technology* not only transforms collections, so that most libraries today are dealing with hybrid print and electronic collections, but also dictates the way we deliver this content and provide supporting services. Blogs, wikis, RSS feeds, Web 2.0 and institutional repositories are just a few examples of technology-based content services that libraries now utilize as a matter of course.

In a world espousing *globalization* as the norm rather than the exception, libraries that struggle to maintain status quo rather than learn from, or indeed dictate to, others at a global level are destined for failure. As we strive to differentiate ourselves we are establishing an environment of *competition* and, certainly in the case of academic libraries, we are regularly assessed in terms of our rival organizations. Coupled with this is the desire to maximize usage of library resources and to *collaborate* with other libraries. The ensuing tension in this competition versus co-operation ('co-opetition'?) situation is obvious.

Budgetary shifts and fluctuations also challenge us to deliver consistency of content to meet users' needs and services to match their expectations. Rigid library budgeting practices are no longer applicable in an era of 'big deals', bundled electronic resources and the growing range of pricing models for print/electronic resources. As *user expectations* for greater quality, accuracy and immediate responsiveness grows, we are asked to be more *accountable* with our funding allocations and to prove our *value* to our organizations. Not only is the volume of change overwhelming, but the rapidity and variety of the impact of this change requires skilled and agile leadership.

The ability not only to survive but, as increasingly expected, to thrive and lead within such a dynamic environment, will distinguish the great libraries from the good. This ability does not necessarily come easily to librarians who are now in leadership roles and whose education in librarianship was undertaken when such issues were rarely, if ever, discussed. Today, the situation is quite different with numerous progressive library schools delivering not only courses in leadership, management, organizational culture and change, but entire doctoral programs.[1] In addition, there are numerous library leadership training opportunities through so called leadership *institutes* or *programs,* to name just two of the labels most commonly assigned to such initiatives. Mason and Wetherbee provide a comprehensive listing of such programs available to librarians worldwide and note that "the majority are located in the United States, but one exists in Australia and another in Canada".[2] Yet despite the fact that Asian librarians are facing the same challenges as those identified above and, in the case of Mainland China, an incredible period of rapid growth and expansion, no similar program of library leadership training was regularly available in Asia for Asian librarians prior to 2003.

---

[1] See for example Simmons College's Ph.D. in Managerial Leadership in the Information Professions <http://www.simmons.edu/gslis/forms/pubs/B_PhDinMLIP.pdf>

In 2002, as the University of Hong Kong Libraries was preparing to undergo significant change through re-engineering its existing, long-standing organizational structure, it became apparent that strong leadership would be a key element in making such changes successful. Our desire to have senior managers attend such a program was soon curtailed by the prohibitive costs that this would entail. Sending librarians to the United States was not a viable option. Investigations revealed that no appropriate library leadership program was available to Asian librarians and that a demand for such a training opportunity would not necessarily be limited to the staff of University of Hong Kong Libraries.

In 2003 the inaugural University of Hong Kong Libraries Leadership Institute was launched. Broadly speaking, the key objectives for the Institute were identified as:

1. To develop and enhance innovative management and leadership qualities in academic and research librarians in the East Asia region including Hong Kong's own librarians, particularly at the University of Hong Kong; and

2. To enhance collaboration and foster relations among academic and research libraries in the region.

LEADERSHIP SKILLS FOR LIBRARIANS

But what represents innovative management and leadership qualities in academic and research librarians? Numerous definitions for what constitutes an effective leader abound. As a long standing and recognized authority on organizational development, leadership and change, Warren Bennis has provided many of these definitions and in his *On becoming a leader*, he highlights some of the key ingredients for successful leadership. Among these are included: having a *guiding vision*; having *passion* which, when communicated correctly, gives hope and inspiration; *integrity* which encompasses self-knowledge, candor and maturity; *trust* which is more a product of integrity; *curiosity* and the desire to learn, and; *daring* or taking risks.[3]

Peter Drucker, another recognized authority on leadership, management and organizations, questions whether specific traits can be assigned to successful leaders. He believes that "'leadership personality', 'leadership style', and 'leadership traits' do not exist" and he demonstrates this by describing conflicting traits/personalities/styles of leaders he has known.[4]

But what about librarians? Is there a recognized style for successful library leaders? In his thought provoking keynote address to the 2006 Shanghai International Library Forum, Steve O'Connor concluded that a major shift in thinking was necessary for the library manager of the future. While O'Connor uses the word manager, these traits may be applied just as meaningfully, if not more so, to library leaders. He strongly emphasizes that library managers/ leaders will need to:

> be global in outlook and will be more flexible than the manager of the past ... work and partner with international people ... be more receptive to that which they do not know or understand ... work confidently with uncertainty ... re-examine their own values; their ability to listen; their ability to keep an open mind; to think heretical thoughts; to think the unthinkable.[5]

But can such qualities be taught through a library leadership program?

Simmons College Dean Michele Cloonan offers a somewhat more pragmatic definition of library leadership. She defines it as:

> the ability to build a shared mission for a library, to foster participatory management, to be innovative and risk taking, to have and communicate ethics and values, to build community relationships, and to possess a sense of humor.[6]

Without losing sight of O'Connor's bold vision for the library leader of the future, it is worth noting that Cloonan's definition is more readily identifiable for librarians, as well as other organizational leaders, since many of the attributes (communication, mission/vision, participation, innovation, risk taking) are widely accepted as key traits required of an effective leader.

LEADERSHIP TRAINING AND THE UNIVERSITY OF HONG KONG LIBRARIES LEADERSHIP INSTITUTE

But is it possible to teach leadership skills? The overwhelming body of literature seems to suggest that such skills *can* be learnt and acquired. But can leadership skills be taught through a three to five-day residential training program? The proliferation of such initiatives, as made apparent by Mason and Wetherbee,[7] appears to testify to the belief that leadership training for librarians can be effective and leadership skills can be learnt through such programs. Bennis, however, argues that "[l]eaders are not made by corporate courses, any more than they are made by their college courses, but by experience." [8] Peter Drucker, on the other hand, in *The Leader of the Future,* questions whether leaders are born or made. He believes, however, that "there may be 'born leaders', but there surely are far too few to depend on them. Leadership must be learned and can be learned."[9]

Both Bennis and Drucker are correct. Their seemingly contradictory views are in fact, I believe, complementary rather than mutually exclusive. The University of Hong Kong Libraries recognizes that end product library leaders are not turned out through its Leadership Institute. However, like so many others, we believe that our institute provides a unique opportunity that is only a stepping stone to new ways of thinking and looking at problems, at the future and at the place and role of participants in a global and local library community. Furthermore, the Institute emphasizes as a basic philosophy an experientially focused and problem based facilitative learning style.

The Institute bears several trademarks of other similar library leadership institutes. Yet we believe that it has several unique features that attempt to address local issues affecting librarians in the East Asia region. The Institute is divided into themed sessions. Each session represents a topic that has been identified as a key issue facing librarians in the region at the time of a particular Institute. The original emphasis, in 2003, was on organizational issues such as changing organizational paradigms, problem solving, performance management, project management and collaboration. By 2006 the Institute had evolved to cover sessions dealing with topics such as technology and converging changes; information management policy; open access publishing; forging new (non-library) collaborations; scenario planning; strategic planning; and project management for an institutional repository.

The planned 2007 Institute will carry the theme of "Redefining Libraries: Web 2.0 and Other Challenges for Library Leaders." Themes to be covered will include: effective leadership; managing technological change; intellectual property in a digital world; the future of library technology; working in groups and teams; optimizing human resources in today's research library; managing your time and managing projects; and benchmarking technology. We annually appraise participants' views of the Institute and administer a questionnaire to prospective attendees to gauge the issues that are of most concern to them. Programs change annually in response to these two measures.

During the structured sessions, facilitators present discussion topics and encourage strong interaction followed by practical exercises that encourage further discussion and teamwork. Facilitators also act as mentors during the Institute by participating in all social activities and offering advice and exchanging views in a less formal setting. All of the Institute's principal facilitators have come from the United States and all have been at the forefront of library leadership in their respective areas of expertise. Over the years, additional facilitators have come from the Peoples Republic of China (four), Hong Kong (five), Macau (one) and Singapore (one), offering a diverse Asian perspective.

Like other leadership institutes, we also run a detailed and complex case study which allows participants to work in teams to develop a solution and, at Institute end, present a solution to the entire group. The case study further emphasizes the Institute's experiential focus. The problem is real and always deemed relevant and identifiable by participants. Furthermore the case study enables a truly collaborative spirit to develop among the assigned teams. It also acts as the glue for the Institute by bringing together the knowledge gained by participants during the structured sessions.

Participants

As the focus of the Institute is aimed at librarians from the East Asia region, the majority of participants come from this region. Table 1 provides a breakdown, by region, of participants in the first four years.

Table 1 Breakdown of Participants by Region

	2003	2004	2005	2006
Fiji		1		
Hong Kong	23	27	26	18
Macau			6	
Malaysia				1
Philippines			1	
PRC	11	13	11	12

Singapore		1	1	1
Taiwan	1	2	5	4
Thailand				2
TOTAL	35	44	50	38

While the Institute was originally aimed at library directors, deputy directors and senior librarians, the applications received over the four years highlight that there is a need to extend this target group. Table 2 provides a breakdown of the seniority level of participants over the four years. While the degree of seniority is broader than anticipated, experience has shown that this range has provided an even greater diversity of perspectives than was originally anticipated.

Table 2 Breakdown of Participants by Management Level

	2003	2004	2005	2006	TOTAL (%)
Director	8 (22.9%)	6 (13.6%)	5 (10%)	6 (16%)	25 (15%)
Deputy Director	9 (25.7%)	7 (15.9%)	6 (12%)	8 (21%)	30 (18%)
Senior Manager	9 (25.7%)	13 (29.5%)	11 (22%)	9 (24%)	42 (25%)
Lower manager	9 (25.7%)	18 (41%)	28 (56%)	15 (39%)	70 (42%)
TOTAL	35 (100%)	44 (100%)	50 (100%)	38 (100%)	167 (100%)

The broadening range of the managerial levels of librarians attending the Institute, while not originally anticipated, demonstrates the need, or perhaps more the desire, to inculcate leadership qualities in a range of levels in the organization. As Budd says, "it is widely acknowledged that leadership can arise from any organizational level." Unfortunately, however, and as Budd agrees "some leading that emerges from the lower levels may be squelched at higher levels."[10]

Challenges faced by participants

As mentioned above, prior to the Institute we administer a questionnaire to prospective attendees to gauge the issues that are of most concern to them and, when possible, attempt to build a program that will address these challenges. As this process was only initiated with the 2006 Institute, the data is somewhat limited. The most recurrent themes are highlighted in Table 3.

Table 3 Major Challenges Identified by Participants (2006 Institute)

Challenge	Number identified
Managing digital/hybrid collections	20
Meeting growing user demands	16
Budget shortages including appropriate distribution	9
Convincing users of the value of the library and its resources	8
Information literacy in an electronic age	7
Personnel issues, staff management, motivation etc.	7
Staff shortages and the need to do 'more with less'	6
Space shortages	6
Keeping current, learning new skills, professional development	5
Collaboration v competition	4
Digitisation issues	3
Maintaining technical infrastructure	2
Virtual reference	2
TOTAL	95

While many of the challenges identified by participants could be easily classified, these classifications (as highlighted in Table 3) do not do justice to some of the descriptions of those challenges. Appendix 1 provides a verbatim selection of the challenges identified by participants and they provide a better illustration of the complexity of some of these. It should be noted that the social and economic environments of the countries from which participants originate vary significantly and therefore a reasonably diverse range of issues have been identified. China's economy, for example, has been expanding at incredible speed while Hong Kong has been negatively affected by the unstable world economy.

At the beginning of the Institute, participants are each provided with a copy of the challenges they have submitted. Each participant is also given a consolidated anonymous version of the challenges, for a broader perspective of the range of issues that challenge their co-participants. They are asked to reflect on these in the context of what they are learning during the Institute.

Overcoming challenges

At the end of the 2006 Institute, we asked all participants to provide responses to two questions: "Based upon what you have heard and learnt at the Institute (1) what can *you personally* do, and (2) what can *your library* do, to overcome the three challenges you identified prior to the Institute?" Some of the responses to these questions reflect an enthusiasm that was less apparent in the challenges identified. For example,

> My library will adopt a management style which takes into consideration humanity. We will create good working relationships among staff and offer awards or encouragement.

This comment is particularly significant as, during the course of the Institute, many librarians (particularly those from mainland China) identified the notions of 'participative management', 'collaborative leadership' and 'caring leadership' (recurrent Institute themes) as being quite alien to their existing practices. A further selection of these responses can be found in Appendix 2.

Institute evaluation

At the end of each Institute an evaluation instrument is administered. Table 4 shows the average scores given by participants for the two questions concerning (1) their satisfaction with the way the event was conducted and (2) the overall usefulness of the event. Since the best possible score was 10, it can be concluded that the Institute has been very well received and is deemed to be highly useful.

Table 4 Average Evaluation Scores for the Four Institutes

	2003	2004	2005	2006
Satisfaction with how event was conducted	8.3	9	8.9	8.73
Usefulness of the event	8.5	8.5	8.7	8.3

Participants are also asked to write a short statement about the impact of the experience on them personally and/or professionally. Some recurring themes appear in these comments. Perhaps most notable of these, and certainly the most frequent, is the opportunity that the Institute has provided for collaboration and learning from different library cultural environments. Comments along the lines of:

> "Gave me greater understanding of how HK & China & Taiwan colleagues think and tackle common problems"; and

> "Gratifying to know that librarians everywhere are open about sharing",

are quite frequent and are particularly pleasing, as one of the objectives of the Institute is "to enhance collaboration and foster relations among academic and research libraries in the region."

A second recurring response, and one that validates part of the initial motivation to develop the Institute, relates to the lack of opportunity for librarians in the region to partake in a learning experience of this kind. For example:

> "As China is in the process of rapid change, the Institute must be useful and relevant to colleagues in China" (2003 participant);

> "It's a good career development activity. For mainland librarians it's a pretty new experience in terms of group discussion, case study" (2005 participant);

"Most of the time in the past, I would listen only, but wouldn't express my own opinions. In this institute, I learned from my team member of Hong Kong to express ideas openly" (2006 participant).

Comments such as these reflect on the need for such a learning experience for librarians in the region and in particular mainland China. The emphasis here is not only on the significance of the content but the manner of the delivery through discussion, teamwork and high interactivity, techniques that proved quite novel for many participants. Appendix 3 contains a further selection of these statements collected since the inception of the Institute in 2003.

Institute success

In terms of evaluations from participants, the University of Hong Kong Libraries Leadership Institute is a great success. However, it is more difficult to ascertain the true degree of success in terms of the two key objectives. Certainly participants' testimonials seem to suggest that they are invigorated and inspired to do things differently upon their return to the workplace but, like many other library leadership institutes, the measure of longer term benefits are more difficult to ascertain. As Mason and Wetherbee note, "participant overviews are of limited value in evaluating the efficacy of leadership training". They further assert that such reviews "do little to address the questions of whether the participants actually learned anything new, whether that learning is retained and applied in the workplace, and whether that knowledge or those skills improved the individual or improved workplace performance".[11]

While Mason and Wetherbee may be correct, we will continue to ask participants to identify their challenges and report on how the Institute helped them to address these challenges. After a few years, we will consolidate these challenges and responses into a publication, in the hope that this will help other librarians facing similar challenges. In order to determine the longer term benefits gained by past participants we will continue to maintain contact with them and survey them on how their attendance at the Institute has helped them in their careers. We hope to be able to ascertain long-term successes of participants and to link these in some way to their participation in the Institute.

CONCLUSION

It is easy to agree with Bennis[12] that experience is key to developing good leadership qualities and with Drucker,[13] that leadership can and must be learnt. The University of Hong Kong Libraries Leadership Institute strives to make the experience for participants as real as possible by drawing upon actual problems and challenges faced by participants, by using a team approach to seek solutions, to ask participants to identify how the Institute has helped them address their challenges and by making the Institute as relevant to their current experience as is possible. It is hoped that participants can actively translate what they have heard and learnt into further meaningful experiences in their respective workplaces. Further analysis will be needed to determine if this has in fact been the case.

REFERENCES

[1] Winston, M.D. & Quinn, S. Library leadership in times of crisis and change. *New Library World* 2005, **106** (1216/1217), 395–415

[2] Mason, F.M. & Wetherbee, L.V. Learning to lead: An analysis of current training programs for library leadership. *Library Trends* 2004, **53** (1), 187–217

[3] Bennis, W. *On becoming a leader*. Updated & expanded ed. Cambridge, Mass.: Perseus, 2003.

[4] Hesselbein, F., Goldsmith, M. & Beckhard, R. (eds). *The leader of the future: new visions, strategies, and practices for the next era (Drucker Foundation Future Series)*. San Francisco: Jossey-Bass, 1997, c1996.

[5] O'Connor, S. The heretical library manager for the future. *Library Management* 2007, **28** (1/2), 62–71

[6] Cloonan, M. Message from the Dean. *The Simmons Librarian* 2006, **38** (1), 2

[7] Mason and Wetherbee, *op. cit.*

[8] Bennis, *op. cit.*

[9] Hesselbein, F., Goldsmith, M. & Beckhard, R. (eds), *op.cit.*

[10] Budd, J.M. *The changing academic library: Operations, culture, environments*. Chicago: Association of College and Research Libraries, 2005.

[11] Mason and Wetherbee, *op. cit.*

[12] Bennis, *op. cit.*

[13] Hesselbein, F., Goldsmith, M. and Beckhard, R. (eds), *op.cit.*

Appendix 1: Challenges identified by participants (2006 Institute)

- Strive to meet increasing demands of a growing student population and increased research projects under severe manpower and financial constraints and price increases. These demands include expanding scholarly information and electronic resources, improving our reference and access services, exploring collaborative programs between libraries, etc.

- Budgeting: Increasing costs of e-resources: allocate library budgets tactfully to meet the ever increasing costs in e-resources under tight budgets; redefine the new role of professional and para-professional staff under organisational change of 'do more with less'.

- The dynamic nature of digital materials provides challenge. As databases add new titles & exclude some titles, the information is not always immediately available or even ever available. To guarantee timely information for changes in resources, communication with database providers seems to be very important. We also need to make decisions in time management and project management to be cost effective. Effective digital resource management also requires cooperation within an individual library, e.g. among library teams such as technical services sections and public services sections.

- Apply latest information technologies and upgrade our service infrastructure to better support user networked information access and library operations under the fast changing technological environment and tight library budget. Boost staff morale under limited promotion opportunities and a further reduction in library staffing due to job freeze on most vacancies.

- The uncertainties of government funding and human resources policy in tertiary section have caused latent psychological frustration among staff. However, it seems to be a norm for all organisations following a trend of 'doing more with less'. How can a library leader lead his team in such adverse context and manage to get result?

Appendix 2: Overcoming challenges (responses from 2006 participants)

- I will help the staff to have a proper concept and perception of 'doing more with less'. Staff are not independent from the adverse context faced by the library. Understanding and cooperation are needed from staff. Frequent briefing should be given to the staff and encourage them to streamline or re-design their daily work.

- My Library will partner with other cultural units (i.e. gallery, museum, etc.) or student service units (i.e. Student Administration Office, Health Centre etc.) to develop into a cultural hub or information hub of the institution. Thus, the access number of the patron could be maintained. And they could have a change of their concept that only books are available in the library.

- I have learnt about opportunities other than fundraising to deal with our budget strain like collaboration, making use of new services and technology provided by other parties.

- I will build networks with other librarians from other institutions so that it will be much easier to collaborate or share the resources that are not physically available in my library.

- Before this Institute, I didn't know how to manage a project. I have wasted much time in a lot of useless things. Now I know how to use my time and energy more efficiently.

- My Library should provide a platform for users to share 'stuff', as an IT hub for exchanging, sharing and retrieving information. Moreover, the library should encourage users to make use of the platform. User education is required too.

Appendix 3: Participants' views of the experience

2003

- I must say that I am very fortunate to be here. It is very stimulating and interesting. I learnt a lot. The chance to interact and share with other leaders is also very rewarding.

- It is a good chance for me to step back and look at myself, and to share experiences with library management in Hong Kong, Taiwan and China. It really is a good experience for my career life.

- The impact will be fairly significant. I will be able to share the experience with other attendees in the future. Also, I will use several techniques myself and I will remind my boss of these techniques.

- The Institute has confirmed that communications is the key to successful leadership and provided a variety of tools, skills, and techniques to help me. I hope by adopting these skills appropriately, I shall become a more effective manager and a better person overall.

- It has made me much more aware of my own position as a leader and the responsibilities inherent in that role. I can take away from this workshop what I have learned, build on by further exploring the topics introduced and refer to them in my working situation in a practical way.

- I agree that the time involved is huge but the benefits are great. As a manager absorbed in daily work, I tend to forget some important ways and concepts in management. Taking a break by learning things new and recapturing old ideas. I believe that I am in a better position to evaluate the requirement of different jobs/staff, design alternative strategies and implement the solutions. More important the achievement honor and reward should be to the whole team.

2004

- The issues covered were very relevant and will help me very much in my work. I also made many new friends and learnt a lot about libraries in China, HK and Taiwan.

- A good occasion for self-refreshment and self-improvement. An excellent opportunity to know people from different areas.

- I have acquired new knowledge and skills in managing change, and of course, made a lot of new friends.

- It has been a valuable experience to work with colleagues from different cities with different library background; Gain acquaintance with local and Mainland and overseas librarians; get to know latest development of libraries and IT.

- As a leader of a library, I must know how to balance my power and democracy. I will be a more facilitating leader.

2005

- The Institute has helped me to rethink and recollect what I personally & my library & colleagues collectively have been doing.
- It gives me a chance to think about the future of the library and how we librarians should prepare for it.
- It helped me by introducing new information & ideas & reinforcing old knowledge. I appreciated the opportunity to meet and work with other librarians from HK, Taiwan, China & other places in the region.
- The Institute provides an excellent wake-up call for librarians about their future work environment.
- I have learnt new techniques which I can adopt and adapt in my leadership role. I can import what I have learnt to my team members at my workplace. Together we can think more creatively to solve problems.

2006

- Provided an opportunity of communication to librarians from different districts; got to know a lot of new friends; discussed some problems which all are interested in.
- Excellent! I've learned a lot. The speaker explains complicate concepts in a simple and easy understanding way, and the examples apply very much to our daily work.
- As an administrative person working in a fast-developing university library, it is good to have a chance to sit down to listen to the experts to talk about the new development of the libraries and new ideas in management; group study provokes thinking and helps to make us think more thoroughly.
- This Institute helps me in choosing/deciding our library direction and how can I work it out to ensure that the library and librarians are still relevant to the institution in future.
- This Institute inspires me to think about the future of libraries and what we should do to face it.
- Other librarians and heads of departments in our library will be able to share the achievement of this institute.

THE OBSERVANT I: SELF-ASSESSMENT AND THE EVALUATION OF LIBRARY LEADERSHIP DEVELOPMENT

Janelle M. Zauha
Reference Team Leader, Associate Professor,
Montana State University Libraries, USA.
jzauha@montana.edu

Abstract

Current popularity of leadership training institutes for library workers is heartening if we believe that such institutes are an effective means of developing leaders. Apparent difficulty in measuring or tracking specific outcomes of such training over time suggests that alternative ways of considering and defining success in leadership training coupled with concerted efforts to increase longitudinal studies are essential if the library profession is to continue its investment.

This paper briefly discusses the costs involved in leadership institutes. It reviews assessment practices for library leadership institutes as reported in the literature, noting that most published studies to date rely heavily on participants' self-assessment. An overview of recent assessment efforts of a new program, the Pacific Northwest Library Association's (PNLA) Leadership Institute (LI), is given, including objectives, methodology, and plans for data analysis and dissemination. Self assessment-focused surveys of leadership participants remain an important tool for determining the value of leadership institutes, especially if these surveys are longitudinal. Assessment plans for leadership institutes must take into account various factors, including the complexity of leadership concepts, and their measurement efforts may need to develop a better understanding and use of participant self-assessment.

INTRODUCTION

Library leadership institutes have become increasingly common in the United States in the past several decades. References to them can be found in the literature as early as 1971 when the Columbia University School of Library Science held its Institute for Library Leadership Development for Inner City Services. In 1978, the Leadership at Leavenworth (WA) workshop spread over three days and included library and media personnel from the unlikely wilds of the west (Washington, Oregon, Alaska, Idaho, and Montana).[1] In 1982 the University of California at Los Angeles delivered its first Senior Fellows Program, a biennial event that will graduate its 14th cohort in August 2007.[2]

Since those early pioneers, leadership institutes have proliferated rapidly, until Mason and Wetherbee's survey of the field, published in 2004, could count 31 such programs in various stages of delivery between 1982 and 2002 in the U. S., Australia, and Canada.[3] At least ten more institutes have appeared subsequently, as evidenced by information gathered from literature and Web sources in spring 2007. These institutes range in origin from academic institutions and individual state associations to regional, national, and international bodies, targeted at all types of library workers, from directors to mid-level managers, non-degreed personnel from staff ranks, and combinations of these.

The current popularity of leadership institutes in the library profession is heartening if we believe that such institutes are a valuable means of developing leaders. Acceptance of these institutes as effective continuing professional development events does appear to depend very much on personal opinion at this point. While it is relatively easy to locate basic information about library leadership institutes, including their individual objectives, statements of philosophy, program outlines, and application materials, it is quite difficult to find much data that objectively measures their effectiveness in developing leaders.

Abundant evidence of participant approval and self-reported gains, however, is everywhere. Participant survey data, articles recounting experiences, testimonials, and other personal statements are thick on the ground. These generally recount the effects leadership institutes have had on individuals' self-awareness as leaders or potential leaders, the impact on their careers, and overall personal growth attributed to the institutes. There has not appeared any clear method for measuring and reporting on the success of these institutes, and those who are currently developing leadership institutes must now consider many factors and options when mapping out evaluation and assessment plans for their programs.

THE COSTS OF LEADERSHIP INSTITUTES

If these institutes were inexpensive and easy to develop and deliver, the difficulty of assessing them would be less troubling. But, like all continuing professional development offerings, leadership institutes come with significant costs. Their length and complexity means that considerable time and money go into their development, delivery, and overall administration. Leadership institutes typically take place over three to five days or longer, requiring absence from regular work for typically 20–45 professionals: the participants, mentors, facilitators, teachers, and administrators involved.

Because of their intensity, focus and, frequently, residential nature, these institutes also require that a new learning space be obtained outside the regular workplace. They are held in locations that ensure a comfortable focus on learning to the exclusion of other work concerns. Mostly this means that accommodation and meeting facilities in resorts, camps, or centers must be purchased so that participants can be removed from their daily professional and familial cares. Fundraising, marketing, application processes, participant screening and selection, communication costs, transportation and learning materials all require time and money. When the cost of creating and delivering a quality curriculum, whether by local leaders or professional facilitators, is added, the result is professional development that is expensive and time consuming.

The apparent inability to definitively evaluate this type of expensive continuing education is problematic in an era of increasing interest in verifiable outcomes for training and education. Is this simply an oversight on the part of the library community or is there another cause? Is gathering assessment data on some types of continuing professional development simply too difficult? Is the kind of learning or development that occurs during and after these institutes so different that there are no tools to track it? Are leadership institutes simply too new, relatively speaking, to have the depth and longevity of participation that such assessment must draw on? Do we already have some of the information we need to assess their worth, but lack conceptual frameworks to analyze and report findings?

REVIEW OF ASSESSMENT PRACTICES AND LEADERSHIP INSTITUTES

When new providers of leadership institutes launch programs, they should decide how to assess the results of their programs in order to justify the expenditure required for developing and participating in leadership institutes. To date, evaluative studies of leadership institutes that have been reported in the literature are typically described as having gaps in knowledge, lacking in depth of data, and providing indefinite conclusions about the meaning or worth of what has been gathered. They are, however, rich in participant testimonials. As Mason and Wetherbee relate, evaluative data in the literature is "primarily focused on self-reports from participants about their learning and their satisfaction with these programs. Systematic evaluation research, particularly utilizing a control group design or providing a longitudinal assessment, has not been widely conducted in the field".[4]

Efforts to measure outcomes of leadership institutes through more extensive surveys of participants and, occasionally, other stakeholders such as supervisors and mentors or assessors, have been published by a few researchers, as Mason and Wetherbee note in their review of the literature. Hiatt's 1992 report on the work of the Career Development and Assessment Center for Librarians (CDACL) of 1979–1983[5] summarizes and evaluates grant-funded leadership training for 89 librarian 'assessees' through an intensive feedback process. Evaluation methods in this study included a pre- and post-test, participant survey, 'assessor' input, but no control group. This work was also reported on by Melber and McLaughlin[6] in 1984, and finalized in the ALA 1993 report *Assessment centers for professional library leadership: a report to the profession from the Career Development and Assessment Center for Librarians.*[7]

Neely and Winston's 1999 survey of 150 Snowbird Leadership Institute participants from 1990–1998[8] relied primarily on self-reported gains and accomplishments of Snowbird graduates as measured by specific professional activities. They conclude that "[i]t is difficult to identify a direct relationship between participation in the Snowbird Leadership Institute and career progression and greater participation in leadership activities".[9]

Hinman and Williams' 2002 unpublished report, "Study of 21st century librarianship initiatives", on three Stanford-California Library Institutes, "provides data on each of the evaluator-administered surveys that were conducted after the institute to identify what participants had learned, how participants intended to apply what they had learned, and how participants intended to use information to change their organizations."[10] Results of an online survey of participants in this institute were also reported by Anne Marie Gold, Executive Director of the institute, at the 2001 IFLA Conference, and published as an Eric Document.[11]

An additional substantive evaluation of leadership institutes not identified by Mason and Wetherbee is the extensive *Narrative Evaluation Report on the Institute For: Library Leadership Development for Inner City Services*,[12] perhaps the earliest of all library leadership institutes. This report, published in 1972 through the Eric Clearinghouse, describes pre- and post-tests of participant attitudes; overall institute evaluation by participants through interviews and other methods; survey input from participants' supervisors; evaluation of resulting programs; and evaluative input from the Institute's advisory committee comprising Columbia University School of Library Services faculty and experts from the field. Although this institute was more narrowly focused on preparing "experienced librarians to take a 'leadership' role in developing innovative library service programs for poverty neighborhoods", than on broad leadership development for the profession, the extensive assessment methods it employed are thorough and instructive for more broadly conceived institutes as well.[12]

More recently, an evaluation of the 2003 Aurora (Australia) Leadership Institute (A6) was conducted by Kay Barney, and selected findings were published in *The Australian Library Journal*.[13] This assessment relies on survey data from the 2003 attendees and, while these self-evaluative responses are very positive, Barney concedes that "[t]his study is not able to demonstrate conclusively that A6 has resulted in behavior changes and any consequent impacts on organizations and communities, but this is not surprising due to the difficulty inherent in measuring such change".[14] Although the Aurora institute has been offered since 1995, Barney's study does not include prior participant cohorts.

Recently launched ongoing evaluations of relatively new institutes include early reporting by Sheehy[15] on Synergy, the Illinois Library Leadership Initiative, an institute that began in 2002. The Synergy study surveys academic participants from two cohorts, their supervisors and their mentors, to determine the value of the experience and the impact on the workplace. Sheehy recognizes that, with such relatively limited data, survey results "cannot be considered statistically definitive but rather indicative of trends,"[16] and calls for more research, including "in-depth statistical investigation ... cost-benefit analysis ... and non-anecdotal measurements of academic library engagement and library leadership".[17]

Another early report of an ongoing survey has been published by Zauha,[18] on the Pacific Northwest Library Association (PNLA) Leadership Institute (LI), a regional institute first delivered in 2004. This research is focused primarily on post-institute surveys of participants and mentors. Further evaluative work on this institute is reported below.

Other leadership-development assessment studies are in process, as grey literature on the Web indicates. Preliminary survey work on the Canadian program, Northern Exposure to Leadership Institute (NELI) can be accessed in the text of a conference presentation published on the Web by Daniel Phelan.[19]

Broader survey work crossing a number of leadership institutes is currently being conducted by Lisa Nickel, Jennifer Arnold, and Lisa Williams, a group of North Carolina librarians who presented an ALA poster session on their work in June 2006.[20] These two research projects appear to be focused on self-assessment and self-reported outcomes gathered through surveys of participants.

The most common mode of assessment, apparent throughout this literature review, is participant self-assessment or self-reporting. A few programs include supervisor and mentor survey data; very few use control groups to provide comparison data. Most are not gathering longitudinal data on specific cohorts. While participant testimonial material abounds, this review could not find any assessment studies that discuss in depth a qualitative analysis of participant or mentor statements or narratives. Interviews of participants and/or mentors appear to be used very seldom as a means of assessment, perhaps because of their time-intensive nature and the difficulty of dealing well with data in text format. Mason and Wetherbee conclude that, "if the designers of leadership training hope to claim that such programs improve productivity and achieve an economic payoff for libraries, better evaluation methods must be developed and used in a systematic way."[21]

THE PNLA LEADERSHIP INSTITUTE

Although some survey research has been completed and published for the PNLA LI (as noted above), much of the gathering and analysis of data still lies ahead for this new leadership program. The PNLA LI is a biennial event inviting degreed and non-degreed library staff from the northwestern US and western Canada for intensive leadership training. First held in 2004, the PNLA LI is focused on providing leadership development to library workers in a large geographic area (Alaska, Alberta, British Columbia, Idaho, Montana, Oregon, and Washington) characterized by considerable distances between metropolitan areas, dispersed rural populations, and scarcity of funding, especially for small rural libraries. Staff who lead these rural libraries often lack professional degrees and have limited access to continuing education.[22]

The first PNLA LI was held in October 2004 in Federal Way, WA, and was entirely funded by seed money from PNLA chapter associations, vendor donations, and registration fees, with mentors, a coordinator, and an administrative assistant all volunteering their time. In early 2006, the LI received partial funding through the U.S. Federal Institute of Museum and Library Services (IMLS) grant program for a second institute, which was held in October 2006 in Donnelly, ID and for a third iteration (planned for 2008). The grant also includes funding for interim year (2007) mentoring activities in which seven participants from the 2006 institute will each be matched with a rural librarian who has not attended the LI and each pair will be sent to their 2007 state/provincial library association conference.

Each institute brings together 32–36 participants and eight mentors from around the region to a central location for five days of intensive group and individual experiential learning led by two facilitators, Becky Schreiber and John Shannon of Schreiber Shannon Associates. Schreiber Shannon are well known consultants in the area of library leadership; they facilitate several other high profile institutes including Snowbird, Aurora, and Library Leadership Ohio. The PNLA LI shares many common characteristics with these other institutes because of this.

PNLA'S ASSESSMENT PLANS AND METHODS

PNLA's assessment plan for its LI has been formed in light of current and past evaluative practices for similar institutes and takes into consideration several other factors germane to the region, the association, and the LI itself. PNLA is fully aware, as are all leadership institute developers, that it cannot prove that the PNLA LI has changed the face or future of library leadership in the region at this stage; no leadership institute could do so after only two or three iterations because leadership development is not a 'magic pill'. The outcomes may be a decade or more in the making.

While some methods of assessment might provide optimal information and more definitive measurement of outcomes, any professional development provider has to decide what assessment is possible and achievable with limited human resources and time, a trade off not unfamiliar to librarians. As a regional professional association with relatively low membership and limited funds, PNLA is certainly no exception. Considerations that have gone into the mapping of PNLA's assessment course include:

- the objectives set out by the association when forming the LI;
- the broad range of participant education, experience, and library position;
- the likely nature of data drawn from small participant pools and limited numbers of cohorts;
- a tight timeline for evaluation required by funding sources;
- administrative limitations for gathering and analyzing data;
- an understanding of the long gestation period for outcomes because of the nature of leadership development.

The evaluation plan that PNLA has implemented is designed to provide information to the association on a number of levels and at different intervals. It will answer more complex questions as time goes on when data from and about the 3 initial cohorts can be combined and compared. The survey schedule is designed to track each cohort at comparable points in their post-institute work and to draw in different types of data at each interval (see Table 1).

Table 1 A time table for survey distribution to the first 3 PNLA LI cohorts

PNLA Leadership Institute Evaluation/Assessment Schedule				
	Immediate: Onsite Evaluations	2 Months: Initial Participant & Mentor Survey	22 Months: In-depth Participant Survey	3 years: Participant Survey & Association Feedback
2004 cohort	Oct 2004 *	Dec 2004 *	July 2006 *	Fall/Winter 2007
2006 cohort	Oct 2006 *	Dec 2006 *	July 2008	Fall/Winter 2009
2008 cohort	Fall 2008	Winter 2008	Summer 2010	Fall/Winter 2011

* Already completed.

Throughout the evaluation cycle, the primary focus is on surveying the participants, with some mentor input and, in the final survey round, input from state and provincial associations. The objectives of the immediate evaluations are to help steer each institute and correct problems with facilities, administration and curriculum before the next institute. This level of evaluation begins with 'Daily Dialogue' input, gathered each afternoon of the institute by the facilitators; this is a hallmark of the Schreiber Shannon style. It encourages reflection on self and group performance, an important tenet of the institute's curriculum, and enables the facilitators and mentors to respond quickly to unmet needs, to talk through issues that come up, and to alter the next day's outline as needed. At the end of the institute, participants are asked to fill out an evaluation form on-site. The questions on this form ask participants to rank the extent to which the institute met its stated objectives, to rank how highly participants valued various activities, to provide feedback on practical arrangements and schedules, to give initial personal impact statements, and to set the stage for further networking with mentors and fellow participants. Results are compiled and distributed to the LI administrators.

Two months after the institute, participants are asked to respond to an online survey of 20 questions administered through SurveyMonkey.[23] These questions ask for participant input in five areas:

- On participants themselves: including choices they made in coming to the institute, their past experience with leadership training, education level, and the types of funding and leave that enabled them to attend (Objectives: to learn what kinds of participants were attracted to the institute and what administrative barriers they faced);

- On participants' experience at the LI: especially what gains were made in specific leadership skill areas such as self-awareness and conflict management, how they have used those skills at work, and what the most important thing learned at the LI was (Objectives: to gauge participants' self-assessment of learning and provide overall curriculum feedback to facilitators and staff);

- On participants' interactions with others during and after the institute: including their small learning groups and mentors, evaluation of progress in learning groups, any impact of various factors on the group experience, amount of contact with participants and mentors after the LI (Objectives: to assess network formation, mentor roles, and the overall group learning experience);

- About the institute generally: including any changes they feel should be considered (Objectives: to improve facilities, scheduling, etc.);

- About leadership and the future: including their own plans for education or training, association involvement, job movement, and their reflections on the importance of leadership training for the future of libraries (Objectives: to gauge participant attitudes, and whether broader PLNA and chapter association objectives, such as increased association involvement and succession planning, may be met by the institute).

At approximately the same time as the second participant survey is distributed online (two months after the institute), a 17-question online survey is sent to the mentors of each cohort, to gain their perspective on administrative and facility details, to learn more about their own personal motivation for participation, and, most important, to gather their observations about the skills advancements they observed in participants within their learning group.

The third survey of each cohort is scheduled for distribution 22 months after graduation, a time frame that is partly determined by administrative availability and partly to avoid too-frequent survey contact with a cohort. This survey is also distributed online using SurveyMonkey. It contains 37 questions grouped into the same basic areas as the second survey, with similar objectives but with an additional interest in charting changes in the cohort. The areas covered by the questions include further education or training acquired; position or institution moves; persistence of attitudes toward gains made in the LI; increased or decreased use of skills; contacts with participants and mentors; professional association involvement; participation in leadership activities on and off the job; impact of the LI on life outside work; and attitudes toward their futures in the profession, including predilection toward moving into higher leadership, managerial, or administrative positions in libraries.

The fourth survey of each cohort is scheduled for the third year after graduation. This instrument has not been designed or delivered at this stage, but preliminary objectives are to continue to gather information about the persistence of skills acquired at the institute, to gauge visible evidence of leadership development through position changes, and specific association and other leadership activities. PNLA and its chapter associations will be tapped for feedback, particularly in terms of LI participants' committee and board leadership activity, as well as conference presentations and other association work. Other means of data gathering may also be considered if time and resources are available. The first cycle of this survey is due to be distributed to the 2004 cohort in fall/winter 2007.

Assessment of mentoring activities for the interim year (2007) is in the exploration and design stages. Input sought from these seven pairs of librarians will need to be significantly different from that gathered from the three LI cohorts, in view of their activities, much smaller numbers, and other factors. Since their experience will revolve around attendance at state and provincial association conferences during this year, all of which occur at different times in the region, scheduling of their assessment may be difficult.

PLANS FOR THE DATA

The assessment of the PNLA LI is still in its early stages. Of 12 scheduled surveys of the three cohorts, only five have been gathered. Some segments are still being designed. Thorough analysis of data is needed.

Response rates to surveys thus far have been very good for both the 2004 and 2006 cohorts. The second survey of the 2004 cohort (conducted in December 2004) had a return of 33 responses out of a possible 36, a rate of 91.7%. The 3rd survey of the 2004 cohort (conducted in July 2006) had a return of 31 responses out of 36, a rate of 86%. The second survey of the 2006 cohort (conducted in December 2006) returned 27 out of a possible 32 for a return rate of 84%.

As PNLA dips into the initial data, it is adjusting the LI curriculum, finding new ways to market the workshop and attempting to diversify the pool of participants by drawing more Canadian and more rural library workers. Initial comparisons of a small sample of the data from the second and third surveys of the 2004 cohort show some positive, although not objectively measurable, evidence of the persistence of the self-reported effects of the 2004 LI (see Tables 2 and 3).

Table 2 Persistence of self-reported gains in leadership skill areas, December 2004 to July 2006, for 2004 LI cohort.

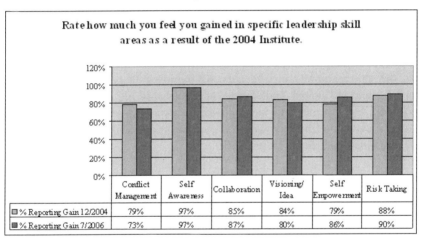

	Conflict Management	Self Awareness	Collaboration	Visioning/ Idea	Self Empowerment	Risk Taking
% Reporting Gain 12/2004	79%	97%	85%	84%	79%	88%
% Reporting Gain 7/2006	73%	97%	87%	80%	86%	90%

Table 3 Change in self-reported use of skills gained during LI, December 2004 to July 2006, for 2004 LI cohort.

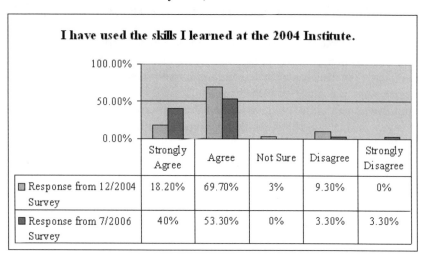

I have used the skills I learned at the 2004 Institute.	Strongly Agree	Agree	Not Sure	Disagree	Strongly Disagree
Response from 12/2004 Survey	18.20%	69.70%	3%	9.30%	0%
Response from 7/2006 Survey	40%	53.30%	0%	3.30%	3.30%

As this data is further collected and analyzed it will be presented to the PNLA membership at annual conferences and published in *PNLA Quarterly*. In addition, the state and provincial chapter associations will be kept abreast of these evaluative efforts through their representatives on the PNLA board and selected local conference presentations.

DISCUSSION

If leadership development were a straightforward employee training endeavor, with easily identifiable and measurable outcomes, PNLA and other leadership training developers might readily turn to the field of human resource development in business and adopt Return on Investment (ROI) evaluation procedures to determine the value of the leadership institutes. However, leadership development is a fuzzy concept in our field, as is 'leadership' itself. Current philosophy and practice often emphasize the idea of leading from any position. This means that outcomes of such institutes as the PNLA LI are likely to be as diverse as the participants in the institute, especially since no specific title, or position, or level of education or experience is a prerequisite for participation.

More traditional human resource training is usually embedded within a specific business or organization and is aimed at employees with a long term specific relationship with the sponsoring body. In these cases, it is easier to determine how one will define and measure success, and to then implement ROI-like evaluations. The employee can be tracked and observed, the environment is understood, products and services are known.

Leadership institutes, on the other hand, are usually sponsored by larger, loosely organized associations and tend to attract participants who do not work in the same teams or even institutions. Seeking such a broad spectrum of participants is often based on sound philosophical reasons such as enhancing learning and encouraging openness in a 'strange' environment, or for very practical reasons such as spreading out the cost of the institute. For these reasons, graduates of LIs are often widely dispersed after their experience and are not readily tracked or observed over time; the environments to which they return are not easily understood, and their positions and backgrounds may differ so widely as to be incomparable.

In addition, acknowledging the ambiguity of what is being imparted is essential in order to understand how difficult it is to measure the results of such training. The number of different definitions of 'leadership' that we find in the library, business, and other literatures should be our first clue that the concept is complex. Mason and Wetherbee acknowledge that "[d]efining leadership seems straightforward, but explaining how leaders lead and, more importantly, what skills they use to lead is a much more complicated and complex issue".[24] Matthew Eriksen writes about these complexities: "There are no natural laws or final, completely adequate understandings of leadership. Rather a leader develops more and more adequate instrumentalities for dealing with always changing and growing leadership situations. In practice, leadership deals with individualized and unique situations that are never exactly duplicable and about which, accordingly, no complete understanding is possible."[25]

CONCLUSION

The difficulty of defining leadership makes it essential for LI developers to be clear about their goals and objectives from the outset, and to plan and design evaluations that can meaningfully measure their success in close relation to these goals and objectives. Those who are developing institutes should determine early on what outcomes they wish to see and how they will monitor or measure them. What are the long and short term goals for the institute as set out by the sponsoring organization(s)? To increase participation in professional associations? To cultivate advocacy activity? To encourage publication in professional journals and newsletters? To create a more diverse mentoring network for a region? To heighten the profile and brand name of the organization(s)? To complement or fill a gap in succession planning?

If long and short term goals are not understood and fully articulated, how will developers know if they have achieved them? Furthermore, defining measurable objectives for these goals and creating a curriculum expressly geared toward achieving the objectives is essential. Leadership institutes that do not establish these foundations at the outset will find themselves faced with a confusing and difficult task when they attempt to measure the outcomes of their work. They might as well try to determine how much sand is on a particular beach—a long, hot, and meaningless exercise with constantly shifting results.

As well as defining their objectives, developers can learn from the assessment efforts that have come before. They should note, as Mason and Weatherbee's review and other subsequent reports in the literature caution, that comparative or baseline data of some kind is as necessary for establishing validity as it is difficult to gather. The developers need to determine how this comparative data will be laid down in their study, whether through control groups, pre- and post-testing, or by some other means.

Participants' self-assessment, thus grounded, will become a more viable component of LI evaluation than it has proven to be in the past. Solid understanding and articulation of how quantitative and qualitative data gathered from participants can fit together in a well-designed, outcomes-focused evaluation will truly be a gift to the profession and to the future of leadership development for libraries.

REFERENCES

[1] Furlong, F., Kerns, M., Rogers, & M. Leadership at Leavenworth. AECT Region IX Leadership Workshop, Camp Field, Leavenworth, Washington, July 12, 13, 14, 1978. Washington, DC: Association for Educational Communications and Technology; 1978 July. Eric Document No.: ED171317.

2. Senior Fellows at UCLA [WWW document]. URL <http://is.gseis.ucla.edu/seniorfellows/index.htm>. Accessed 10 Feb 2007.

3. Mason, F.M., & Wetherbee, L.V. Learning to lead: an analysis of current training programs for library leadership. *Library Trends* 2004, 53(1), 187-217.

4. *Ibid.* p. 187.

5. Hiatt, P. Identifying and encouraging leadership potentital: assessment technology and the library profession. *Library Trends* 1992, 40(3), 513-42.

6. Melber, B.D., & McLaughlin SD. Evaluation of a career development and assessment center program for professional librarians. *Library and Information Science Research* 1984, 7(2), 159-81.

7. Hiatt, P., Hamilton, R.H., & Wood, C.L. *Assessment centers for professional library leadership : a report to the profession from the Career Development and Assessment Center for Librarians.* Chicago: American Library Association, 1993.

8. Neely, T.Y., & Winston, M.D. Snowbird Leadership institute: leadership development in the profession. *College and Research Libraries* 1999, 60(5), 412-425.

9. Neely & Winston, *op.cit.,* p. 424.

10. Mason and Wetherbee, *op.cit.,* p. 208.

11. Gold, A.M. Developing leaders for libraries: the Stanford-California State Library Institute on 21st Century Librarianship. In: *Libraries and Librarians: Making a Difference in the Knowledge Age. Council and General Conference: Conference Programme and Proceedings* (67th, Boston, MA August 16-25, 2001). Eric Document No: ED459787.

12. Prentice, A.E. Narrative evaluation report on the Institute For: Library Leadership Development for Inner City Services. Columbia University School of Library Service. Report period: September 1971 to January 1972. Bureau of Libraries and Education al Technology, Washington, DC. Eric Document No: ED096994.

13. Barney, K. Evaluation of the impact of the 2003 Aurora Leadership Institute – 'the gift that keeps on giving.' *The Australian Library Journal* 2004, 53(4), 337-48.

14 *Ibid,* p. 346.

15 Sheehy, C.A. Synergy: The Illinois Library Leadership Initiative and the development of future academic library leaders. *College & Undergraduate Libraries* 2004, 11 (1), 61-75.

16 *Ibid,* p. 66.

17 *Ibid,* p. 71.

18 Zauha, J.M. Leadership training for all: providing opportunities for degreed and non-degreed librarians in a regional institute. In Genoni, P. and Walton, G (eds.) *Continuing Professional Development – Preparing for New Roles in Libraries: A Voyage of Discovery. Sixth World Conference on Continuing Professional Development and Workplace Learning for the Library and Information Professions* [International Federation of Library Associations and Institutions]. Munich: Saur, 2005: pp 245-55.

19 Phelan, D. Creating leaders: a study of the Northern Exposure to Leadership Participants – before and after. February 3, 2005. [WWW document] <http://www.accessola2.com/superconference2005/thurs/docs/108/creating.ppt> Accessed February 12, 2007.

20 Nickel, L., Arnold J., & Williams, L. Follow me! Are leadership institutes creating the next generation of library leaders? American Library Association Annual Conference, New Orleans, LA, June 24, 2006. Poster Session II-3. [WWW document] URL <http://www.lib.jmu.edu/org/ala/abstracts/default.aspx> Accessed February 10, 2007.

21 Mason & Wetherbee, *op.cit.,* p. 214

22 PNLA Leads: The Pacific Northwest Library Association's leadership institute project narrative. Submitted to the Institute of Museum and Library Services, December 2005. [WWW document] URL: <ttp://www.pnla.org/institute/IMLSNarrative06.doc> Accessed February 13, 2007.

23 SurveyMonkey. URL: <http://www.surveymonkey.com> Accessed March 15, 2007.

24 Mason & Wetherbee, *op.cit.,* p. 187

25 Eriksen, M. Developing the ability of proactive reflection. *Academic Exchange Quarterly* 2004, June 22.

LEADERSHIP SKILLS: WHEN ARE THEY TAUGHT, WHEN ARE THEY USED

Blanche Woolls
Professor and Director Emerita
School of Library and Information Science
San Jose State University, USA
bwoolls@slis.sjsu.edu

Nancy Zimmerman
Associate Professor
School of Library and Information Science
University of South Carolina, USA
nzimmerman@gwa.sc.edu

Abstract

This study was designed to determine the perceptions of new and graduating students and recent graduates in U.S. schools of library and information science (LIS) towards leadership. Specifically it addresses whether or not leadership is taught and when or if it is used in practice. An electronic questionnaire was sent to students and recent graduates from two large LIS programs in the United States accredited by the American Library Association, one on the east coast and one on the west coast, to learn when and how often they received leadership training and when they put their leadership skills to work.

LEADERSHIP SKILLS

The phenomenon called *leadership* is a continuing discussion topic at library and information science (LIS) meetings as trustees of library systems attempt to replace retiring library directors in all types of libraries. Middle managers, secure in their positions as second in command, do not relish the thought of moving into the role of the person who makes the final decision. This is not unique to LIS. In 1985, Warren Bennis and Burt Nanus wrote:

> *Leadership* is a word on everyone's lips. The young attack it and the old grow wistful for it. Parents have lost it and police seek it. Experts claim it and artists spurn it, while scholars want it. Philosophers

reconcile it (as authority) with liberty and theologians demonstrate its compatibility with conscience. If bureaucrats pretend they have it, politicians wish they did. Everybody agrees that there is less of it than there used to be.[1]

The lack of persons with an interest in leadership in LIS is pointed out by Rosie Albritton and Thomas Shaughnessy in their foreword to *Developing Leaderships Skills:*

> Leadership, or the lack of it, is one of the most discussed topics in the library community today. Turnover in the ranks of library directors is high, and university officers are concerned about the difficulty they have in identifying and recruiting excellent candidates. Simultaneously, library administers report a similar difficulty in recruiting middle- and upper-level managers who can successfully balance the many demands of the job.[2]

Brooke E. Sheldon used the Bennis and Nanus qualities of vision, communication, positioning, and self confidence to assess to what degree librarians in leadership positions have these qualities.[3] She added mentors and networking as variables in her interviews and ended with some implications for library education. Sheldon's chapter on library education suggests:

> The neglect of leadership issues is due primarily to the fact that leadership and related issues have not been studied in any concerted way by our profession, nor have leadership concepts been integrated into the mainstream of library and information science education.[4]

Donald Riggs agrees with her when he states:

> Few, if any schools of information and library science are teaching leadership classes. These schools were teaching administration classes while business schools were teaching management classes; now SLIS programs are teaching management classes while business schools are teaching leadership classes. Should we not expect more emphasis on leadership from schools preparing our future library leaders?[5]

The literature search for this paper found very few research reports or articles. The search for doctoral students' studies in this area found a surprising number of dissertations and theses done outside programs accredited by the American

Library Association. A great many writers were interested in public schools and academic libraries, but they did their research at other universities and were not students in LIS schools at the time they conducted the research.

RESEARCH REPORTS

The research reports that discuss leadership did not indicate where it is taught. Studies concerning leadership in libraries include Young, Hernon and Powell's study[6] of the perceptions of Gen-X (Generation X) academic and public librarians, about the attributes essential for both types of library leaders. Little agreement was found between the perceptions of these two groups concerning the attributes needed. Rosie Albritten[7] tested a model of transformational vs. transactional leadership. Leadership is identified as a role in team management by Marie A. Kascus.[8] Susan Davis[9] sought to learn about leadership roles of persons acting either independently or on behalf of their institutions or professional associations, and found that individuals who became involved in early stages in association membership kept their involvement and were viewed as more influential by their peers.

When higher education was charged with educating students to become culturally competent global citizens, strategies of Australian academic librarians to assist in this goal were tested by Linda K. Becker.[10] Catherine Matthews[11] describes four stages of transition cycles to becoming a chief or lead librarian. In Mary Somerville's study[12] of ways to get long-time employees to reconsider traditional roles, systems thinking became a successful pedagogical strategy.

The leadership behavior of immediate supervisors was studied by two persons. Darlene Parish[13] looked at the organizational commitment and job autonomy of information services librarians in relation to their perceptions of supervisors. Dana Boden[14] investigated perceptions of department chairs' leadership practices in faculty development. Patha Suwannarat[15] reviewed library leadership of directors in 29 research university libraries using Bass's Model of Transformational Leadership, and found that directors thought they exhibited transformational leadership behaviors and were able to encourage extra effort from their subordinates. This perception was not confirmed by questions asked of their subordinates. Diane Kazlauskas[16] asked librarians in the State University System of Florida their perceptions of their managers' leadership practices and of the employees' job satisfaction. She discovered that autonomy in the work setting was more closely related to job satisfaction than leadership practices.

Three studies report management strategies used in library organizations undergoing major changes and innovations. Lois Little[17] found that the degree of innovation is related to the leader's vision and change strategy. Charles D. McCowan,[18] testing whether leadership styles were affected before, during, and after a major organizational transition, found that leaders' styles remain consistent. The growth of leadership in Czech public libraries was reported by Andrew Hess[19] as he traced the adoption of information technology and how it created new public library roles.

School librarians most often work as single professionals and do not always have clerical staff to assist them. Their leadership takes the form of working with teachers and administrators and is most often shown in leading teachers to collaborate with student assignments or with implementing change. Jean Brown and Bruce Sheppard[20] equate showing teachers how to use new technologies with leadership. Their research includes three studies of leadership for change in schools and districts: a five-year study of eight schools, a case study of two schools, and the third of seven schools. Catherine Edwards's study[21] of successful practice in integrating technology into classrooms confirms that teachers are most receptive to learning from their peers. Brenda McCoy[22] found that librarians show a "high degree of general interest in technology integration and implementation" which would indicate that they are prepared to take a leadership role in staff development.

The findings of Linda Underwood's study[23] of leadership roles suggest that leadership of the school librarian could place the school library as the instructional hub of the school. Anne Carroll[24] describes the role of the secondary school librarian in the curricular integration of technology through staff development. Elizabeth Greenan[25] found that school library leadership is vital in collection development. The need for continuing professional education is pointed out in Li-ling Kuo's study[26] of high school library directors in the Republic of China.

Special libraries are discussed in two research studies. Beatriz Cendon[27] looked at the critical factors in making a medical library powerful in the parent organization and found the characteristics of leadership include vision, inhibited power motive, linguistic abilities, and cognitive complexity. Adrian Dale analyzed leadership in special libraries during a conference in Stockholm. He found that "90% of TLS delegates wanted libraries to take a leadership role in information management in their organization, but only 29% of delegates thought this was likely."[28]

When one views leadership in light of the problem of libraries keeping adequate staff, or, in the case of school librarians, keeping their jobs, it would seem that the lack of leadership skills might be the cause when practitioners lament the poor image of librarians. 'Image' is a topic more often found in the LIS literature than leadership. Ideally leadership competency should be acquired as part of the curriculum of a graduate program, but research suggests this happens infrequently. If leadership training is lacking in library education programs, then it becomes essential that library staff and professional associations conduct the necessary training to prepare their future leaders. Two reports suggested how this could happen.

Dan Gjelten and Teresa Fishel[29] identified two leadership institutes for librarians in the U.S., the one-week ACRL (Association of College and Research Libraries)/Harvard Leadership Institute (Cambridge, MA) and the two-week Frye leadership Institute (Atlanta, GA). Programming at these institutes could provide a model for other organizations planning leadership programs. Sharyn Milnar's master's thesis[30] details the method, research, delivery and evaluation of a one-week training course complete with training modules on a compact disk.

How continuing professional development programs can build leaders is the purpose of this continuing professional development conference. The profession faces many challenges. Libraries today compete with other departments or agencies for limited funds, increasing the difficulty of providing service and information for patrons and professional development opportunities, particularly leadership development, for staff. In addition, the need to increase membership in professional associations and to get members to accept leadership responsibility for activities is daunting, given this decreased funding for professional development. Ever-increasing travel expenses and staff shortages that make covering leave time difficult contribute to the problem of providing leadership education from the workplace.

So what is the solution? In an attempt to shed light on leadership education, this study sought to capture, through a survey, a snapshot of students and graduates of two accredited LIS programs in the U.S. and if, and in what courses, leadership is taught, and if and how this education is applied.

LEADERSHIP TRAINING

A questionnaire was submitted electronically to current students and recent graduates of two LIS education programs in the U.S. Both are accredited by the

American Library Association, have distance programs and large enrolment. Three groups, new students (103 at one school and 535 at the other), those who had completed fewer than three courses, and students ready to graduate (71 at one school and 220 at the other), each completed one questionnaire. Accurate figures for the middle group were not possible to obtain because students in both locations are distant and attending only part-time.

Graduates from the last five years who were members of the alumni association lists completed another. Again, it was not possible to get accurate figures here because, while numbers of graduates are available, this does not translate into the same numbers because not all graduates join the alumni lists. Questionnaires were posted at the end of the fall semester with only a short period for response and at a holiday time for potential respondents. No follow-up request was made. In spite of these limitations, a total of 299 student returns and 87 alumni returns was tabulated.

Students were asked to indicate the type of LIS position in which they planned to work and whether they were new students; had taken between one and three courses or were nearing graduation. Responses for students attending the two schools shown in this and further tables, are pooled because there was no significant difference between students attending the two schools. Results are shown in Table 1 below.

Table 1 Students and Number of Courses Taken in Program (n = 299*)

Type of library	New Student	Has taken 3 or less than 3 courses	Nearing graduation	Total	%
Academic	8	26	21	55	19
Archives	1	15	9	25	8
Public	7	38	32	77	26
Special	4	15	14	33	11
School	3	36	13	52	19
Self-employed	0	1	2	3	0
Undecided	7	28	14	49	17
Total	30	159	105	294	100

*While 299 students completed the survey, five students did not indicate the number of courses taken in the program: one each in academic, public, or school, and two students were undecided. A total of 19% chose academic libraries.

Thirty students, less than 10%, indicated they were new students, while 105 (36%) were graduating. The largest number, 159 (54%), were just beginning their programs. Their probable choice for type of library after graduation was 19% academic, 8% archives, 26% public, 11% special, 19% school, less than 1% would be self-employed, and 17% were undecided. It was interesting to note that 14 (5%) of those graduating had yet to make a decision about a type of library.

Student responses were then sorted according to whether the students were new; had taken fewer than three courses or were nearing graduation; and to see the number of courses they had taken which specialized in management. The responses for two categories are shown in Table 2 below. New students were not tabulated here.

Table 2 Time in Program and Courses Taken Specializing in Management (n = 264)

Time in Program	None	Only core	Core +1	Core +2	Core +3	Total
3 or < 3	63	92	4	0	0	159
Graduating	1	74	21	6	3	105
Totals	64	168	27	6	3	264

Of those students with not more than three courses, 63 (24%) had not yet taken a management course and 92 (35%) had completed only the core. Of the 106 graduating students, 74 (28%) had taken only the core, 21 (8%) had taken the core and one additional management course, while only nine (3%) had taken the core and two additional courses.

Students were then asked how many of their non-management courses offered management components. Their responses are in Table 3.

Table 3 Percentage of Time Spent on Management in Non-Management Courses (n = 260)

Time in Program	No Answer	None	5% One	5% +1	10% One	10% +1	50% One	50% +1	Most	Total
3 or < 3	9	53	42	15	21	7	5	2	2	156
Nearing Graduating	2	18	17	18	16	18	6	5	4	104
Total	11	71	59	33	37	25	11	7	6	260

Eleven (4%) did not answer this question, and 71 (27%) had no management instruction in non-management courses. Less than 10% of the students have had more than minimal time spent on management in non-management courses.

Students were then asked how many courses they had taken that specialized in leadership. Their responses are found in Table 4.

Table 4 Courses Taken Specializing in Leadership (n = 269)

Time in Program	None	Only core	Core +1	Core +2	Core +3	Total
3 or < 3	65	78	15	1	0	159
Graduating	2	67	22	8	7	106
Totals	67	145	37	9	7	265

Of the students with one to three courses, 65 (24%) had taken no course specializing in leadership, and 78 (29%) had leadership only in the core. Graduating students (69 or 26%) had no course or only the core, and the remainder (37 or 13%) had core and one to three others.

Students then indicated how much of their courses, other than management, had leadership components. Their responses are found in Table 5.

Table 5 Percent of Time Spent in Leadership in Courses other than the Core (n = 264)

Time in Program	No Answer	None	5% One	5% +1	10% One	10% +1	50% One	50% +1	Most	Total
3 or < 3	15	45	47	13	16	12	5	0	5	158
Nearing Graduating	1	30	17	18	8	18	4	6	4	106
Total	16	75	64	31	24	30	9	6	0	264

Several students (16 or 6%) did not answer this question, and 75 (28%) had no course with a leadership component other than their core management course. Only 15 (5%) had more than 10% of any class other than the core with a leadership component.

The next question asked how soon they expected to manage after they graduated. Those responses are found in Table 6.

Table 6 How Soon They Expected to Manage (n = 294)

Time in Program	Never	Immediately	1-3 Years	3+ Years	Total
New Student	1	23	5	1	30
3 or < 3	5	90	49	16	160
Nearing Graduation	5	56	32	10	104
Total	11	170	88	29	294

Most of the students (287 or 96%) expected to manage at some point. For 170 (57%) that would happen immediately; 88 (29%) would wait one to three years, and 29 (9%) felt they would not manage for three years. Only 11 (4%) felt they would never manage. Students were also asked how soon they expected to take a leadership role. Their responses are shown in Table 7.

Table 7 How Soon they Expected to Take a Leadership Role (n = 294)

Time in Program	Never	Immediately	1-3 Years	3+ Years	Total
New Student	1	26	3	0	30
3 or < 3	3	125	26	5	159
Nearing Graduation	4	72	27	1	105
Total	8	226	56	9	294

Only eight (2%) did not think they would take a leadership role. Most of the students, 226 (76%) thought they would do so immediately while 65 (22%) thought they would wait at least three years or even more than three.

Students were asked to say where they would be starting their leadership roles and they were given the option of choosing more than one place. Table 8 provides their answers.

Table 8 Where Would They Lead?

Time in Program	Will Not	Professional Association	Social Assn	Religious Assn	Neighborhood Assn
New Student	1	25	17	8	4
3 or < 3	16	123	70	30	11
Nearing Graduation	18	73	43	18	12
Total	25	221	130	56	27

Although only seven respondents suggested they wouldn't accept a leadership role when choosing a place to begin leadership, 25 indicated that none of the choices given them would be their choice. Most of the students thought they would join a professional association and 130 would join a social group. A much smaller number thought they would choose a religious group, and even fewer, 27, would choose a neighborhood or community role.

ALUMNI RESULTS

Alumni who had graduated within the past five years were asked exactly how many years it had been since they graduated. They were also asked to indicate the type of library or information agency in which they were presently employed. Two categories were general: 'self-employed' and 'working in another occupation'. Their responses are shown below in Table 9.

Table 9 Number of Years since Graduation and Type of Library (n = 87)

Type of Library	1 year	2 years	3 years	4 years	5 Years	Total	%
Academic	2	2	5	4	2	15	17
Archives	0	0	2	0	0	2	2
Public	12	5	9	1	3	30	34
School	3	2	2	2	2	11	13
Special	4	2	3	2	1	12	14
Self-Employed	1	0	2	0	0	3	3
Another Occupation	5	1	4	0	0	10	12
Not working	2	1	0	1	0	4	5
Total	29	13	27	10	8	87	100

Of the respondents, 48% graduated within two years and only 9 % had to search their memories for five years. Of those responding, 15 (17%) were academic librarians, two (2%) were archivists, 30 (34%) public librarians, 11 (13%) school, 12 (14%) special, three (3%) were self-employed, ten (12%) in an occupation other than LIS, and four (5%) were not working.

Respondents were asked to state the type of position they presently held and to indicate the number of courses they took in the program that specialized in management. While 'records management' was a choice on the questionnaire, no respondents replied that they were working in that area. The results of this question are shown in Table 10.

Table 10 Positions Held and Number of Courses Specializing in Management (n = 87*)

Position	Core Only	Core + 1	Core +2	Core +3	Total
Reference	23	4	1	0	28
Cataloging	5	2	0	0	7
Automation/Technology	4	0	0	0	4
Youth Services	11	2	1	0	14
School Librarians	3	3	2	2	10
Archive	2	1	0	0	3
Self-Employed/Consultants	1	1	0	0	2
Another occupation	6	2	2	1	11
Not working	3	0	0	0	3
Did not specify job title	2	1	0	0	3
Totals	60	16	6	4	86

*One person 'not working' didn't provide number of management courses.

Almost 70% of the graduates from these two programs completed only a core course in management. Of the remaining 30%, 20% had taken a second course specializing in management.

Respondents were asked to indicate the percentage of their non-management courses that had management components. The results of this are shown in Table 11.

Table 11 Percentage of Non-Management Courses with Management Components (n = 87*)

Position	None	5% One	5% +1	10% One	10% +1	50% One	50% +1	Most	Total
Reference	8	9	1	2	5	2	0	0	27
Cataloging	2	1	1	0	3	0	0	0	7
Automation/Technology	3	1	1	0	0	0	0	0	5

Youth Services	1	5	1	1	3	1	0	2	14
School Librarian	3	2	0	1	2	1	0	1	10
Archives	1	1	0	0	1	0	0	0	3
Self-Employed/ Consultant	1	0	1	0	0	0	0	0	2
Another occupation	0	0	2	3	4	1	0	1	11
Not Working	1	0	0	0	3	0	0	0	4
Did not specify job title	0	1	2	0	0	0	0	0	3
Total	20	20	9	7	21	5	0	4	86

*One respondent didn't specify number of non-management courses with management components.

Of these graduates, 23% had no management in any of their other courses and 23% had less than 5% of one other course. Two youth librarians, one school librarian, and 1 respondent working in another occupation felt that most of their courses had management components. A total of 89% had at the most, 10% of one class teaching management.

Respondents were also asked how many courses they had taken which specialized in leadership. Their answers are shown in Table 12.

Table 12 Type of Position by Number of Courses Specializing in Leadership (n = 87*)

Position	Only core	Core +1	Core +2	Core +3	Total
Reference	23	3	0	2	28
Cataloging	6	1	0	0	7
Automation/Technology	3	2	0	0	5
Youth Services	12	2	0	0	14
School Librarian	4	2	1	2	9
Archives	2	0	1	0	3
Self-Employed/Consultant	2	0	0	0	2
Another Occupation	9	1	0	1	11

Not Working	3	1	0	0	4
Did not specify job title	1	2	0	0	3
Totals	65	14	2	3	86

*One school librarian did not indicate the number of courses specializing in leadership.

Table 13 shows respondents answers to how many of their courses other than the core, offered leadership components and how much dealt with leadership.

Table 13 Number of Other Courses with Leadership Components (n = 87)

Position	None	5% One	5% +1	10% One	10% +1	50% One	50% +1	Most	Total
Reference	10	9	2	1	5	1	1	0	29
Cataloging	3	0	1	0	2	0	0	0	6
Automation/ Technology	2	2	1	0	0	0	0	0	5
Youth Services	5	2	2	1	1	1	0	2	14
School Librarian	3	2	0	1	3	0	0	1	10
Archives	1	0	0	1	1	0	0	0	3
Self-Employed/ Consultant	1	0	1	0	0	0	0	0	2
Another Occupation	3	1	1	1	3	1	0	1	11
Not Working	1	1	0	0	2	0	0	0	4
Did not specify job title	1	1	0	0		0	0	1	3
Total	30	18	8	5	17	3	1	5	87

Thirty (34%) had no courses with leadership components and 48 (55%) had up to 10% of one or more classes teaching them leadership skills. Four (5%) had 50% of one or more classes and five (6%) had leadership components in most of their classes. Youth services and school librarians indicated they had more leadership components than other graduates.

Respondents were asked the number of persons who reported to them before they took their present position and how many they currently manage in their present position. The chart also shows which respondents had an increase in the number of persons to supervise, which had fewer, and which had the same number. Results are shown in Table 14.

Table 14 Number of Persons Supervised Before Graduating and at the Present Time (n = 87*)

	# Before				# After						
Position	None	1–3	3+	Total	None	1–3	3+	Total	+	-	Same
Reference	13	7	8	28	18	5	5	28	6	12	10
Cataloging	1	2	4	7	3	0	4	7	1	2	4
Automation/Technology	4	1	0	5	2	1	2	5	3	0	2
Youth Services	6	3	5	14	9	3	2	14	1	4	9
School Librarian	6	1	3	10	3	1	6	10	4	1	5
Archives	2	0	1	3	1	0	2	3	2	1	0
Self-Employed/Consultant	0	0	2	2	1	0	1	2		1	1
Another Occupation	3	4	4	11	4	1	6	11	6	4	1
Not Working	3	0	1	4	X	X	X	X	X	X	X
Did not specify job title	0	1	2	3	1	1	1	3	0	1	2
Total	39	19	37	87	52	12	29	83*	23	26	34

*One reference librarian did not indicate the number before and did say 3+ after graduating.

**This total is less because the four not working would not be supervising.

While 34 (40%) of graduates were supervising as many employees after graduation as they did before, 23 (28%) were supervising more and 26 (31%) were supervising fewer. It seemed that reference librarians and youth librarians were most likely to find that their new professional positions had different reporting structures. School librarians had more employees to supervise than before they received their degrees. This may be explained that a professional school librarian may have a clerk, and before, this person was the clerk.

Table 15 shows respondents' replies concerning their holding a management position or how soon they would seek a position that required them to use management skills.

Table 15 Moving to a Position Requiring Managing Skills (n = 83)

Position	Presently Manage	Never	Immediately	1–3 Years	3+ Years	Total
Reference	7	4	1	7	9	28
Cataloging	4	0	0	1	2	7
Automation/Technology	2	0	0	2	0	4
Youth Services	2	0	1	4	6	13
School Librarian	7	0	0	3	0	10
Archives	2	0	0	1	0	3
Self-Employed/Consultant	0	1	0	0	0	1
Another Occupation	4	0	2	3	1	10
Not Working	1	0	2	0	1	4
Did not specify job title	2	0	0	1	0	3
Totals	31	5	6	22	19	83

While 31 (37%) presently manage, five (6%) did not choose to manage ever. Six (7%) would manage immediately, but 41 (49%) would wait at least one year and perhaps longer than three years.

Respondents were also asked how soon they would be exercising their leadership skills. Their responses are shown in Table 16.

Table 16 Exercising Leadership Skills (n = 87)

Position	Never	Immediately	1–3 Years	3+ Years	Total
Reference	1	22	5	0	28
Cataloging	1	4	2	0	7
Automation/Technology	0	0	3	1	4
Youth Services	1	9	2	1	13*
School Librarian	0	10	0	0	10

Archives	0	2	1	0	3
Self-Employed/Consultant	1	1	0	0	2
Another Occupation	2	8	1	0	11
Not Working	3	0	0	0	3
Did not specify job title	0	3	0	0	3
Total	9	59	14	2	84

*One respondent did not answer.

Answering about leadership, 59 (70%) would be exercising these skills immediately. Nine (10%) never planned to lead, and 16 (19%) would wait to do that for at least one year.

Responses for where they would lead are shown in Table 17, whether in a professional, social, religious, or neighborhood association. Respondents were not limited to a single choice. Two answers are represented by P/S for professional/social association, P/R for Professional/Religious, S/R for Social/Religious, and O for a different combination.

Table 17 Positions Held and Number of Courses Specializing in Management (n = 76)

Position	None	Prof	Social	Relig	Neigh	P/S	P/R	S/R	O	Total
Reference	1	9	2	2	2	5	3	1	0	25
Cataloging	2	1	2	0	0	2	0	0	0	7
Automation/Technology	0	2	0	0	0	3	0	0	0	5
Youth Services	1	5	1	0	0	0	4	0	0	11
School Librarian	2	2	1	0	0	2	2	0	0	9
Archives	0	1	0	0	0	1	0	0	0	2
Self-Empl/Consultants	1	0	0	0	0	1	0	0	0	2
Another occupation	3	2	1	0	0	4	0	0	1	11
Not working	2	0	0	0	0	0	0	1	1	4
Totals	12	22	7	2	2	18	9	2	2	76

Prof = Professional Association, Relig = Religious Association

By far the largest number chose a professional association or two associations, one professional and one social. While only nine responded that they would never lead, three respondents did not like their choices for this question and said they would not lead. This does not seem to be reflected by those information professionals in all types of libraries and information agencies who talk frequently about the need for new leaders in the field of library and information science. In the U.S., and possibly other countries, it would be interesting to find out; it is often difficult to get employees in middle management positions to apply for higher positions. They do not seem willing to manage or lead others. Determining what is taught and what has been learned in formal education in this study begins the search and will be helpful in establishing continuing professional education development needs.

SUMMARY

This survey of the perceptions of present students and recent graduates of the two LIS programs bears out the premise that they were not receiving or had received very little management and even less leadership training in their coursework. The two groups which seemed to be exposed to more management and leadership in their courses were the youth and school librarians. It may be that their instructors recognized the challenges they would face and prepared them for leadership roles and/or that the leadership role articulated in *Information Power*,[31] the standards for school librarians published by the American Association of School Librarians, provides a strong impetus for the provision of leadership education in their course work.

While library schools may be covering the theory of management and leadership and allowing students in some measure to assess their leadership potential, it is clear that students are not opting for courses in these two areas. In both schools, students have a great deal of choice for their courses. Learning why students do not choose to take more management courses before they graduate would be helpful to library educators designing curriculum and revising accrediting standards. Knowing students do not take many management courses and that leadership components are minimal in the management courses they do take, means that continuing professional development is needed.

Because the respondents indicate willingness to take on leadership roles in professional associations, it is clear that professional associations can play a critical role in leadership education. As professional association leaders conduct workshops to train their members, they should publish just how they conduct these sessions and try to conduct appropriate research to track the success of such professional development. Sheldon's work tells us that:

> Librarians and information professionals are needed who are prepared and positioned so that they can influence the character of institutions. If libraries are to be fully recognized as agencies essential to the cultural, educational, and economic life of their communities, then they must be staffed with vigor and assistance.[32]

The review of the literature, coupled with the findings of this study, indicates that there is great need for improved leadership education and research to ensure that librarians *do* possess the leadership vigor necessary, as Sheldon suggests, to influence the character of their institutions to make libraries recognized essential community agencies.

REFERENCES

[1] Bennis, A. and Nanus, B. *Leaders: The strategies for taking charge.* New York: Harper & Row, 1985.

[2] Albritton, Rosie L. and Shaughnessy, Thomas W. *Developing leadership skills: A source book for librarians.* Englewood, Colo.: Libraries Unlimited, 1990. p. xi.

[3] Sheldon, B. E. *Leaders in libraries: Styles and strategies for success.* Chicago: American Library Association, 1991.

[4] *Ibid.,* p. 69.

[5] Riggs, D. E. "The Crisis and opportunities in library leadership," *Journal of Library Administration* 2001, **32** (3/4), 8.

[6] Young, A.P., Hernon, P. and Powell, R.R. "Attributes of academic library leadership: An exploratory study of some Gen-Xers." *The Journal of Academic Library Leadership* 2006, **32** (5)**,** 489-502.

[7] Albritton, R. L. *Transformational vs. transactional leadership in university libraries: A test of the model and its relationship to perceived library organizational effectiveness.* PhD Dissertation, University of Illinois at Urbana-Champaign, 1993.

[8] Kascus, M.A. *Effect of the introduction of team management on the leadership role and skills needed to lead teams: A case study.* DA dissertation, Simmons College, 2004.

[9] Davis, S.E. *Organization and influence in professional standards development: The case of archival description.* PhD dissertation, The University of Wisconsin-Madison, 2003.

[10] Becker, L.K. *Globalization and structural change: Internationalization and the role of librarians in Australian universities.* EdD dissertation, University of Massachusetts.

[11] Matthews, C.J. Becoming a chief librarian: An analysis of transition stages in academic library leadership. *Library Trends* **50** (4), 578-602.

[12] Sommerville, M.M., Schader, B., and Huston, Malia E. Rethinking what we do and how we do it: Systems thinking strategies for library leadership. *Australian Academic & Research Libraries* **36** (4), 214-227.

[13] D.A. Parrish. *The Impact of leadership behavior on organizational commitment and job autonomy of information services librarians.* PhD dissertation. The Florida State University, 2001.

[14] Boden, D.W.R. *Department chair faculty development activities and leadership practices: University libraries faculty perceptions.* PhD dissertation, The University of Nebraska-Lincoln, 2002.

[15] Suwannarata, P. *Library leadership in research university libraries.* EdD dissertation, Peabody College for Teachers of Vanderbilt University. 1994.

[16] Kazlauskas, D.W. *Leadership practices and employee job satisfaction in the academic libraries of the State University System of Florida.* EdD dissertation, University of Florida 1993.

[17] Little, L.F. *Innovation and change as strategies in library management with special reference to New South Wales Tafe Library Services from 1985 to 1989.* PhD dissertation, University of New South Wales (Australia), 1994.

[18] McCowan, C.D. *Leading before, during, and after a Major organizational transition.* EdD dissertation, East Tennessee State University, 2004.

[19] Hess, A.J. *Born-digital: Information technology discourse and the transformation of Czech Public Library roles.* PhD dissertation, New York University, 2001.

[20] Brown, J. and Sheppard, B. Teacher-librarians: Mirror images + the spark," *Emergency Librarian* 1998, **25**, 20-7.

[21] Edwards, C.A. *Successful integration of Internet technology in the K-12 classroom: Trends, perceptions, and successful practice.* EdD Dissertation, East Tennessee State University, 2002.

[22] McCoy, B.S. *A Survey of practicing school library media specialists to determine the job competencies that they value most.* Ph.D. Dissertation, Georgia State University, 2001.

[23] Underwood, L. J. *A Case study of four school library media specialists' leadership in Louisiana.* EdD Dissertation, West Virginia University, 2003.

[24] Carroll, A. M. *Professional development and the teacher-librarian: An Internship report* Med. Thesis, Memorial University of Newfoundland (Canada). 1995.

[25] Greenan, Elizabeth Ann. *Today we're Better: The process of collection development in a Prince Edward Island elementary school library.* MEd Thesis University of Prince Edward Island (Canada), 2002.

[26] Kuo, L-L. *Factors related to management skills of high school library directors in the Republic of China.* PhD Dissertration. The Ohio State University, 1997.

[27] Cendon, Beatriz Valadares. *Power and technology in medical libraries: A study of selected participants in the IAIMS program.* PhD dissertation. The University of Texas at Austin, 1996.

[28] Dale, Adrian. Transforming the future of library and information science units. *Tidskrift for Dokumentation* 2003, **58** (1) 21.

[29] Gjelten, D. and Fishel, T. Developing leaders and transforming libraries: Leadership institutes for librarians. *College & Research Libraries News* 2006, **67** (7), 409-12.

[30] Milnar, S.E. *The Planning and execution of a one-week leadership workshop: Leading into the future.* M.S. Thesis, California State University, Dominguez Hills, 2002.

[31] American Association of School *Librarians* and the Association for Educational Communications and Technology. *Information Power: Building Partnerships for Learning.* Chicago: American Library Association, 1998.

[32] Sheldon, B.E. *Ibid.*, p. 71.

DEVELOPING A NORTH/SOUTH LEADERSHIP DIALOGUE: BUILDING ON THE EXPERIENCE OF THE NORTHERN EXPOSURE TO LEADERSHIP INSTITUTE (NELI)

Ernie Ingles
Vice-Provost and Chief Librarian
Cameron Library, University of Alberta, Canada,
ernie.ingles@ualberta.ca

Karen Adams
Director, Library Services and Information Resources
Cameron Library, University of Alberta, Canada,
karen.adams@ualberta.ca

Mary-Jo Romaniuk
Associate Vice-Provost, Learning Services
Cameron Library, University of Alberta, Canada,
mary-jo.romaniuk@ualberta.ca

Abstract

Library leadership development and leadership training must respond to the basic components of leadership programming generally, including such leadership attributes as the creation of inspiring visions, the nurturing of passion, curiosity and imagination, personal self-assessment and understanding, the fostering of ethical practices, and the appropriate blend of symbols, ceremony and the physical environment. Programmes frequently blend these elements in a gestalt experience, combining both classroom and experiential learning techniques. However, programming must also take into consideration the cultural context of the targeted audience, as well as the evolving generational differences of that audience. The Canadian Northern Exposure to Leadership Institute (NELI) is explored as an exemplar of such programming. The paper not only describes the NELI experience, but explores elements of the NELI that might be appropriately exported to different geo-political jurisdictions. It further explores the current evolution of the programme in response to the profiles of Generation X and the Millennials. The export that is the success of the NELI is the understanding of the dynamic interactions that define the nexus between culture, community and the continuously evolving generational personae of the librarian.

BACKGROUND

In response to concerns in the Library profession, the past two decades have seen an increase in the worldwide development, but particularly throughout North America, of library leadership programming. Some programmes established have been general in nature, intended to address shared concerns such as the availability of candidates for leadership positions and succession planning. One of the first such programmes was the Snowbird Leadership Institute in the United States. Another example is the more recently conceived Aurora Library Leadership Institute patterned after Snowbird and intended to serve the library communities of Australia and New Zealand.

Other programmes have been socially motivated, for example, to address diversity considerations. The Association of Research Libraries (ARL) has been particularly effective in addressing diversity concerns, as has ARL in type-of-library based programmes. The Research Libraries Leadership Fellows Program and the National Library of Medicine/Association of Academic Health Sciences Libraries Leadership Fellows Program are best practice examples in this arena. Another similar model is the Association of College and Research Libraries/ Harvard Leadership Institute.

Finally, there are geographically-based programmes intended to address local leadership concerns. Here we would find such examples as the TALL Texans Leadership Development Institute, the Pacific Northwest Library Association Leadership Institute, the Florida Library Leadership Program, or the Nevada Library Leadership Institute. Whatever the reason, whatever the place, library communities have drawn upon their renowned imaginations and have created responses to a shared concern that the future of the profession must be built by librarians able to create bold visions underpinned by curiosity and daring, and delivered with passion by trusted individuals. In short, most North American programmes focus on the basic ingredients of leadership described by the eminent authority Warren Bennis.[1]

THE NORTHERN EXPOSURE TO LEADERSHIP INSTITUTE (NELI)

The first Northern Exposure to Leadership Institute (NELI) in 1994 was a Canadian response to a perceived need. Succession planning was seen to be an issue of national concern, reinforced by stories that suggested an increasing shortage of individuals prepared to assume leadership roles in Canadian libraries. These early perceptions have been the subject of a research project and found to be valid. Two studies, *The Future of Human Resources in Canadian Libraries*[2] and *Training Gaps Analysis: Librarians and Library Technicians*[3] reinforced the need for leadership development with 60% of librarians agreeing that enhanced leadership skills would greatly enhance professional performance, and 76% of library employers reported leadership potential as important to look for when hiring.

The NELI drew its initial inspiration from the Snowbird Institute. The late Dennis Day, Chief Librarian of the Salt Lake City Public Library and founder of the Snowbird Institute, was generous with his advice and counsel. His enthusiasm was infectious. Library leadership advocates, wherever they may be, owe Day a debt of gratitude. Though Day and his Snowbird Institute provided inspiration, the NELI quickly determined its own character.

The underpinning principles were simple. First, the NELI was created to provide a leadership development experience of the highest quality. Such a statement seems basic in expression but it has remained the first priority in every decision associated with the experience—from nomination to graduation, from programme to location.

Second, the targeted audience is professional librarians with a minimum of two years and a maximum of seven years experience. The NELI continues to identify and then support emerging library leaders, rather than assist mid-career librarians or refresh senior librarians in management positions. Our goal was to provide an identifiable pool of potential leaders as a service to the Canadian library community.

Third, participants were to enjoy an experience that approached similar types of programmes available to the highest levels in the business sector. Experience had shown that library professional development programmes rarely achieve the same level of distinction as do those in the business sector. Leadership begins with self-assurance. This, in part, is a product of feeling 'special'. Librarians are special, but rarely are pampered. The NELI makes no apology for creating a feeling, although it may be fleeting, of elitism in its participants. In large measure this goal is achieved by the intimate involvement of three committed sponsors, SirsiDynix, EBSCO Information Services and YBP Library Services. Their commitment to the wellbeing of the library community and to the development of leader librarians is truly commendable.

The vision of the NELI is to contribute to the vitality, growth and success of the library profession well into the 21st century. How? By positioning professionals to be proactive, effective and important voices in a dynamic and sophisticated information environment. The mission is to motivate librarians in order to assist them in developing, strengthening and exercising their individual leadership abilities—curiosity, enthusiasm, teamwork. Why? So they are better prepared to create, articulate and achieve organizational visions for the benefit of library service, initially, and society at large, ultimately. The vision and mission are achieved by situating the Institute where nature's beauty and grandeur, combined with its intrinsic spirituality, become part of the programme itself. Where? At a remote resort in the heart of the Canadian Rocky Mountains, a location that was historically a meeting point between European and aboriginal cultures, each with their own world views, both of which are represented within the NELI programme.

The programme combines experiential and theoretical learning, with emphasis on the former. It consists of related modules that combine in a gestalt to focus on defined objectives. The programme:

- models leadership, group work, team building and collegiality;
- engages participants in a discussion about leadership, what it means, how it is recognized, developed and sustained;
- exposes participants to a variety of leadership styles, including those that are innovative and may fall outside of cultures based on Western Europe;
- initiates a discussion about vision and passion, what they mean, how they are achieved and communicated;
- assists participants in making creative and sustainable connections; and
- instills a readiness and willingness for continued professional development and professional contribution.

This programme is delivered by a team of dedicated instructors and facilitators. Integral to their success is the involvement of specially selected librarians who serve as mentors. Mentors have a strong support relationship with instructors and facilitators. They are chosen for their demonstrated leadership in a variety of areas and the breadth of their personal and professional experience. They contribute to the NELI by bringing experiences that lend practical balance to the theory and concepts associated with all facets of the programme. Mentors share responsibility for the success of the Institute. Working with participants in groups, mentors advance, agitate or calm the discussion as required. They also share their personal and professional experiences, successes, failures, joys, frustrations, wisdom, perspectives and advice.

Most importantly, there are the librarian participants. In age they reflect the demographics of those entering the profession in Canada and range from those in their mid-twenties to those with considerable life-experience. Participants are nominated either by employer organizations, institutions, or by library associations. Before being nominated many participate in competitive processes within their home institutions to earn the right of nomination. A Selection Committee reviews hundreds of nominations and selects twenty-six individuals. Thus, each NELI is guaranteed twenty-six librarians who have demonstrated leadership potential, strong academic performance, excellent communication skills, genuine performance accomplishment, and a successful employment experience.

The success and longevity of the NELI are the result of something that is itself special. Its programme was developed by Canadians for Canadians and, as a result, blends traditional approaches to leadership programming with the unique requirements of Canadian librarianship, and the attributes of the cultural construct that is Canada. Its applicability in other geo-political or professional contexts thus poses an interesting question that does not have a clear answer. Success can be attributed to the interplay of people of different ages and backgrounds (organizers, instructors, facilitators, sponsors, mentors and participants) with programme and location.

THE CULTURAL SETTING FOR THE NELI AND ITS ASSUMPTIONS

There appears to be no research with respect to library leadership and culture across nations. Looking at business and industry models in 62 different cultures, the Global Leadership and Organizational Behavior Effectiveness Research

Program (GLOBE) reports some preliminary findings with respect to culture and leadership. GLOBE's research indicates a strong relationship between societal culture and organizational culture.[4] While there are many questions still to be answered, the Program has concluded that as cultures are different, so will be their culturally implicit theories of leadership. Education for library leadership needs to take place within a cultural context.

Within the NELI, leadership is viewed as the ability to influence people and events, from whatever position one holds in the organization. The underlying concept is that a 'new' librarian can lead from below to contribute to the improvement of the library and its services. In Canada, the context for most organizations, including libraries, is hierarchical structures based on military command-and-control models, with a sprinkling of sports concepts like coaching and teamwork. Canadian organizations operate within an industrial paradigm and a democratic society. The NELI presumes that someone relatively new to the profession of librarianship is operating in an environment where new ideas and ways of working could be welcomed, although this may not be the case in every library. The NELI is based on the idea that knowing oneself enables a better awareness of the work environment, and a more effective way of operating within it. The only research on the Institute is a 2000 PhD thesis by Brockmeyer-Klebaum that has surveyed participants from the NELI. This research found that the experience moved the participant learners in an "emotional, soulful and spiritual way".[5] This portion of the paper explores the elements that create this impact at the individual and personal level, so that readers from other countries can think about whether similar elements might have the same impact in their own setting.

The elements that Brockmeyer-Klebaum identifies as nurturing the soul include: relationships with mentors, peers and self; risk; struggle and disclosure; ceremony, symbol and the sacred; ethics; creativity and imagination; physical environment; residential factors of seclusion and shared accommodations; and the use of a variety of teaching methods with a concentration on experiential learning.[5] These elements interact with each other, and do not have simple linear connections to what happens during the days of the programme. Some of these elements also form part of other recent leadership events targeted at librarians from outside North America.

THE RELATIONSHIPS WITH MENTORS, PEERS AND SELF

Part of the NELI experience is the opportunity to develop relationships between the participants, the mentors and the organizers who are senior members of the North American library community. The sense of unique opportunity begins with the process of gaining entry to the Institute. The University of Hong Kong's 4th Annual Library Leadership Institute, aimed at library directors and senior librarians, also used the device of limited intake to ensure a committed and elite cohort.[6]

Because the Institute provides an exceptional opportunity to build relationships with peers and mentors, the sense of uniqueness begins upon arrival. The welcoming events create a sense that the Institute is special, and that individuals selected to go to it are as well. Establishing active participation from arrival until departure and making people feel that they are special people at a special event are both easy to duplicate in other countries and cultures.

THE PHYSICAL ENVIRONMENT

In the case of the NELI, the venue is also special. The lodge and the surrounding mountains provide a different atmosphere from the city. Some people find the interior and exterior silence uncomfortable at first because the rooms have neither radio nor television. There is no road noise. The setting is designed to uplift and nourish the soul as one looks automatically upward when outdoors. However, only one of the programme activities takes place outdoors. Here too, the provision of an uplifting, out-of-the-ordinary venue and the sense of continued engagement can be created in other cultures. The South African Library Leadership Project (2002-2004) organized by the Mortenson Center for International Library Programs at the University of Illinois took its participants to another continent![7] That is a very special venue, indeed.

THE PROGRAMME

As noted, the programme creates a gestalt: "a structure, configuration, or pattern of physical, biological, or psychological phenomena so integrated as to constitute a functional unit with properties not derivable by summation of its parts".[8] So, it is not useful to describe each activity in each day. The programme does involve risk, struggle and disclosure, creativity and imagination. The programme has evolved in response to mentor and participant feedback. The educational sessions may be the most significant elements of the Institute with cultural dependency. For example, at the first NELI, there was an activity involving risk. The risk involved participants, mentors and organizers disclosing personal information; for example, "How many times have you been married?" This exercise was a Canadian version of the risk element that was also part of the United States' Snowbird Institute, but in the U.S. risk was a physical activity. In spite of continuous change in the NELI risk exercise, it remains a topic of discussion for mentors and organizers every year. Canadians do not have the same approach to taking risk as do our neighbours to the south.

The programme includes self knowledge using the Myers-Briggs Type Indicator, collaborative work on building a preferred future/vision for libraries, the application of creativity to dress at one evening's dinner, the use of creativity and imagination for skits at another dinner, approaches and case studies in ethics, and a concluding exercise to help participants transition back to work. By the end, many participants have developed a new approach to a matter that may have been troubling them before they arrived. The NELI uses learning that supports understanding of self and others, that provides a mix of learning methodologies, and that provides tools that can be used after the Institute is over and the participant has returned to his or her home environment. At a broad level, any leadership programme could benefit from these three elements.

THE CEREMONY AND THE SACRED

The final element in the Institute's programme is an honouring ceremony that is conducted partially outdoors and reflects the spirituality of Canada's First Nations. This is a form of spirituality that is generally unfamiliar to participants. The ceremony is entirely appropriate to the physical setting and, once again, emphasizes the sense of an extraordinary event. In a similar way, the Workshop on Leadership Development for Directors of National Libraries in Developing Countries (2004) had a closing ceremony with a cultural component reflecting participating nations in Kuala Lumpur.[9]

THE PEOPLE

In terms of the people who make up the Institute, the principle of 'most variety' is important. Although the organizers are all from one place, the mentors are chosen to provide a balance of men and women; to be from different types and sizes of libraries; and to be from different places. Similar guiding principles apply to the participants themselves, with initial selection reflecting gender, place and type of library as well as the quality of the application and nomination. Where mentors are likely to be older, participants are likely to be younger.

THE NELI AND OTHER CULTURES

In summing up the elements of the NELI that contribute to its success in Canada, we have an inspiring venue that supports a spiritual dimension; a sense of participant and mentor engagement from the beginning; people with varied backgrounds and experience; creating a sense that the event and the people are special; and a varied programme that promotes self awareness, risk-taking, ethics, teamwork, and creating a vision. While a special venue, engagement and a varied programme are likely to contribute to the success of any learning event, it is unlikely that the NELI could be transferred exactly as it is to another country. The Aurora Foundation's Institutes are "modeled on the Snowbird Leadership Institutes in the USA, with some adjustments to suit Australian and New Zealand circumstances."[10] The NELI also had to change the U.S. programme to Canadian. The evidence provided by the GLOBE project indicates that adjustments must be made to reflect local culture and context.

Finally, the NELI targets a cohort in the early years of their professional practice; they do not necessarily hold management positions. Most library leadership programmes cited in this article target participants already in managerial positions, and the difference between established and emerging professionals may also mean that the format and content of the NELI would be less successful if the cohort were all in senior management positions. The NELI may again have to adapt to changes in its own culture as the Millennials join Generation X and ultimately replace Baby Boomers as participants.

THE LEADERSHIP PROGRAMMING OF THE FUTURE

The success of the NELI has been an ability to adapt to the unique personae of the changing demographics from which its candidates are drawn. Until now, the NELI, created in 1994, by Baby Boomers, and originally for Baby Boomers, has had to respond only to the new demands of Generation X. A successful leadership programme must continually resonate with its participants. The ability to resonate with both Generation X and Millennials, is dependent on the leadership styles and characteristics of these generations, and the ability of the programme to adapt the context and delivery of content to complement the learning and leadership qualities of the participants. An examination of Generation X, those born between 1965 and 1976 and of Generation Y or the Millennials, those born between 1977 and 1998, as defined by Thielfoldt and Scheef, aids understanding of future leadership and relevant mentoring opportunities.[11]

THE GENERATION X AND THE MILLENNIALS – WHO ARE THEY?

Generation X, like every other generation, is influenced by the political, economic and sociological events occurring in their formative years and youth. Generation X is a denotation associated primarily with North America and Western Europe. They encompass a demographic of about 11 years but numerous other definitions suggest that Generation X includes anyone born after 1960 and before 1980. They grew up in the seventies and eighties, when the economy was in crisis, mothers went to work, latchkey kids prevailed, divorce rates rose rapidly, AIDS emerged as the Vietnam War ended. Generation X watched the Cold War end and the Berlin Wall fall. They had cable television, video games, and computers. Each of these occurrences was to shape this generation and influence how they would lead, how they would learn and how they would be led.

The Baby Boomers (1946–mid1960s) are characterized by Raines as having an optimistic outlook, a 'driven' work ethic, a team oriented perspective and are typically believers in leadership by consensus.[12] Contrast those Boomer characteristics with those possessed by Generation X: skepticism, a need for a balanced life, self-reliance, a failure to be impressed by authority and a belief that leadership should be a function of competence. These characteristics have often been misconstrued, so that Generation X has often been mislabeled as 'slackers' by the Baby Boomers. Research by Bengtson, Biblarz and Roberts suggests that Generation X are not underachievers but rather that they have higher education and occupational aspirations than did their Baby Boomer parents.[13] Furthermore, this research suggests that in spite of differences in the family model, Generation X has higher levels of self-esteem than their parents.

The attributes of Generation X clearly result from their environment. Skepticism or cynicism is largely directed at institutions and conventions. The generation witnessed political and workplace mismanagement and scandal. Mass layoffs characterized the workplace. It is no wonder that this generation harbours distrust and demands a flexible and responsive work environment so that work does not become their life. For Generation X competency, not title, must drive organizational leadership.[14] That said, they are not inhibited by traditional institutional authority and, as such, are innovators and creative problem solvers who move forward without permission and without delay, and who propose creative solutions to strategic problems.

Independence and self-reliance exhibited by the generation results in part from their acceptance of responsibility at an early age when both parents entered the workforce. Furthermore, independence has fostered the understanding of risk and its importance in innovation noted by Tulgan.[14] Independence contributes to a desire for opportunity and a demand for collaborative participation in goal setting and strategic planning.

They have experienced a proliferation of information and technological change. They are thus analytical and collaborative decision-makers, who expect answers to questions, an exchange of ideas, information and ongoing feedback. Information abundance and technological advances are likely to have fostered the desire for constant learning and skill development that Tulgan reports as an attribute of this generation.[14]

Like Generation X, Generation Y, better known as the Millennials, has also been influenced by a succession of events and factors that transpired during their early years and youth. Growing up in the 80s and 90s, Millennials grew up in times of economic prosperity, in a society that valued children and the family. Parents became pre-occupied with child-rearing. As Raines suggests, Millennials have been the busiest generation ever, with highly scheduled and structured lives, little free time, and with continual involvement and advocacy by parents and teachers.[15] Changes to the education curricula had finally occurred so Millennials were immersed in a team-learning pedagogy.

Terrorism plagued their formative years as they witnessed violent and tragic events, including the destruction of the World Trade Center on September 11, 2001. They have witnessed political uprising and natural disasters such as Hurricane Katrina and the Indian Ocean Tsunami. They have been bombarded with information not only in the media but on the Internet as they are the first truly digital generation exposed to the proliferation of home computers.

Immigration and world events heightened their awareness of multiculturalism and ethnicities.

Millennials are characterized as hopeful; optimistic yet practical and inclusive; favouring a team structure to accomplish any task. [15] These traits are similar to those possessed by the Boomers but dissimilar from Generation X. Like Generation X they have high self-esteem and demand a balanced life with flexibility in the workplace. They also want the workplace to be fun and collegial; a place to work with friends.[16] While extremely goal oriented, Millennials are reluctant leaders, desiring mentoring and role models. [15]

As with Generation X, Millennial attributes are a by-product of their environment. The most significant influence has been that of their parents who have encouraged them and instilled self-confidence and self-esteem. Thus, Millennials believe their ideas should be heard. Parents expected achievement, which is manifested in their goal orientation. Their highly regimented childhood has created a need for ongoing structure, schedules, progress measures and feedback. They were always learning and continually challenged, so they expect learning opportunities and new challenges to combat boredom. Parents were their role model, so they continue to expect role models who have integrity and trustworthiness. They respected their parents, who encouraged conversation, and thus they continue to respect authority as long as those in authority respect their ideas. Obviously the impact of parents has been even more pervasive, as McGlynn indicates, "research shows that the great majority of them get along with their parents and that 75% of them share their parents' values."[17] Their parents were predominantly Boomers.

The Internet has provided a gateway to the world and multi-tasking. Millennials were quick to explore other cultures and see events from a global perspective. Technology has been a world wide unifier of this generation. [15] The global perspective and parental encouragement have instilled a civic-mindedness. [15] They were treated to authentic learning, not just active learning. Millennials demand authenticity of their experiences.[18]

LEADERSHIP, GENERATION X AND THE MILLENNIALS

The unique characteristics of both Generation X and of the Millennials influence their respective leadership styles and qualities. Because the NELI subscribes to the leadership ingredients proposed by Bennis it is most relevant to review

Generation X and the Millennials in light of those attributes. The characteristics themselves and the attributes embodied therein are timeless and transcend generations. As noted previously, Bennis suggests that vision, curiosity and daring, passion and trust through integrity, along with the additional competencies of self-knowledge, mastery of the context, communication with meaning, and realization of intentions through action and the additional values of ethics, diversity and recognition are all characteristics of leaders.[19]

Tulgan best describes the leadership style of Generation X in suggesting that "Gen X managers and leaders are intent on being the kind of managers they always wanted to have: facilitative."[14] Facilitative leadership implies that formal or 'titled' leadership is not required but can come from anyone within an organization or group who has the competency to perform. The facilitative style suggests that Generation X leaders address mastery of the context through collaboration, sharing of information and brainstorming. They realize intentions by communicating a clear mission, directions and expectations and by promoting independence of action. Both meaningful communication and recognition are very important to this cohort. These attributes manifest themselves in Generation X leaders through their emphasis on feedback. The ongoing exchange of feedback responds to the Generation X belief in continuous development and the importance of meaningful recognition for accomplishments. The high levels of self-esteem in Generation X are indicative of self-knowledge, a critical component of self-esteem.

None of the literature characterizes this group as particularly visionary. However, the characteristics of curiosity and daring are exhibited in Generation X by their comfort in risk-taking and their understanding of the relationship between risk and innovation. Furthermore, Generation X believes that trust is critical to performance.[14] Their natural distrust of authority and institutions must be mitigated by a clear demonstration of ethics and integrity by leaders. Generation X leaders are likely to possess integrity and ethics and see the importance of building trust. Finally, from a generation that demands flexibility, Generation X leaders will be flexible.

Millennial leaders will have a different style than that exhibited by their Generation X predecessors. Millennials are reluctant leaders until they gain experience and are mentored. As leaders they will be eager mentors who demonstrate ethics, integrity and respectfulness. Once they are ready to lead, their high self-esteem enforces their belief that there is nothing that they cannot accomplish. They bring optimism to every situation. They will always be seeking another new opportunity or challenge and have passion and curiosity. Their emphasis will not only be on a global vision but on a practical strategy to respond to optimistic goals. They will have a logical, organized and methodical 'roadmap' for everything they do.

They will continue to identify with teams. As leaders, they will surround themselves with colleagues to exchange ideas. Teams will have a greater importance than the individual, as they will be the vehicle to discuss solutions, analyze information and exchange knowledge. They will encourage feedback and share recognition with their team. Millennial leaders will be inclusive; age, gender, ethnicity, culture, or experience will not be barriers to participation. Millennials will lead with a social conscience and diversity will be encouraged. As they have a profound need for life balance, work will be efficient. Flexibility, fun and friendships will characterize any organization they lead.

THE IMPACT OF GENERATIONAL DIFFERENCES ON THE NELI

When the NELI began, the participants at the first two Institutes were predominately Baby Boomers. By the third Institute the number of Generation X participants surpassed the number of Boomers. Generation X participation continued to grow through the next five Institutes, so that in the last three Institutes they have enjoyed almost exclusive participation. Throughout this period Baby Boomers have predominated as mentors, leaders and as the programme developers. By the tenth Institute in 2008, the NELI will see Millennials as participants. Over time, the demographic profile of the mentors too will change. For the first time, the NELI will entwine the leadership potential, values and attributes of three diverse generations.

Brockmeyer-Klebaum summarized the participant feedback from the first four Institutes.[5] An analysis of these summaries, together with the transcripts of the participant feedback from the fifth and sixth Institutes and the corresponding agendas, supports the assertion that programmatic modifications were responsive to the characteristics of the participants, who were primarily Generation X. Predictably, Generation X participants were enthusiastic about programme elements that encouraged brainstorming, discussion and the exchange of ideas both in groups and in one-on-one settings. When feasible, the programme changed to accommodate more discussion time and interaction between mentors, leaders and participants. They were appreciative of visioning and creating strategic direction and discussing the ethics of the profession; they also appreciated receiving formal and informal feedback. The programme was tweaked several times to expand the feedback sections and to enhance the ethics area. Experiential learning, inherent in the programme, has been well received. The programme elements that encouraged honesty and integrity established the mentors and leaders as trustworthy and competent. For Generation X, this was undoubtedly most critical to the success of the Institute.

THE PROGNOSIS FOR THE FUTURE

As the NELI prepares to offer programming to a new generation the Institute will retain those elements important to Boomers and X'ers while incorporating content that responds to Millennial needs. This is consistent with the finding of Partridge and Hallam, who suggest that library education should respond to the unique learning styles of the Millennial student.[20] Every leadership programme needs to undertake a similar exercise. Generational differences may significantly impact programme elements. Key elements for review and consideration should include:

1. *Authenticity of the experience.* The exercises and feedback must be about their 'real life' environment. For a generation that would rather work in a soup kitchen than make a donation to a faceless charity, authentic experience is everything.[18]

2. *Experiential learning.* While Boomers are happy with a mix of active and traditional learning and Generation X favours experiential learning, Millennials will demand authentic experiential learning.

3. *Role of mentors.* Millennials respect trustworthy and credible role models. There has never been a generation previously who prefers not to lead without adequate mentoring. Mentors and leaders will need to stay actively engaged with Millennial participants, at least for some period subsequent to the programme.

4. *Team building exercises.* Teams for Generation X are no more than a sum of the distinct and individual parts. Teams do not have identities separate from the constituent individuals. For Millennials, teams are defined as the 'whole', and the team identity is that of team. However, they do not want to be confined to participation on a single team. Millennials, while enjoying a team building exercise, may wonder why something as self-evident as teamwork occupies the curriculum. They know no other way.

5. *Feedback.* Generation X prefers the individual feedback. Millennials too will want a lot of individual feedback and also from the team perspective. Team feedback and potentially feedback between teams will be increasingly important. To benefit Millennials, feedback exercises must relate to real experiences, not just role plays or case studies.

6. *Visioning.* Visioning exercises will continue to be important, particularly if they relate to the profession or are otherwise authentic.

7. *Ethics.* Integrity and ethics are imperative for Generation X and Millennials.

8. *Brainstorming, group discussion and sharing.* The exchange of ideas will continue to be important for both Generation X and the Millennials. Both generations need to be heard, and both need to participate in the creation of ideas and concepts.

9. *Programme structure – balance.* Like their counterparts from Generation X, Millennials demand balance and want to have fun with ample time for friendships, even at a leadership programme.

10. *Diversity.* Given globalization and the appreciation of diverse cultures and lifestyles by Millennials; elements on diversity should be considered.

As with culture, the impact of generational differences on library leadership development programming must be considered from the perspective of the programme and the geo-political jurisdiction in which it resides. While globalization and technological advances have contributed to worldwide homogeneity of Millennials, every programme needs to assess its target audience to determine generational predominance. Effective library leadership programmes must be created, and reviewed not from the perspective of the creators, but from that of the potential participants.

REFERENCES

[1] Bennis, W. *On becoming a leader.* New York: Basic Books, 2003.

[2] Ingles, E., De Long, K., Humphrey, C. & Sivak, A. *The future of human resources in Canadian libraries.* Edmonton (Canada): University of Alberta, 2005.

[3] Ingles, E., De Long, K., Schrader, A. M. & Sivak, A. *Training gaps analysis: librarians and library technicians.* Ottawa (Canada): Cultural Human Resources Council; 2006.

[4] House, R.J., Hanges, P.J., Javidan, M., Dorfman, P.W. & Gupta, V, editors. *Culture, leadership, and organizations: the GLOBE study of 62 societies.* Thousand Oaks (CA): Sage Publications, 2004.

[5] Brockmeyer-Klebaum, D. Education to nurture the soul: an interpretive study of a professional leadership institute for librarians. Vancouver (Canada): The University of British Columbia, 2000. PhD thesis.

[6] The University of Hong Kong Libraries. Leadership Institute 06.[Online]. Hong Kong: The University; 2006. [cited 2006 Dec 28]; [about 6 screens]. URL: http://lib.hku.hk/leadership/2006.html

[7] Library & Information Association of South Africa. South African library leadership project. [Online]. Pretoria (South Africa): LIASA; 2004. [cited 2006 Dec 12]; [about 6 screens]. URL: http://www.liasa.org.za/partnership/sallp/accomplishments.php

[8] Merriam-Webster Online. Gestalt. [Online]. Springfield (MA): Merriam-Webster; 2006-2007 [cited 2006 Dec 29]; [1 screen]. URL: http://www.m-w.com/dictionary/gestalt

[9] Zawiyah Baba, Dato'. Report on workshop on leadership development for directors of national libraries in developing countries 2004. [Online]. The Hague: IFLA National Libraries Section; 2007 [cited 2006 December 12]. URL: http://www.ifla.org/VII/s1/pub/leadership_malaysia.pdf

[10] Aurora Foundation. Aurora Leadership Institute. [Online]. Ainslie (Australia): The Foundation; 2001-2006 [cited 2007 Jan 27]. [about 2 screens]. URL: http://www.alia.org.au/~aurora/aurora.html

[11] Thielfoldt, D. & Scheef, D. Generation X and the Millennials: what you need to know about mentoring the new generations. Law Practice Today [serial

online]. 2004 Aug [cited 2007 Jan 12]; Nov 2005:[about 3 p.]. URL: http://www.abanet.org/lpm/lpt/articles/mgt08044.html.

[12] Raines, C. *Beyond Generation X: a practical guide for managers.* Menlo Park (CA): Crisp Publications, 1997.

[13] Bengtson, V., Biblarz, T., & Roberts, R. *How families still matter: a longitudinal study of youth in two generations.* Cambridge: Cambridge University Press, 2002.

[14] Tulgan, B. *Managing Generation X: how to bring out the best in young talent.* Revised ed. New York: Norton, 2000.

[15] Raines, C. Managing Millennials. Generations At Work: The Online Home of Claire Raines Associates [Online]. 2002 [cited 2006 Dec 27]. Articles: Managing Millennials;[about 9 p.]. URL: http://www.generationsatwork.com/articles/millenials.htm

[16] Heathfield, S. M. Managing Millenials: eleven tips for managing millennials. About: Human Resources [Online]. New York: The New York Times Co; 2007 [cited 2007 Jan 12]; 2005 Aug 18 [about 3 screens]. URL: http://humanresources.about.com/od/managementtips/a/millenials.htm

[17] McGlynn, A. Teaching Millenials, our newest cultural chort (sic). Education Digest [serial online]. 2005 [cited 2006 Dec 29]; 71(4): 12-16. Available from: TOC Premier.

[18] Johnson, L. *Mind your X's and Y's .* New York: Free Press, 2006.

[19] Bennis, W. & Goldsmith, J. *Learning to lead: a workbook on becoming a leader.* 3rd ed. New York: Basic Books, 2003.

[20] Partridge, H. & Hallam, G. Educating the Millennial Generation for evidence based information practice. *Library Hi Tech 2006,* **24** (3), 400-19.

LOCATION, LOCATION, LOCATION: A LIBRARIAN'S GUIDE TO ISOLATION

Liz Burke
Associate Librarian (Reader Services),
The University of Western Australia, Australia
lburke@library.uwa.edu.au

Abstract

The library and information services profession faces many challenges in developing leaders and leadership potential. Such challenges can be particularly confronting to those living and working in geographically remote regions. This paper uses examples from a geographically remote region in Australia to outline possible approaches to attracting, retaining and developing leaders.

The author fills a senior leadership role at the University of Western Australia (UWA) Library in Perth, one of the most remote capital cities in the world. Attracting, retaining and developing leaders in the library profession in Perth can be challenging.

In response to the challenge of geographic remoteness, the author describes an initiative adopted by the UWA Library to develop leadership. In a fast changing and demanding environment, it is essential that all managers be forward thinking, pro-active and ready to lead others. 'Taking the Lead' is a programme designed to provide continuing professional development opportunities for senior library staff in leadership positions. The author also outlines some of the strategies adopted by the library professional association in Western Australia. The author is convenor of one of the local groups which co-ordinates and communicates strategic professional issues and organises continuing professional development activities state-wide and sector-wide.

INTRODUCTION

Developing leaders and leadership potential is a particular challenge to the library and information profession. The 'greying' of the profession and the anticipated rate of retirements over the next ten to fifteen years present particular challenges. To geographically remote regions is added the challenge of physical isolation from peers, colleagues and mentors. This paper explores some of these issues in Western Australia and also examines a particular leadership programme at UWA Library. Some of the key lessons from this programme are identified and shared. Librarians from other geographically remote areas may benefit from hearing what worked and what did not and the impact the programme has had on library staff.

General management and business texts state that the most important skills for leaders are being honest, forward-looking, inspiring, and competent. Mason and Wetherbee[1] outline important leadership skills, including the ability to create a vision for the future, engage others in the co-creation of that vision, describe it in compelling and powerful ways, and create an environment where stakeholders work together productively and effectively to implement the vision successfully. Articles within the library professional literature suggest that leaders should be flexible, energetic, empathetic, wise, creative, courageous, principled, gregarious, determined and possess a sense of humour.

Being or becoming a leader comes naturally to some but others need to learn the necessary skills. Hill[2] observes that "the process of becoming a leader is an arduous, albeit rewarding journey of continuous learning and self-development". Those aspiring to leadership positions can identify the skills they need and locate appropriate training or other opportunities to assist them in developing these skills. Hill believes that learning to lead is a process of learning by doing, that it cannot be taught in a classroom, but is a craft acquired through on-the-job experiences.

There are significant leadership development opportunities which take place in the workplace.[1] Some people take on 'acting' roles to increase their exposure to greater levels of responsibility within the organisation. These can be very useful opportunities to learn new skills and face new challenges, without committing to such a role for an indefinite period.

Leadership is a particular issue within the library profession at present as the number of anticipated retirements over the next ten to fifteen years is significant. In Australia, it is anticipated the population demographics will place pressure on the labour force: "Demographic change will develop into the challenge of replacing skilled older workers from a much smaller pool of younger workers."[3] Hernon and Schwartz[4] observed that the number of librarians entering the profession cannot match the number of those retiring.

They also noted that "tomorrow's leaders ... will need the knowledge, experience, and skills to cope with directing institutions and managing change in increasingly complex organisations, constantly evolving services, and an environment of globalization". Talking about the library profession in Canada, Abram[5] noted that a primary concern was that "of having a sufficient number of adequately trained and experienced staff that could succeed a senior librarian workforce poised to retire in large numbers in Canada over the next five to ten years".

A collaborative project was initiated in 2006 in Australia to explore this issue. The Australian Library and Information Association (ALIA) in association with Queensland University of Technology and CAVAL Collaborative Solutions[6] is addressing this concern by commissioning research into workforce planning issues by the ALIA immediate past president, Dr Gillian Hallam. The project aims to foster an awareness of the importance of workforce planning and to develop a collaborative framework for career-long learning for the library profession.[3]

A similar research project was undertaken in Canada in 2004, resulting in the report *8Rs Future of human resources in Canadian libraries*.[7] This study focuses on eight key elements: recruitment, retention, retirement, remuneration, rejuvenation, restructuring, repatriation, and re-accreditation. It emphasises the need to ensure there are sufficient numbers of adequately trained and experienced library and information workers. It also highlights the critical need to rejuvenate mid-level staff who may not have had the opportunity to develop leadership or managerial skills due to hierarchical flattening and organisational down-sizing.

As a result of the significant exodus anticipated from the profession due to retirements, there will be a variety of leadership opportunities for younger members of the profession. It will be important for these younger members of the profession to take up continuing professional development and workplace learning opportunities to ready themselves for these leadership roles. Assuming 'acting' positions, arranging secondments, attending relevant training, or undertaking formal continuing education qualifications are all ways to prepare for such opportunities. Those who are willing to go beyond their 'comfort zones' will reap the benefits of learning news skills and taking on new challenges.

BACKGROUND TO WESTERN AUSTRALIA

The library profession in Western Australia faces some particular challenges. Attracting library professionals to Western Australia and retaining those who work there, can be challenging due to the geographic isolation. The state of Western Australia is a vast land mass, covering one third of the continent of Australia. It covers 2,532,400 square kilometres with 12,500 kilometres of coastline, making up 34% of the entire coastline of Australia. As an indication of the size of the state, the UK, Texas and Japan could all be fitted into its borders.[8] The capital city, Perth, located in the south-west of the state, is described as the most isolated capital city in the world and is closer to Jakarta in Indonesia than it is to Sydney. 2,050,000 people live in Western Australia with 1,477,815 in Perth itself.

Table 1: Distance from Perth to Other Cities

Perth to:	Km
Adelaide, South Australia	2,716
Brisbane, Queensland	4,363
Canberra, Australian Capital Territory	3,741
Darwin, Northern Territory	4,049
Hobart, Tasmania	3,720
Melbourne, Victoria	3,456
Sydney, New South Wales	3,972
Jakarta, Indonesia	3,004
Singapore	4,722

Geographic remoteness is compounded by the fact that the vast area of Western Australia is not densely populated. Black[9] reports Australian Bureau of Statistics figures which show that at June 2005, capital cities in Australia account for 64% of the nation's population – almost two thirds of the Australian population. He also noted that the areas with the largest or fastest growing population centres in each state and territory tended to be inner cities, outer suburbs and certain regional centres especially those located along the coast. This trend is evident in Western Australia where the highest population centre is clustered around Perth and some regional centres, particularly those along the coast.

Knight[10] investigated the provision of public library services to remote, regional communities and how these areas deal with service withdrawal and population decline. He discovered that the situation in rural New South Wales, Australia had a lot in common with the situations in remote, rural regions of Montana and North Dakota in the United States and in Saskatchewan, Canada.

The library profession in Western Australia incorporates librarians with professional qualifications at either undergraduate or postgraduate level, library technicians who graduate with a diploma, and library aides or officers who receive on-the-job training. Library services are delivered throughout the state from public libraries, special libraries, school libraries, university libraries, and government department libraries. The vast distances and lack of population density in Western Australia create a number of challenges for the library profession. For employers it can present challenges to recruiting and retaining staff with the appropriate skill set. For librarians located in Western Australia the challenge can be combating a sense of isolation and distance from colleagues and training opportunities.

Librarians wishing to maintain their own continuing professional development or those seeking opportunities to develop and demonstrate leadership may find this harder to achieve in geographically remote areas. Shipherd[11] notes that librarians in larger population centres are usually able to pursue a comfortable and satisfying career structure with job advancement without changing other elements in their life style whereas, for librarians in smaller more isolated areas, opportunities for advancement or for change are more limited. Librarians in remote regions tend to be disadvantaged because the region often lacks a critical mass of other library professionals to share knowledge, expertise and provide support and advice. Burke, Dazkiw and Sheridan[12] found that opportunities to move to new positions in a regional area or to build opportunities for career building are limited. Many library staff in a geographically isolated area have chosen to live in the region and are committed for the long term to the locality. Accepting an opportunity to work elsewhere may involve long distance travelling or the relocation of an entire family. These may not be attractive alternatives.

It is important for librarians to experience the stimulation resulting from attendance at conferences and visiting other libraries. Participation in such continuing professional development activities can be limited when the librarian lives in a geographically remote region and travel can be prohibitive both in terms of cost and time. Leary[13] observed in the case of rural librarians trying to maintain their professional skill level, that many training courses are conducted in capital cities and the cost of accommodation as well as travel can quickly eat away at training funds. Burke, Dazkiw and Sheridan[12] observed a similar issue in their study of the efforts of one university library to encourage opportunity and innovation in the workplace across metropolitan and regional settings.

Schmude[14] notes that one of the key challenges for library staff in a rural setting is coping with the realities of isolation and that geographic remoteness has particular significance for Australia due to the size of the country, the relatively small population, and its pattern of concentrated settlement in the cities and on the coast. He notes that rural librarians tend to lack access to professional development opportunities readily available to their metropolitan counterparts. Cox and Hawkett[15] observed that working in isolation can erode morale and diminish effectiveness when there is little opportunity for face-to-face discussion prior to decision-making and no local opportunity for informal discussion of library matters.

There are numerous strategies which can be adopted to overcome or minimise the isolation which may result from living and working in a geographically remote region.

TECHNIQUES FOR INDIVIDUALS TO ADDRESS GEOGRAPHIC ISOLATION

Communication is the key to minimising the disadvantages of geographic isolation. Shipherd[11] describes communication as the 'oxygen' needed to maintain professional stimulation for librarians located in geographically remote areas. All forms of communication may be useful: mail, telephone, travel and using the Internet.

Telecommunications obviously play a significant role in minimising the 'tyranny of distance'. In a study examining the use of the Internet by academic staff at the University of the South Pacific[16], Mamtora[17] concluded that the majority of respondents considered themselves to be geographically isolated from information resources but that most of them felt connecting to the Internet helped them overcome the isolation.

Peer support is important to all professionals, and the geographically isolated librarian, especially, may feel the lack of physical contact with colleagues. Subscribing to relevant listservs and discussion lists is a useful way to stay in touch with peers and keep on top of relevant and developing issues. While face-to-face interactions might be the favoured method for maintaining professional contacts, for librarians in remote regions of the country, teleconferences, email and other forms of virtual communication are equally useful tools for maintaining contact.

To maintain what Shipherd[11] described as a 'professional edge', it is vital for library staff to develop and maintain professional contacts and to see how other library systems and services operate. When opportunities arise to attend relevant professional conferences, incorporating professional visits to similar organisations may be very useful. In this way individual librarians can extend their own network and maintain that 'professional edge'.

Many universities now offer degrees in a fully online mode. For librarians located in regional and remote areas, enrolling in postgraduate studies may be a very useful way to stay connected with the latest developments in the profession. While in the past distance education often required some attendance on campus by students, today's suite of online degrees and continuing professional development activities offer many options including fully online courses.

In geographically remote areas it is important for the library professional association to be active and supported by members, probably more so than in metropolitan areas. According to Abram,[5] library professional associations exist for three main purposes: to provide networking opportunities for members, to provide professional development opportunities, and to provide a vehicle for advocacy on behalf of the profession and library users. The Australian Library and Information Association (ALIA) has a number of branches in Western Australia: Academic and Research Libraries (WA), ALIA WA Library Technicians, ALIAWest, and ALIA Mentoring Program (WA).

Table 2: ALIA Branches in Western Australia

Group Name	Purpose
ALIAWest	Co-ordinates and communicates strategic professional issues and organises continuing professional development activities across the large state of Western Australia. Co-ordinates a social and networking program across groups in WA.
ALIA Academic & Research Libraries (WA)	Is a forum for tertiary, research and academic librarians to discuss ideas and practices and foster collaboration.
ALIA Mentoring Program (WA)	A facilitated mentoring program for members in Western Asutralia.
ALIA WA Library Technicians	Promotes ALIA and library technicial activities, encouraging professional development and communication within the local area and nationally.

The author is convenor of ALIAWest[18] which is not sector-specific or aimed at a particular group of library professionals. It was formed in 2001 and introduced an online newsletter, held regular functions to keep members in touch, and maintained an Award[19] established by the Western Australia Branch Council for the most promising graduand each year. As a non sector-specific group, ALIAWest has a great deal of freedom in choosing event topics and themes and working collaboratively with other groups. Such a non-partisan group is important to a geographically remote region where there are fewer opportunities for professionals to network and attend relevant events.

One of ALIA's Principles[20] is: *Library and information professionals have a responsibility to commit to professional development and career-long learning.* Similarly, their employers and the Australian Library and Information Association have a responsibility to provide opportunities which enable library and information professionals to maintain excellent service delivery. ALIA encourages members to take responsibility for their own continuing professional development. The ALIA groups in Western Australia organise events and activities which provide many continuing professional development opportunities for members. ALIAWest for example, has been exploring the concept of an 'unconference'[21] and is likely to facilitate such an event during 2007 in association with the State Library of Western Australia.

TECHNIQUES FOR LIBRARY ORGANISATIONS TO MINIMISE GEOGRAPHIC ISOLATION

One strategy to ensure library staff will be interested in seeking employment in a regional setting, is for library staff to participate in the professional community, to become known and convey the attitudes and values of their home library. In this way, when a library is recruiting, librarians from other regions already know about it and may be interested in applying for the position.

Co-operative activities also help to minimise the isolation experienced in geographically remote regions. One example in Western Australia is the Skills for Teaching and Learning (STIL) Advisory Group.[22] This group is a collaboration between the five Western Australia universities: Curtin, Edith Cowan, Murdoch, Notre Dame, and UWA. Representatives from each university library develop and maintain learning resources for reference librarians to develop their teaching skills. It is important for libraries to support staff participation in such activities by way of release from work to participate, and the use of work resources and time to organise events.

Teleconferencing provides opportunities for librarians in remote and isolated regions to participate in real-time discussions. Burke, Dazkiw and Sheridan[12] describe the use of teleconference equipment augmented by software which allows staff to view remotely the screen of another computer workstation. The adoption of innovations such as this is crucial in addressing the 'tyranny of distance'.

LEADERSHIP DEVELOPMENT AT UWA LIBRARY

The preceding sections outline the geographic isolation of the state of Western Australia, the context within which the University of Western Australia operates. Situated as it is in the most remote capital city in the world, the University deals with the realities of geographic isolation every day. As an essential part of the University, the UWA Library is also challenged by the constraints of such isolation and this requires library managers to be creative in attracting, retaining and developing leaders. This section outlines one strategy adopted by the UWA Library to develop leadership amongst its existing staff.

Stephens and Russell[23] pose the question "what is good leadership?" They admit it is difficult to define leadership and consequently difficult to design programmes for developing the leaders of the future. Nevertheless, the University of Western Australia Library has designed a continuing professional development programme for senior library staff titled *Taking the Lead*. This programme is designed to ensure that library managers have the skills and knowledge required to drive the required changes and achieve positive and high performance workplaces.

In 2006 The University of Western Australia published the document *Working at The University of Western Australia – Expectations of staff in leadership and management roles*.[24] In general it requires leaders and managers to be innovative and committed to high performance in their own work and to encourage it in others. In a fast changing and more demanding environment it is essential that all managers, including library managers, have and use the broad range of skills required by the University.

Members of the millennial generation now form the majority of users at the University of Western Australia Library. Described as the "demographic tsunami that will permanently and irreversibly change the library and information landscape",[25] these users have greater expectations of library services than perhaps previous generations of students demonstrated. New library services and new ways of delivering these services demand a management team that is forward-thinking, pro-active and ready to lead staff in addressing the challenges that change involves. As the solutions to satisfying client needs become increasingly expensive it is also important that operational efficiencies are achieved through prudent management. *Transforming the Organisation* is one theme within the UWA Library's Strategic Plan[26] and *Taking the Lead* forms one of the projects within this theme.

Taking the Lead identifies the management skills required by individual library staff at level 7 (2) and above and delivers the training required to address their skills gap. The identification of the management skills gap utilises a 360-degree feedback instrument and a behavioural style inventory. A 360-degree feedback instrument combines evaluations of the programme participants by their supervisors, peers, and the staff who report directly to them. The feedback is voluntary, anonymous and confidential and the tool employed by UWA Library uses an on-line questionnaire, the Quality Leadership Profile (QLP)[26] developed by Queensland University of Technology specifically for the university context. The report received by each participant includes the average scores for managers from the higher education sector throughout Australia. These scores can be used as a baseline against which an individual's response can be compared.

DiSC Classic[27] was used as a behavioural style inventory. It is designed to be self-scored and self-interpreted because the respondent is regarded as the expert on him or herself. It is a tool designed to help an individual develop a broader understanding of their behavioural tendencies and those of others. This instrument divides behaviour into four dimensions:

- **Dominance:** Direct and Decisive. D's are strong-willed, strong-minded people who like accepting challenges, taking action, and getting immediate results

- **Influence:** Optimistic and Outgoing. I's are 'people people' who like participating on teams, sharing ideas, and energizing and entertaining others.

- **Steadiness:** Sympathetic and Cooperative. S's are helpful people who like working behind the scenes, performing in consistent and predictable ways, and being good listeners.

- **Conscientiousness:** Concerned and Correct. C's are sticklers for quality and like planning ahead, employing systematic approaches, and checking and re-checking for accuracy.

The programme also identifies which skills are best addressed in a group setting, determines a training plan for each participant, sources and schedules the training, evaluates the project including a repeat of the 360-degree feedback process for each participant and provides an ongoing forum for participants to discuss management issues. The ongoing forum, titled *Leading into the Weekend* is a monthly Friday afternoon one-hour session. All participants take turns organising the event; these vary widely and include guest speakers, discussion of leadership case studies, and experiential opportunities in leadership. The very act of organising a session for peers around the issue of leadership is of itself an opportunity to demonstrate leadership.

One important aspect of the programme is the support from senior Library managers. When launching the programme, the University Librarian indicated that he and his executive team would participate fully. This contributed to universal 'buy-in' to the voluntary programme.

Taking the Lead commenced in August 2006 and is expected to run through to August 2007, so no formal evaluation has yet been conducted. In preparing a nomination for an Australian Industry Training Development Award, however, participants were asked to comment on any notable differences they had observed, any lessons they had learnt, and what they would do differently next time. Many staff commented on how useful the DiSC behavioural style inventory was, especially for understanding colleagues' communication styles and their ability to work more effectively with a variety of people. Some staff noted that they were attempting to adjust their own communication style in an effort to accommodate the various styles of their colleagues and staff in their teams. Reactions to the 360-degree feedback exercise were mostly cautious. A few staff noted that the report they received was the basis of useful conversations with their immediate supervisors. One observed, after discussing the feedback with her supervisor, that a comment she had taken as critical was seen in a more positive light, possibly even as a complement on her management style. In commenting on the overall programme, one staff member described it as "useful, enjoyable and even, dare I say, inspirational".

Towards the end of the project, participants will repeat the 360-degree feedback exercise. This is intended to provide an opportunity for individuals to monitor any changes and improvements in their behaviour on-the-job. It will also provide participants and their supervisors, with useful information to discuss during the University's performance and professional development review procedure, the annual Professional Development Reviews. A further intention of the programme is for participants to gain improved insight into their leadership style and role in the organisation and to foster the leadership skills of all those in leadership positions. It is hoped that those new to leadership will develop greater skill and confidence, and those who have been leaders for some time, will be exposed to new ideas, inspiration, and greater understanding. In this way, the UWA Library is proactively developing and 'growing' their own leaders, and retaining staff who might otherwise seek opportunities elsewhere.

CONCLUSION

This paper has explored some of the challenges faced by librarians and information professionals living and working in geographically remote areas.

Examples from the author's own experience living and working in Perth, Western Australia, have formed a basis for identifying how individuals and employers can address some of the issues that overcome the 'tyranny of distance'. Employers have the added challenge of attracting, retaining and developing staff with the right skill set and aptitude.

Leadership is a particular issue for the library and information profession because of the anticipated gap which will be created by large numbers retiring over the next ten to fifteen years. Succession planning is an activity that increasing numbers of libraries and professional associations are starting to address.

Unpacking the issues which geographic remoteness presents, perhaps provides an opportunity to see a way forward, and to suggest ways of minimising the isolation. Identifying the issues and starting to address them in forums such as this international one, provides a better opportunity to identify some of the answers.

The library and information profession needs people who are willing to be leaders. To step out in front and successfully take a leadership position requires courage, confidence, and a significant level of self awareness. Without such individuals as leaders, the library profession may dwindle and disappear as a result of the combined effects of a significant number of retirements and the lower numbers of students enrolling in library degrees.

It is our responsibility to demonstrate librarianship as an interesting and challenging career choice and to foster and support staff who could enrol in a course of study to qualify as librarians. It is also our responsibility to encourage and support those who may be the library leaders of tomorrow. They need challenging opportunities to realise the leadership potential they hold; they need support from employers and mentors to take advantage of those opportunities; and they need role models who demonstrate a variety of leadership styles.

Most importantly, we need to be audacious in our approach to succession planning and leadership development. In not responding to this issue, libraries may wither into 'dignified irrelevance'.[26] Instead, let us be proactive rather than reactive; let us take the initiative and create the future we would like to see.

REFERENCES

[1] Mason FM, Wetherbee LV. Learning to lead: an analysis of current training programs for library leadership. *Library Trends* 2004, 53 (1), 187-217.

[2] Hill LA. Becoming the boss. *Harvard Business Review* 2007, 85 (1), 49-56.

[3] Hallam G. Future perfect – will we have made it? Workforce planning issues in the library and information sector. [document on the Internet]. In: *Click06: ALIA Biennial Conference* 2006 September 19-22; Perth, Australia. [cited 2007 Jan 25]. URL: http://conferences.alia.org.au/alia2006/Papers/Gillian_Hallam.pdf

[4] Hernon P, Schwartz C. Leadership: a unique focus: guest editorial. *Journal of Academic Librarianship*. 2006, 32 (1), 1-2.

[5] Abram S. Technoschism: the real world and libraries, librarians, and our associations: a view from Canada. *LMT* 2006, 27 (1/2), 14-25.

[6] CAVAL Collaborative Solutions is a company owned by ten Australian universities and established in 1978. CAVAL initiates, encourages, promotes and develops all forms of collaboration and coordination in the establishment, improvement and development of libraries. [document on the Internet]. Melbourne: CAVAL, 2007; [cited 2007 Jan 25]. URL: http://www.caval.edu.au

[7] Ingles E, De Long K, Humphrey C, Sivak A. The future of human resources in Canadian libraries [document on the Internet]. Edmonton: 8Rs Canadian Library Human Resource Study; 2005 [cited 2007 Jan 25]. URL: http://www.ls.ualberta.ca/8rs/8RsFutureofHRLibraries.pdf

[8] Ward PL. Developing education programmes in the most isolated city in the world. *Library Assocaition Record* 1985, 87(5), 191-192.

[9] Black G. Is life in the fast lane always the best lane? In: The New Librarians Symposium; 2006 Dec 1-2; Sydney, Australia. [cited 2007 Jan 11]. Available from: URL: http://e-prints.alia.org.au/archive/00000129/01/black%5Fg%5Fpaper.pdf

[10] Knight R. Last one turn off the lights: the influence of geographic, demographic and economic factors on the provision of library services in rural and remote communities. *Rural Society* 2002, 12(3), 273-284.

[11] Shipherd A. Providing library services to isolated areas. In: *Libraries: after 1984. Proceedings of the LAA/NZLA Conference; 1984; Brisbane.* Sydney: Library Association of Australia; 1985; 367-370.

[12] Burke L, Dazkiw J, Sheridan L. Big ideas in a shrinking world: encouraging opportunity and innovation in the workplace [document on the Internet]. In: Continuing Professional Development Conference 2006: Out of bounds and borders: a trans-Tasman Collaboration; 2006 Apr 19-20; Auckland. [cited 2007 Jan 18]. Available from: http://www.lib.latrobe.edu.au/about/publications/burke-dazkiw-sheridan-ripplepaper.pdf

[13] Leary J. Library services for isolated communities: a western New South Wales perspective. *Australian Public Library and Information Services* 1991, 4(3), 150-154.

[14] Schmude K. Library staff development in an isolated environment. In: Henri J, Sanders R. editors. *Libraries alone: proceedings of the Rural and Isolated Librarians Conference; 1987 July, Wagga Wagga NSW*: Libraries alone; 1988; 17-19.

[15] Cox K, Hawkett M. Professional isolation and networking: our experiences. In: Henri J, Sanders R. editors. *Libraries alone: Proceedings of the Rural and Isolated Librarians Conference; 1987 July; Wagga Wagga NSW*: Libraries alone; 1988; 34-38.

[16] Kennedy J. Collection development: is the isolated university library a special case? *Australian Association of Research Libraries.* 1996 27(2):132-138. Kennedy describes the University of the South Pacific as one of the most geographically isolated university libraries in the world in terms of distance from other major research collections.

[17] Mamtora J. Pacific academics and the Internet. *Australian Association of Research Libraries* 2004, 35(1), 35-52.

[18] Australian Library and Information Association – Description of Groups [document on the Internet]. Canberra: ALIA; 2003 [updated 2006 Dec 8; cited 2007 Jan 11]. URL: http://www.alia.org.au/groups/aliawest/

[19] The F.A. Sharr Medal is named after Francis Aubie (Ali) Sharr, State Librarian of Western Australia from 1953 to 1976, in recognition of his contribution to libraries and librarianship in Western Australia and to the profession [document on the Internet]. Canberra: ALIA; 2003 [updated 2007

Mar 29; cited 2007 Jan 30]. URL: http://www.alia.org.au/awards/merit/sharr.medal/

[20] Australian Library and Information Association – Professional Development for Library and Information Professionals [document on the Internet]. Canberra: ALIA 2003 [updated 2005 Aug 10; cited 2007 Jan 11]. URL: http://www.alia.org.au/policies/professional.development.html

[21] The principles of the unconference are:
- Whoever comes is the right person
- Whatever happens, that's the way it's supposed to happen
- Whenever it starts, it's the right time to start
- When it's over it's over

Modelled on Library Camps held in 2006 in the US, the idea is that participants shape the agenda and are responsible for the day. An unconference focuses on who's going to be at the event and what they're interested in. The organisers provide space, enough blank surfaces to write on so that people can self-organise, and a general theme for the day.

[22] The University of Western Australia Library. Skills for teaching information literacy (STIL) [document on the Internet]. Perth: The University of Western Australia, University Library. Information Services Coordination Team; 2006 [cited 2007 Jan 11]. URL http://www.library.uwa.edu.au/education_training_and_support/information_skills/skills_for_teaching_information_literacy_stil

[23] Stephens D, Russell K. Organizational development, leadership, change, and the future of libraries. *Library Trends* 2004, 53(1), 238-257.

[24] The University of Western Australia. Working at The University of Western Australia – expectations of staff in leadership and management roles [document on the Internet] . Perth: The Library: University of Western Australia; 2005 [cited 2007 Jan 30]. URL: http://www.hr.uwa.edu.au/policy/toc/performance_management_of_staff/professional_development_review/working_at_uwa

[25] Sweeney RT. Reinventing library buildings and services for the millennial generation. *Library Administration and Management* 2005, 19(4), 165-175.

[26] The University of Western Australia Library Strategic Plan 2005-2007 [document on the Internet]. Perth: The Library: University of Western Australia; 2005 [cited 2007 Jan 30]. URL:

http://www.library.uwa.edu.au/__data/assets/pdf_file/3039/library_strategic_plan05-07.pdf

[27] Library staff in Australian university libraries span a classification scale encompassing ten levels, Level 1 being the entry level and Level 10 covering executive management positions.

[28] The QLP was designed by Queensland University of Technology [document on the Internet]. Brisbane: Queensland University of Technology [updated 2006 March 30; cited 2007 Jan 24]. URL: http://www.hrd.qut.edu.au/planning/externalrelations/product/qlp/

[29] DiSC Classic information [document on the Internet]. Leadership Resources and Consulting [cited 2007 Jan 15]. URL: http://www.lrandc.com/

TWO X'ERS TELL WHY AND HOW: SUCCESSION PLANNING FOR THE FUTURE

Perri-Lee Sandell
Macquarie University Library
Sydney, NSW Australia
perrilee.sandell@library.mq.edu.au

Susan M. Vickery
Macquarie University Library
Sydney, NSW Australia
susan.vickery@library.mq.edu.au

Abstract

A number of reports within the international library and information sector are highlighting the need for succession planning within this sector, particularly in response to the disproportionate numbers of librarians expected to retire within the next twenty years. There is a call for organisations to understand the new generation that is currently entering the workforce—Generation Y. The library and information sector can draw from the current research into generation theory to review their organisations' strategies to attract and retain this new workforce. Current human resources and management literature examines the different styles of work and underlying behaviours of the different generations. This paper focuses specifically on the attributes of Generation Y and Generation X in relation to professional development, and retention of talent within an organisation. In particular the authors draw on their own personal experiences and the case for job sharing at management level is examined as a strategy to contribute to a flexible workforce whilst providing a means to develop Generation X and Y leadership skills.

AN AGEING WORKFORCE

It is predicted that the international library workforce is about to enter a period colloquially known as the 'brain drain'—a time when the impact of an ageing workforce will begin to take effect within the library and information sector. An

Australian Labour Force Survey in 2005[1] revealed that the median age of librarians in the workforce is 48, with 65% of Australian librarians over 45, compared to the national average of 35% for all occupations. Only 32.2% are aged between 25–44 followed by a small 2.7% under 24 years of age. Refer to Table 1.

Table 1. Share of employment (%) by age group for Librarians compared with all occupations[1]

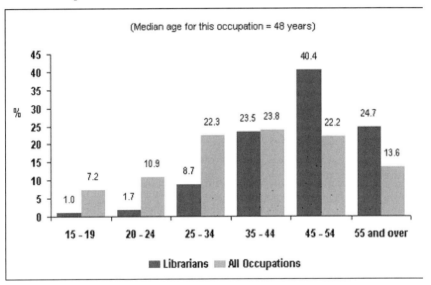

Similar demographic patterns have been observed in the US, Canada, the UK and NZ. In the US, 24% of librarians in the US workforce will retire between 2005 and 2010 and a further 27% between 2010 and 2020.[2,3] Encel's 2003 report on the mature workforce notes that Australia has developed a culture of 'early exit', voluntary or otherwise, with some superannuation schemes creating a financial incentive for people to leave full-time work at age 55. Surveys indicate that over 75% of males and around 95% of females intend to retire from full-time work before reaching age 65, and over 50% of women indicate that they intend to retire from full-time work before age 45. However Encel notes that given financial considerations "the realism of these intentions, both at the level of the individual and from the perspective of the broader community, is open to significant doubt".[4 (p3)]

Within twenty years it is predicted that over half of the current librarian professionals will have left the workforce, and finding replacements for these positions will have become increasingly difficult. In Australian libraries only 11.4% of librarians are under 35 years of age, whereas the number of workers in other occupations under 35 is 40.4%.[1] In addition, the number of graduates in the Australian library and information sector has stagnated and in the case of undergraduates has decreased by 54% since 1997.[5] In the US the total number of MLIS graduates has also been described as 'stagnant', whilst in Canada, which has recently recorded an increase in numbers of students enrolling, 45% of the students enrolled were over 35 years of age.[3]

Australia has also reported a skills shortage with the number of positions available exceeding the number of applicants. Avril Henry, an HR consultant who has surveyed Generation Y extensively, refers to the current situation in Australia as an 'employees market', or from the employers' perspective a 'war for talent', as candidates can pick and choose from a range of positions.[6,7] The library sector is competing within this arena and is further hindered by its small pool of talent. In addition to this, the information skills of new graduates are transferable to a range of industries (records management, IT), and consequently the library sector needs to re-examine its recruitment policies, and revamp its image in order to attract these new graduates into the industry.

Examining the attributes of this new group highlights a whole range of issues that need to be considered in succession plans for the library and information sector. Instead of looking at who will *replace* those leaving the profession, we should be looking at who will be *succeeding* them.

WHAT IS SUCCESSION PLANNING, AND WHY BOTHER?

Succession planning is defined as "a deliberate and systematic effort by an organisation to ensure leadership continuity in key positions, retain and develop intellectual and knowledge capital for the future, and encourage individual advancement".[8 (p10)]

Succession planning should be a proactive process rather than a reactive response. It goes beyond replacement planning and instead attempts to ensure the continuity of leadership by cultivating talent from within the organization through planned development activities. Rothwell delineates between managerial succession planning and technical succession planning, with the latter focussing on retaining organisational knowledge and expertise through knowledge management.[9] A comprehensive succession plan provides strategies to ensure business continuity including: the retention of organisational knowledge; the replacement of future vacancies; a way to meet future skill and talent needs; competitiveness as an employer and an increased ability to attract and retain talented staff.

The Librarians of the Australian Technology Network group (LATN), an Australian and New Zealand Technology Universities group, recently contracted Whitmell & Associates to develop a workforce succession plan to consider how they can best prepare their workforce and be competitive in the hiring market.[10] The report presented seven key recommendations for organisational succession and workforce planning:

1. Develop a written plan;

2. Change recruitment, hiring and retention practices (reduce hierarchies, provide career paths and opportunities for multi-skilling including job rotation or job swap);

3. Recognise good work and abilities;

4. Encourage professional development and higher education;

5. Develop leaders and managers, through mentoring programs for example;

6. Work with the Library information education sector; and

7. Work with other libraries within the industry.

The Australian Library and Information Association (ALIA), Queensland University of Technology (QUT) and CAVAL Collaborative Solutions are currently undertaking a major collaborative research project to examine the library and information services workforce in Australia: the neXus census. Two of the key goals of the project are to foster a deeper understanding and awareness of the importance of workforce planning and to develop a collaborative framework for career-long learning for the library profession, bringing together employers, educators, trainers and individual practitioners.

WHO IS SUCCEEDING?

The literature of human resources and management reflects studies of the four generations currently believed to coexist in the workforce. Each of these generations has particular working styles and characteristics. (See Table 2.) This paper recognises that not every person born within these generations demonstrates all of their supposed attributes. However, generational theorists such as Howe and Strauss agree that these characteristics are useful in providing a general description of the generations.[11] This is helpful when understanding the needs and wants of the generations and how they are motivated. As an industry we need to pay attention to generational issues and intergenerational interactions in the workplace.

Rachel Singer Gordon notes "as a library manager part of your responsibility toward your staff is to bring out their best and respect their individual needs. Paying attention to generational concerns is just one facet of being a good manager, paying attention to generational trends that affect your institution is just one part of securing your library's future".[12, (p181)]

A comprehensive coverage of the attributes of the four main generations, and the rationale behind them, is outside the scope of this paper. Papers and books, such as Sheahan's *Generation Y: thriving (and surviving) with Generation Y at work* and Huntley's *The world according to Y: inside the new adult generation*,[13,14] provide a comprehensive analysis of the causes of these behaviours. Henry states "each generation has its own distinct set of values, views of family, work/life balance, career, training and development, loyalty, and expectations of leaders and the work environment".[6]

This paper focuses specifically on the new generation coming into the workforce, Generation Y. They are also known as Gen Y'ers; Generation whY; Gen Y; Ultra Gen X; Millennials; Nexters; Generation next; Echo Boomers; Boomlets; the I Generation; the Net Generation; and Netizens. As two Generation X managers, we, the authors, also examine how an understanding of Boomers, Generation X, and Generation Y can help an organisation in recruiting and retaining staff and developing leaders within the organisation.

DON'T FOCUS JUST ON GENERATION Y.

Although current numbers of Gen Y'ers in the library and information workforce are low, this generation cannot be ignored. The literature is consistent in the recognition that core Generation Y traits are *different* from any other generation in the work force. A better understanding of these traits will help us understand their behaviour, rather than rejecting it or ignoring it. Zemke, Raines and Filipczak in *Generations at work: managing the clash of Veterans, Boomers, Xers and Nexters in your workplace* examines how each of the generations interacts with each other and looks specifically at the type of clashes or misconceptions that occur between the generations.[15]

In recognising these interactions, a learning organisation can maximise the effectiveness of these intergenerational relationships. For example Gen Y'ers respect the Veterans and Boomers,[16] and consequently there is the potential for a mentoring relationship by these two groups in which the Boomers and Veterans can pass on the organisational history and their own experiences. In return the Gen Y'ers can share their technological expertise and inject their creativity to brainstorming and organisational planning. Y'ers can also be useful sharing their technical confidence and ability with youth-to-youth or peer-to-peer IT skills training. As Boomers prepare to exit the workforce (often through contract work after retirement) they too can share their skills and knowledge such as through project work. Encel's report on the mature workforce recommends that organisations and government develop policies that engage and encourage Boomers to continue in the workforce.[4]

Table 2. Comparison of attributes of current workforce generations. (Adapted from Eisner, Henry, Sheahan & Zemke[6, 7, 13, 15, 16])

	Veterans/Traditionalists: pre 1946* (60yrs +)	Boomers: 1946–1964* (43–61 years)	Generation X: 1965–1979* (42–28 years)	Generation Y: 1980+ * (under 28 years)
Overview	Grew up in war time	Largest generation in the workforce. Grew up post World war II	Known as 'latchkey kids'	Told they 'Can do anything', optimistic, confident, sociable; strong morals and ethics; conservative

Characteristics in workplace	Disciplined; they respect law and order	Open minded and rebellious in their youth, more conservative in their 30s–40s	Resourceful; individualistic; self reliant; sceptical of authority; hardworking, enthusiastic; excited by challenges	Expect greater workplace flexibility; creative; enjoy brainstorming, thrive on challenges
Work needs	Loyal; self-sacrificing	Optimistic; ambitious; loyal; workaholics; known as superwoman; driven to succeed	Focus on relationships (at home and work) and outcomes, their rights and skills in the workplace	Need a positive work environment; a competent inspiring manager and a work/life balance
Respect	Directive, command management style; they respect positional power	Crave job status; status symbols are important	Are not interested in long term careers, and not into corporate loyalty or status	Like an inclusive style of management; involved in their career plan; value honesty
Work styles	Fixed views on roles; inform other on a need-to-know basis. Lead by hierarchy.	Good technical skills; may micro manage others; were not formally trained in leadership skills. Lead by consensus.	Comfortable with technology; easy to recruit—hard to retain; will have at least 3 careers in their lifetime; will self educate for leadership skills (MBA) if necessary. Lead by competence.	Grew up with technology (live and breathe it); expect to make decisions and be involved in decision making; will have up to 25 different jobs in their lifetime. Lead by cooperation.
Orientation to change	Not comfortable with change	Resist change, are loyal to the old ways	Accept change	Want/expect change

*Exact dates vary amongst different theorists.

INTRODUCING THE NEXT GENERATION: GENERATION Y.

Initially, Gen Y was viewed as 'Gen X on steroids'. Before writing this paper the authors were also under the misconception that Generation Y's attitudes to work and life were the same as theirs (Generation X). In their readings and experience as managers, they have now come to realize that they were wrong in their assumptions. As Huntley, a fellow self-confessed Gen X'er, observes "despite a few similarities in behaviour and attitudes, Gen Y actually represents a sharp break from Generation X. Instead of imitating us, Y'ers have reacted to our moods and our failings."[14 (p5)]

In an Australian 2005 survey of Generation Y workers, Henry recorded their top three values as loyalty, honesty, and trust.[16] They are specifically loyal to their team (home or work) and to a good manager, not necessarily their organisation. They also expect these values to be reciprocated by those around them. The same survey found that Generation Y'ers rated the following as the most important factors in terms of careers:

1. Positive work environment;

2. Working for a good manager/supervisor;

3. Having a work/life balance;

4. Access to training and development.

Generation Y workers are motivated by: a good manager whom they respect and look to for guidance; recognition for a job well done; a need to feel valued by the organisation; having a job with purpose and meaning (client satisfaction); and challenges and responsibility.

Gordon reports that job fulfillment is fundamental to this group.[12] Gen Y'ers are unwilling to stay in less than satisfactory conditions as they are transient and are continually scoping the job market for 'the best job'. They view their employer as a hub of new resources or opportunities for themselves, and will not stay if they feel that they are not getting enough from a job.

Other work/lifestyle conditions considered important by Generation Y, as reported by Sheahan, are: flexible work arrangements (this does not necessarily mean working part-time); promotional/career progression opportunities;

considerable remuneration; integrity (no empty promises); corporate social responsibility, morals and ethics and a social or fun workplace.[13]

WHAT IS THE MOST EFFECTIVE WAY TO BRING OUT THE BEST IN GENERATION Y?

Armed with the knowledge of what generation Y needs in the workplace, their managers/supervisors can use the following to produce a work environment that is attractive and responsive to the new generation.[13, 16]

Trust them.

Trust them to work in the way that suits them best, such as in a loud talkative team environment, or working from home. Don't be afraid to challenge them or give them opportunities to perform at higher then expected levels. Demonstrate fairness in how you treat them, and how they see you treating others.

Empower them.

Generation Y respond well to personal plans, which gives them a job purpose. They expect to be involved in decisions across the organisation, and have their feedback recognized and valued. Generation Y are confident in their abilities and therefore can be assertive, ambitious, and expect instant gratification. Their manager needs to be able to harness their ideas, without discouraging them. For example, they may expect the latest technology in the office; the manager might redirect their enthusiasm to sharing their expertise with others (e.g. technology training, peer-to-peer) and deal with any unrealistic expectations through articulation of the organisation's strategic focus. Gen Y may lack direction and focus, but they cope well under pressure and respond to deadlines and short-term goals. Finally, giving Gen Y accountability will help keep them focused and also feel valued.

Communicate with them.

Generation Y are sometimes referred to as the "whY generation", as they are not afraid to openly question the rationale of a policy or decision or direction—be it from their peers, supervisors or managers. They will respond well to forums that involve them in all levels of strategic discussion and planning. Communication needs to be immediate and open. They respond well to personal communication including one-on-one, face-to-face and team meetings. They need to hear and share others' opinions and they will respect a manager who develops a personal connection with them.

Train and develop them.

Because of their informal tendencies, Generation Y will benefit from business skills development, such as public speaking, business writing, business etiquette, conflict resolution, time management skills, negotiation skills and relationship building. They need to recognise the value of history and tradition, but they are receptive to coaching and mentoring rather than to a directive style. They value a supportive, inspirational role model with vision, who leads by example.

Gen Y'ers are independent in thought and confident enough to express it. At the same time, however, they enjoy the security (both emotional and financial) that comes with living with parents, or from belonging to an organisation. This 'independent dependence' means that in the workplace they can be coached and desire empowerment. "Emotionally intelligent managers will find Generation Y are tremendous assets to the team and workplace, as they are willing to develop and improve. Managers with the confidence to empower their Generation Y staff will find them, if managed properly, willing and able to meet the challenge."[13] (p48)

WHY DEVELOP GENERATION Y, WHEN THEY WILL LEAVE ANYWAY?

The thought that arises at this point is that perhaps an organisation is wasting its time on developing these individuals, especially if they are not going to stay and repay the investment. There are however five facts that cannot be ignored.

- Their potential is great, they are receptive to change and development. A smart organisation will know how to harness energy of Gen Y'ers and promote their development.

- Addressing what motivates them will help attract and retain Gen Y'ers in the industry. This is important in boosting the number of new graduates in the library and information sector.

- An understanding of their strengths and weaknesses, like and dislikes, will help when developing and managing intergenerational workgroups.

- If and when they leave, they will promote you to their peers (via word of mouth).
- They are the future of our organisations. They cannot be ignored.

SKILLS NEEDED BY A MANAGER OF GENERATION Y

In order to facilitate the development of the Generation Y worker, future managers need to develop their own skills in: listening; responding to being questioned and challenged; giving and receiving feedback; emotional intelligence and an ability to recognise Generation Y'ers mood cycles; managing Generation Y's high expectations; personal involvement and interest in career development of staff; mentoring and coaching; creative leadership; and up-to-date technology skills. [7,13,17]

GENERATION X AS MANAGERS

Generation X have received their fair share of criticism. They have been described as the slack generation and have sometimes been referred to as cynical and self-centred. Eisner describes Generation X managers as lacking in social skills and reluctant to network.[16] These skills will need to be developed in order to communicate effectively with Generation Y. However they are also flexible, technologically savvy and resourceful. As managers, Generation X tend to be fair, competent and straightforward leaders. Those in leadership roles tend to choose them and be chosen for them.[15] Although different from Generation Y, Generation X share some similar values and may act as a bridge between the Boomers and Generation Y. Successful Generation X managers who achieve the work/life balance need to take the lead in demonstrating the attainability and sustainability of flexible work practices. As Hutley notes, "Generation X could hold the key to the survival of our profession as this group may have the insights into Generation Y to recruit enough new librarians from this age range to fill the void created by Boomers' retirements." [18 (p4)]

WHAT THE LIBRARY AND INFORMATION SECTOR NEEDS TO DO

Job fulfilment and work/life balance are very important to Generation Y workers. This group is more likely to change jobs than any other generation in the workforce. Henry[6] predicts that Generation Y'ers will have up to 29 different employers within their career span. "Information skills are in demand and transferable, if traditional libraries are to keep younger workers, they need to find a way to remain attractive in the face of non-traditional opportunities"[12 (p2)]

To address this, library and information organisations need to consider the following in their succession planning:[7, 13]

- Providing opportunities for Generation Y'ers to express and share ideas, to enable them to feel valued (via open forums and staff meetings);

- Flexibility: for example job swap, rotation, part time, or sabbaticals;

- Remuneration based on accountability and responsibility, rather than seniority, or time in the organisation;

- Articulating the strategic direction and expectations of the organisation;

- Providing personal and professional education and training (not just basic skills) and making it relevant, interactive and with their peers;

- Reviewing Y'ers' expectations regularly, focusing on their aptitudes and abilities not their demonstrated skills (ignore the corporate ladder approach, Y'ers do not have time);

- Providing a career path;

- Developing and demonstrating a social conscience or corporate responsibility (to recruit and retain);

- Being sincere, modern, 'edgy', passionate, and optimistic;

- Becoming a learning organisation; asking at exit interviews if they have any good ideas before they go and if they would recommend the company to a friend? Asking if they know anyone who wants the job.

- Addressing Generation Y's needs in your advertising; illustrating that you provide support and training;

- Making sure technology is up-to-date, including information on your websites;

- Having a brand strategy to help with recruitment.

The library and information sector can also employ strategies to attract this generation's loyalty to the profession:

- Reach out to library and information studies schools, and start building relationships before they graduate;

- Offer internships;
- Revamp the industry image.

Kate Davis, a self titled 'Millennial Librarian', recently presented a paper at the Australian New Librarians Symposium (NSL2006) on the work profile of Generation Y and its implications for the library workforce. Like Sheahan's work, this paper is written from the perspective of a Generation Y'er and offers some useful insights into this perspective. Davis notes that the library workplace fosters the characteristics that Generation Y staff seek, including diversity, collegiality and flexibility. However, she predicts that this Generation will not be attracted to libraries with a hierarchical environment.[11]

AN EXAMPLE OF WORK/LIFE BALANCE WORKING AT MACQUARIE UNIVERSITY LIBRARY

As a result of a recent restructure (2004–2006) Macquarie University Library has already begun to employ the strategies of succession planning. The aim of the change was to create a structure that would simplify and improve services for clients. The restructure was based on six guiding principles: the Library needs to be agile, resilient, informed, connected, successful and responsible. The focus of the restructure was to contribute to the development of a flexible organisational structure, create promotional opportunities across the Library, 'future-proof' jobs via a multi-skilling approach, and retain the skills and knowledge of existing staff, incorporating best practice standards. There was a focus on becoming a 'thinking and learning organisation', as well as a 'doing' organisation.[19]

The Library's newly created structure and position descriptions have been developed to maximise cooperation across library departments, resulting in multiple opportunities for development. Secondment to project positions within the Library's newly created Project Office also offers unique opportunities for individual growth and development. Each position description now focuses on abilities and responsibilities rather than the previous task/skill based format.

Another benefit from the restructure was the increase of Liaison Librarians from one per faculty to two or more per faculty. This model incorporated the principle of connectivity. The aim was to create flexibility in the structure to build partnerships and share knowledge by increasing the number of staff involved in liaising with the academic community. The authors' job-sharing model provided an example of how these partnerships could work.

What follows is a case study of how Macquarie University Library successfully employed some of the above-mentioned considerations to the benefit of both the employee and the organisation. It is the authors' own experiences as two Generation X workers who felt a need to reduce working hours, and how management within the Library has supported the work/life balance need.

A PERSONAL CASE STUDY OF JOB SHARE IN PRACTICE

Returning from parental leave, the authors felt unable to cope satisfactorily with balancing home commitments and a family, with having a career. They were both in their thirties, having chosen like many Generation X'ers to start a family later in life. Together they had twenty-eight years of library experience, including eight years at Macquarie University Library. Their immediate manager and the University Librarian agreed that they could exchange their two individual full time positions as Academic Outreach Librarians (AOL), to job share in one position of AOL (the equivalent of a faculty librarian position).

In doing this the organisation retained the expertise and organisational knowledge that they had acquired. Interestingly, their career choices thus far were not motivated by remuneration, but rather by positions that offered greater job satisfaction and developmental opportunities. This is behaviour typical of both Generations X and Y. Feyerherm and Vick's study of high achieving Generation X female managers found that "personal fulfilment was intrinsically connected to professional success and that they wanted support from their companies in terms of mentors for guidance and development, opportunities to excel, recognition for efforts, relationships and flexibility to achieve work/life balance."[20 (p216)]

After two years of successful job share they applied jointly for an opportunity to act in their manager's position for ten months. The Library Management Team was initially concerned at the prospect of job share at management level but agreed, on condition of a three month trial/probation period. The experience was successful and they went on to job share the position of another department manager for seven months. Finally, they were successful in the permanent appointment to their current job share position (Manager, Liaison & Research

Services). This arrangement has enabled them to remain with the organisation and, in addition, has given them the opportunity to continue their professional development and career path with Macquarie University.

Flexible work arrangements do not only mean working part time or job share; this also includes working from home, leave in lieu, variable work hours, job swap, job rotation, or secondments. In response to the increasing demand by Gen X and Gen Y, males and females, for more flexible working conditions and a greater balance of their home and work life, job sharing in management has been much of the focus of recent human resources and management literature. Most of the literature on job share in management, however, resides in business or retail, with only a few examples of senior job share in the library sector.[21]

ORGANISATIONAL AND PERSONAL BENEFITS OF JOB SHARE AT MANAGEMENT LEVEL

The cost to the organisation for this flexibility is well documented.[21] The organisation has to cover the cost of training and development of two staff instead of one. Conversely, this results in a larger talent pool. There is also the administration and employment duplication, double the demands upon the supervisor/manager of the job sharers and the consequences should one of the partners leave. The success of job share is also dependent upon the individuals involved and their ability to communicate and work as a team, and on their own flexibility. At a management level there is also the issue of having two personalities in charge, and clear communication strategies are therefore essential, both for staff reporting to them and for their own line managers.

The benefits to the employer, however, are also to be considered. The obvious one is having, within one position, the skills of two individuals, two different approaches, and sometimes a more rounded or balanced perspective. "You access the skills of two individuals rather than one, giving greater scope and flexibility. For this to work the individuals need to share values and agree on common principles, but there is no need to be halves of the same clone ... it is the diversity that gives the greatest gains as the extremes of opinion on both sides tend to become more centred". [22 (p432)]

The other benefit for job share is the opportunity for the organisation to retain their assets, valued employees who might have otherwise left in search of part-time work. A 2001 WorkLife report[21] revealed that flexible working arrangements could significantly improve performance. The authors' experience supports these findings. They feel less stressed, and more energetic when at work, compared to their experience when working fulltime. They also believe that they are now more efficient in their work style, and home life has benefited too. However they recognise that there is some duplication in workload, for example reading emails, memos, minutes etc.

The success of the authors' job share experience has been attributed to their complementary work styles. They use their strengths in one partner to develop or mentor the other. For example: Susan's strengths include manipulating data and budgets; whereas Perri-Lee's strength is looking at the bigger picture and translating the organisational vision. On some projects, time permitting, they will reverse tasks to allow each other's weaknesses to strengthen. They also brainstorm, share ideas and use each other as a 'sounding board' creating a very healthy environment with mutual respect and trust. Feedback from their staff and peers has been that they enjoy working with 'both', and that their different styles of people management are welcomed. Staff are also encouraged by how well they communicate the issues to each other without people needing to repeat everything twice.

CONCLUSION

Generation Y have needs and wants that are different from the generations that have gone before them. Developing them with mentoring and encouragement and offering an organisation that is appealing as a whole package will help to attract them to, and retain them within, our profession.

Although different from Generation Y, Generation X share some similar approaches and may act as a bridge between the generations. Understanding how they think and behave will enable us to redirect our foci in regards to human resources, organisational change and succession planning for the library and information sector.

Job sharing is a strategy worthy of consideration in succession planning. It maximises Generation Y's openness to coaching or mentoring, need for a work/life balance, desire to work collaboratively, and their attraction to developmental opportunities. Additionally job sharing at the management level provides a means to develop Gen X and Gen Y's leadership skills, retains talent within an organisation and contributes to a sustainable flexible workforce.

REFERENCES

[1] ABS. *Australian Labour Force Survey, Australia—average 2005*. [WWW document] URL <http://jobsearch.gov.au/joboutlook/default.aspx?pageId=KeyInfo3&AscoCode=2292>. Accessed 15 January 2007

[2] Wilder, S.J. *The Age demographics of Academic Librarians: a Profession Apart. A report based on data from the ARL Annual Salary Survey*, Washington DC: ARL, 1995

[3] Ingles, E. Towards a national strategy for library human resources in Canada. *24th Annual Conference of International Association of Technological University Libraries* 2003 June 2, Ankara, Turkey 2003 [WWW document]. URL <http://www.iatul.org/conference/proceedings/vol13/papers/INGLES.ppt>. Accessed 19 January 2007

[4] Encel, S. (2003) *Age can work: The case for older Australians staying in the workforce. A report to the Australian Council of Trade Unions and the Business Council of Australia*. [WWW document]. URL <http://www.bca.com.au/Content.aspx?ContentID=89175>. Accessed 01 February 2007

[5] Hallam, G. Future perfect—will we have made it? Workforce planning issues in the library and information sector *2006. ALIA 2006 Biennial Conference Click06* 2006 Sept 19–22, Perth, [WWW document] URL <http://conferences.alia.org.au/alia2006/Papers/Gillian_Hallam.pdf>. Accessed 12 December 2006

[6] Henry, A. (2006) *Motivating & Managing Different Generations at Work*. AH Revelations [WWW document] URL<http://www.mskills.com.au/downloads/Manuf2020_Avril%20Henry.pdf>. Accessed 12 December 2006

[7] Henry, A. *Gen Y in the workplace with Avril Henry* [Podcast on the Internet] URL <http://www.roberthalf.com.au/Site/showpage.jsp?p=PODCAST_ARCHIVE&s=RHM_AUS>. Accessed 12 December 2006

[8] Rothwell, W.J. *Effective Succession Planning: ensuring leadership continuity and building talent from within*. 3rd ed. AMACOM, 2005

[9] Rothwell, W.J. Introducing Technical (not Managerial) succession planning. *Public Personnel Management* Winter 2004, **33** (4), 405–429.

[10] Whitmell, V. Workforce and succession planning in the libraries of the Australian Technology Network: preparing for demographic change. In: Huthwaite, A. (ed.) *Managing information in the Digital Age: The Australian Technology Network Libraries response*. Adelaide: University of South Australia Library, 2005: pp 157–178.

[11] Davis, K. (2006) *whY Generation: the Millennial Librarian, or the Future of Library Management*. [WWW Document] URL< http://e-prints.alia.org.au/archive/00000135/01/davis_k_paper.pdf> Accessed 19 December 2006

[12] Gordon, R.S. *The nextgen librarian's survival guide*. Medford (NJ): Information Today. 2006

[13] Sheahan, P. *Generation Y: Thriving (and surviving) with Generation Y at work*. Prahran (Victoria): Hardi Grant Books. 2005

[14] Huntley, R. *The world according to Y: inside the new adult generation*. Crows Nest (NSW): Allen & Unwin, 2006

[15] Zemke, R., Raines, C., Filipczak, B. *Generations at work: Managing the clash of Veterans, Boomers, Xers and Nexters in your workplace*, New York: AMACOM. 2000

[16] Henry, A. *The Who What When and Y of Generation whY?* Macquarie Centre, (NSW). AH Revelations Pty. Ltd., February 2006

[17] Eisner, S.P., Managing Generation Y. *SAM Advanced Management Journal* 2005, **70** (4), 4–15.

[18] Hutley, S., Solomons, T. Generational change in Australian Librarianship; Viewpoints from Generation X. *ALIA 2004 Biennial Conference: Challenging ideas,* 2004 Sept 21–24, Gold Coast, [WWW document]. URL <http://conferences.alia.org.au/alia2004/pdfs/hutley.s.paper.pdf>. Accessed on 19 December 2006

[19] Pearson, K., Kelly, J., Martinelli, M., Not the "r" word! Or a breath of fresh air"—the impact of organisational restructure at Macquarie University Library. 2006. *ALIA 2006 Biennial Conference Click06,* 2006 Sept 19–22, Perth, [WWW document] URL

<http://conferences.alia.org.au/alia2006/Papers/Kathryn_Pearson.pdf>. Accessed 01 February 2007

[20] Feyerherm, A., Vick, Y.H. Generation X women in high technology: overcoming gender and generational challenges to success in the corporate environment, *Career Development International* 2005, **10** (3), 216–227.

[21] Brocklebank, J., Whitehouse, H. Job sharing in academic libraries at the senior management level: experiences of job sharing at deputy and director level. *Library Management* 2003, **24** (4/5), 243–251.

[22] Tiney, C. Job share: can this work in management? *International Journal of Retail & Distribution Management* 2004, **32** (9), 430–433.

DEVELOPING THE CONCEPTS OF 'LEADERSHIP FOR ALL' IN LIBRARY AND INFORMATION SERVICES: EXPLORING THE RATIONALE AND MAKING IT HAPPEN

Dr Graham Walton
Service Development Manager
Library, Loughborough University
j.g.walton@lboro.ac.uk

Abstract

The aim of the paper is to look at the concept of 'leadership for all' within both the wider management and library management arenas. The main driver for 'leadership for all' is the rate and level of change in the 21St century. Having leadership skills across all employees in the organisation is seen to help sustainability. Apart from change, other theoretical perspectives will be examined which inform 'leadership for all'. These include developmental leadership, transformational management vs. transactional management, vision, motivation and innovation. The ideas around 'leadership for all' in libraries are then described within the context of the wider perspectives. In terms of achieving 'leadership for all' in libraries, the following strategies are considered: sharing the vision, trust, action learning and managing communication.

INTRODUCTION

Trying to produce a definitive breakdown of the skills and roles of the leader (never mind the library leader) is not straightforward. This is primarily because the views and definitions of what constitutes effective leadership skills changes with time. These views and definitions will also vary across countries. In what can be seen as the first leadership manual, Machiavelli[1] advocates that leaders should exercise brute power and rewards wherever appropriate to preserve the status quo. This may have worked in medieval Europe, but may not be entirely appropriate in the 21st century. Metaphors to inform the role of the leader based on war, games/sport, art, machines and religion/spirituality abound.[2] One metaphor recommends that the leader should take on the same role as that of the orchestral conductor. They should be at the front, deciding who is involved, when they are involved and what the score (agenda) should be. Another metaphor likens the leader to that of a midwife, facilitating the birth of change.

The purpose of this paper is to explore in detail the metaphor of the leader as 'servant', whose role it is to support employees developing leadership skills. There will be a discussion and analysis of the general theories that support leadership skills being present in all employees. This will be followed by reflection on the implications for the library manager. Developing leadership skills across library staff will then be discussed along with the barriers that may exist. Four practical library management scenarios will be identified to illustrate how 'leadership for all' could be used to address them. It does not take too much historical insight to feel that Machiavelli would not have been comfortable with the 'leadership for all' approach!

CHANGE, ORGANISATIONS AND 'LEADERSHIP FOR ALL'

The nature of change in the 21st Century is the overarching driver for leadership skills to be present across all staff. Theorists like Drucker have examined how change manifests itself in the current world. It is unpredictable, occurring all the time and is felt most acutely at the individual level. Smith and Sharma[3] have proposed that with this rate of change in organisations there should be 'every person exhibiting leadership not just the leaders'. They have also produced an alignment-autonomy framework to develop their perspective (Figure 1). Change as described above means that organisations should position themselves in the 'innovative organisation' and 'collaborative culture' quadrant. This position allows people to be responsible for their work and also ensures their actions are targeted to the overarching strategic direction of the organisation. The concept of 'leadership for all' is entirely focussed on ensuring the top right quadrant in Figure 1 is achieved. Supporting a collaborative culture within an innovative organisation is achievable if 'leadership for all' is present.

Figure 1: Autonomy Alignment Framework (Smith and Sharma[3])

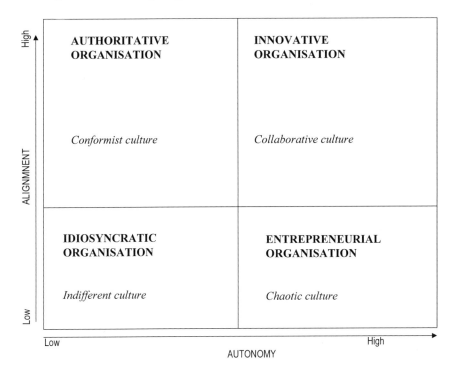

DEVELOPMENTAL LEADERSHIP

A related theory to 'leadership for all' is the concept of developmental leadership. Van Nickerk and Wagh[4] have argued that the concept of developmental (or servant) leadership is very important. There has to be a realisation by leaders that unless employees are prepared for lifelong learning, ready to take on challenges and more competition, the organisation will be unable to renew itself. This means that managers must develop characteristics of 'servantship'. This is interpreted as putting employees needs, growth and development above their own. Managers must also be able to engender trust through their own actions, beliefs and values. Further examples of developmental leadership practice are provided by Wallington.[5] Much value is attached to finding, recognizing and nurturing leadership across the organisation. Included in these approaches are encouraging participation, soliciting views, never being disparaging, letting others lead and using failure to teach.

TRANSFORMATIONAL MANAGEMENT VS. TRANSACTIONAL MANAGEMENT

Related to the ideas around developmental leadership are those to do with the concepts of transformational management vs. transactional management [4,6]. Within the whole development of leadership skills across employees, the transformational approach is proposed as being appropriate. The manager is aiming to empower staff to question old assumptions within the transformational framework. Their purpose is to allow other staff the opportunity to express themselves. Employees have to be helped to work towards the long term strategic goals of the organisation (rather than their own short term self interest). The focus is on allowing staff to acquire leadership skills previously seen as the prerequisites of the staff at the top of the hierarchy. In contrast, transactional management is assignment and task oriented. There are organisational rewards and punishment which are used to make sure staff comply and perform appropriately. Staff have to work to specified objectives they may not have been involved in formulating. Transactional management may have worked well in the past for libraries but this is no longer the case.

VISION

The concept of vision has also been seen as important in the debate on 'leadership for all'. In the transactional management model, the vision is developed by a select few and handed down from on high to the rest of the staff for them to take forward. This way to develop the vision has been questioned by various authors considering 'leadership for all'[6,7,8]. They argue that the emphasis should be on the organisation itself and the people that make up that organisation to develop the vision. Within the transformational model, importance is attached to people expressing themselves and developing their vision for themselves and the other organisational stakeholders. This means there has to be a process that facilitates not only the sharing of the vision but also to ensure it grows and develops. Smith[9] argues that the vision is at its strongest when it results from the 'sharing of individual yearnings of employees'.

MOTIVATION

Another theoretical perspective that informs the discussion around 'leadership for all' is the debates around motivation[10]. People are motivated either intrinsically (outside in) or extrinsically (inside out). In management terms, this means that with extrinsic motivation people are supervised or managed and with intrinsic motivation they manage themselves. With extrinsic motivation, the push to work hard comes from earning rewards and avoiding punishment. In contrast, when intrinsic motivation is present people are rewarded by the challenge of work and pride in their job. If just short term results are required, extrinsic motivation may be best. Again, the fast rate of change means that if sustainability is the aspiration, looking for employees who are intrinsically motivated is more likely to be successful. For sustainability, people need to be self-monitored, self-managed and self motivated. It is impossible to have employees who are both intrinsically and extrinsically motivated.

People are either trusted or they are not trusted. Managers have to trust the workforce to be prepared to take on leadership skills so they can do their own jobs and create long term relationships with colleagues and customers. Where staff are extrinsically motivated, it is the managers who are trusted to verify results. In comparison, when intrinsic motivation is present the general workforce are trusted to assess their own results and performances by their own measures. The intrinsically motivated employee will be a major facet of the freedom-based workplace. In this workplace, the leadership function and remit are present in all staff.

INNOVATION

The development of the innovative work place is another driver to achieve 'leadership for all'. The level and pace for change are also the main drivers for innovation. The European Commission[11] concludes that innovation is to do with:

- renewal and enlargement of the range of products and services and the associated markets
- establishment of new methods of production, supply and distribution

Most tellingly for 'leadership for all', innovation is also about changes in management, work organisation and the working conditions and skills of the workforce. If innovation is sought, managers[12] have to be candid, highly communicative and open to participation by others in decision making (i.e. allow people to become leaders themselves). If the driving force of innovation is mobilized, then there will be positive outcomes.[6]

IMPLICATIONS OF 'LEADERSHIP FOR ALL' FOR LIBRARY MANAGEMENT

Very little has been written in the library management literature which explicitly advocates that leadership skills are generic and should be present in all staff. There is an acknowledgment by Stephens and Russell[13] that there is pressure to look at this approach. When reviewing the recent ideas about leadership they found a focus on leadership development in all employees. Their support was less than fulsome when they advocated that 'libraries should broaden their efforts to embrace experiments in the use of these newer approaches to leadership'. They did state that they were 'intrigued by the work of several employers who view every employee as a leader (at one level or another, in various ways) and who recommend leadership training for everyone'. What does come through very clearly in the writings about library leadership is that previous approaches to leadership are not appropriate in times of massive change. One observer[8] argues that between 1876 and the mid 1970s the leadership and managerial skills needed for libraries remained unchanged. The invention of the personal computer and the Internet alongside the development of digital resources has changed this stability. Libraries have gone through the same level of continuous change as health care, telecommunications, insurance and advertisng[7]. With this rate of change, the library manager has to shepherd the service through tumultuous times whilst at the same time balancing change with continuity. The previous approaches of 'command and control' are being jettisoned in favour of library managers ensuring there is effective communication, that people collaborate easily and have input to the decision making process. For library and information services in the commercial sector, the 'command and control' principle was once seen as increasing competitiveness.[4] This has now been disproved and there is a need for libraries to move away from this. The library manager has to focus more on giving employees the flexibility to adapt to an environment where there is constant change.

This departure from 'command and control' is directing library managers to become the facilitative leader. The essence of the facilitative leader has been well captured by Rees[14]:

> The leader who can take the role of a facilitator blends his or her role of visionary decisive leader with that of listening and empowering leader. As a facilitative leader he or she involves followers as much as possible in creating the group's vision and purpose, carrying out the vision and purpose and building a productive and cohesive team.

Facilitation skills are becoming recognised as part of the repertoire of the new library managers. Moore[15] argues that facilitative leadership fits well into libraries because it is compatible with other tools and principles in libraries. The mangers role is to create the facilitative environment in the library where individuals at every level can:

- have some individuality of thought and actions
- set some standards to monitor their own performance
- be able to interpret events without fear of making mistakes
- respond to events without having to follow the rulebook all the time

The advantage that accrue from library managers showing facilitation skills is that people can do things that otherwise would not be possible. Common goals are more likely to be developed because people will understand each other more.

There are barriers to effective 'leadership for all' in libraries. There may be some resistance from employees as they will have differences in how they wish to be treated. There are some library staff who would like top-down, directive leadership as they just like to be told what to do. Over the years, most libraries have developed very powerful hierarchies and also rigid traditions which do not allow the concept of 'leadership for all' to flourish. If the hierarchy is very influential, there will be little room for development and creativity. The hierarchy forces people to create boundaries around their different needs and relationships.

As Shoaf also points out, 'libraries seem to attract the risk averse'.[22] The culture of 'leadership for all' struggles to come through within this setting. If this culture does not change, employees will not think creatively or relish risk taking. Neither will they show enthusiasm or passion about their work and library.

DEVELOPING 'LEADERSHIP FOR ALL' IN THE LIBRARY

'Leadership for all' as a principle will not develop organically in a library. There have to be various explicit commitments and strategies to allow it to flourish. Included in these are:

- **sharing the vision**: the importance of the shared vision has already been alluded to. The facilitative manager supports the library staff develop a single vision together. This does not happen easily as developing the vision takes more time this way and it also loses some of its crispness, as there are always diverse interests in the library. The library manager has to be patient as the vision is identified, developed and refined. There is every likelihood that the sharing of the vision will produce the willingness to innovate as well as the enthusiasm and belief in the service that 'leadership for all' is intended to achieve. There are some tensions here as the strong manager also should have a vision. This may (or may not) be the same as employees. The skills of negotiating and influencing then come to the fore as the manager tries to ensure there is consistency between their own vision and that of the rest of the library staff.

- **trust**: unless the manager trusts the library employee, 'leadership for all' will never materialise. Libraries have traditionally found it difficult to allow their staff to be able to interpret events themselves and have individuality of thought and practice. After years of telling people what to do, library managers have to have a belief that their employees are responsible and committed. If the trust does not exist, any semblance of 'leadership for all' will soon disappear.

- **Action learning**: when considering 'leadership for all', having action learning in place is seen as a very effective way to support its development. Action learning as a concept developed on the UK as a way to improve coal production.[16] The job environment becomes the classroom where people learn through experience. The process allows people to learn through their own personal reflection and also by questioning fellow action learners. This approach encourages the enhancement of traits of leadership and personal responsibility. In terms of leadership development, action learning allows competencies such as 'adaptive thinking, building relations, inspiring trust, aligning the organisation, fostering open and effective communication, demonstrating vision and focusing on quality and continuous improvement'.[17] For a library, a major strength of action learning is that it does not require any special set of conditions, it works just as well in a bureaucracy as it does in a flat organisation.

- **Making communication work**: libraries are organisations which employ social animals (staff) who ensure the service is delivered. As social animals, interaction and communication takes place all the time in formal or informal meetings. These meetings are very important within the context of 'leadership for all'. If people are to be encouraged to work collaboratively, to communicate effectively and agree on shared actions and visions they have to be able to function well in meetings. If they do not have these skills, then there will be a lack of comprehension and the quality of interactions will plummet.[9] The library manager has to therefore ensure employees have enhanced interpersonal and communication skills. If they understand each other more and are comfortable in opening up to their colleagues, the underpinning 'leadership for all' should emerge.

PRACTICE IMPLICATIONS OF 'LEADERSHIP FOR ALL'

This paper so far has taken a theoretical stance on exploring 'leadership for all' within the library context. This section will consider how these concepts could apply in practice. Four scenarios are given that describe practical management challenges in libraries where qualities of leadership are needed. Suggestions will be given on how these challenges could be addressed using the principles of 'leadership for all'.

Scenario 1: the University Librarian is concerned that the Library web site looks tired, it conveys neither the required message nor the range of services provided.

- A recently appointed library assistant who has lots of ideas about how electronic services can be improved has come to the Librarian's attention. This person is seconded as project manager to oversee the development and production of the new web pages.
- The brief drawn up for the project allows the library assistant to choose who will be on the project team and also makes it clear the high level of autonomy

- The Librarian volunteers to help by looking at the web metrics of the current site.
- Funding is released by the Librarian to send the library assistant on a project management course

Scenario 2: A city council authority has produced a work/ life balance strategy that all sections of the council have to adopt and implement. This includes the public library service and the 12 libraries within that service.

- The City Librarian sets up a steering group to oversee the implementation of the work/ life balance strategy. Representation includes staff from each of the 12 libraries
- A member of staff recently returning from maternity leaves is asked to chair and oversee the steering group
- The City Librarian is not on the steering group but ensures regular meetings take place with the steering group chair. The City Librarian also makes sure minutes from meetings are distributed effectively and that the steering group produces a regular news sheet
- An expert in work/ life balance is brought in to advise the steering group on the relevant issues and approaches
- The City Librarian gives a clear steer that the recommendations from the steering group should be allocated to specific individuals in the public library system to implement

Scenario 3: A large hospital library has decided to move over completely to e-journals. This will mean that significant physical space will be freed up as the paper journals are discarded. The space will need to be used effectively to support future library service.

- The Librarian arranges for library staff to visit other hospital libraries that have already moved in this direction to identify how space has been used
- After the visits, library staff are charged with collaborating and producing recommendations and timescales
- These recommendations are then given to a two library assistants to oversee and manage

- Regular progress reports take place between the Librarian and the library assistants on the development of the space

Scenario 4: The large public library authority is introducing Radio Frequency Identification (RFID) tags. This will vastly reduce the need for library staff to be involved in the issuing and discharge of books.

- An open meeting is held for all staff where the Librarian makes it clear from the outset that this will lead to opportunities for role development (as opposed to redundancy)

- An 'away' day is then organised for the staff most likely to be affected by the introduction of the technology

- People at this meeting are split into three groups, each charged with areas of responsibility: one will look at how other libraries have developed roles, the second will produce the RFID implementation plans and the other will establish and deliver the relevant training

- A convenor for each group is identified. These three people will oversee the implementation of RFID in the library

The intention of these library management scenarios has been to encapsulate the practical implications of 'leadership for all'. The various situations do capture the implications for the library manager if 'leadership for all' is the aspiration. Managers have to recognise leadership skills in others and ensure they are nurtured. A facilitation role is necessary as they empower colleagues and also encourage people to express themselves. Effective communication channels need to be in place so library staff are informed and aware of recent developments. The library managers themselves also have to be prepared to take on visions that they may not have originated. Mutual trust has to be present between managers and other library staff. There is tension for the library manager in having a background profile whilst at the same time being highly sensitive and aware to what is currently happening. The major challenge for the library manager is determining the actions they need to take when trust or communication or intrinsic motivation etc is not present in the library.

CONCLUSION

A side effect of 'leadership for all' in the library context is that it could address the issue of effective succession planning.[18] There is a concern that the ageing library workforce will mean that there will not be enough appropriate individuals in the future to take over the management roles. 'Leadership for all' could be the way this possible problem is solved. It brings a level of sustainability that is often difficult to achieve otherwise.

The purpose of this paper has been to explore the concept of 'leadership for all' within the library context. There are signs that having all staff demonstrate leadership skills that were previously seen as being needed only by the few is becoming recognised as important in libraries. Moore[15] outlines how the Wake Public Library system in the Unites States has trained 40 staff in 'leadership for all' skills. Included in its achievements are:

- Helping people do things they could not do on their own
- Ensuring people understand each other better
- Allowing common goals to be established, agreed upon, committed to and reached
- Helping people reach better decisions, learn from their mistakes and engage in more meaningful conversations than before

The challenge for the library manager is to have the courage, the belief and the trust to take the principles of 'leadership for all' and apply them to their own library.

REFERENCES

[1] Machiavelli, N. *The prince* http://www.gutenberg.org/etext/1232 (accessed 14th January 2007)

[2] Oberlecher, T. and Schonberger, V. *Towards a new understanding of leadership through metaphor*, Center for Public Leadership, Harvard University, 2003. http://www.ksg.harvard.edu/leadership/pubs/papers/index.php?itemid=199 (accessed 14th January 2007)

[3] Smith, P.A.C. and Sharma, M. Developing responsibility and leadership traits in all your employees: part 1—shaping and harmonizing the high performance. *Management Decisions* 2002 **40** (7/8), 764–77.

[4] van Niekerk, H.J. and Waghid, Y.. Developing leadership competencies for the knowledge society: the relevance of action learning. *South African Journal of Information Management* 2004, **6** (4), n.p.

[5] Wallington, P. Leadership from below: tap into talent at all levels on the organisation, *CIO* 2002 **16** (2). 1–2.

[6] Castiglione, J. Organisational learning and transformational leadership in the library environment, *Library Management* 2006 **27** (4/5), 289–299.

[7] Shoaf, E.C. New leadership for libraries: who has the right stuff? *College & Research Libraries News* 2004 **65** (7), 363–365, 375.

[8] Schulz, P.W. Competitive edge *Leadership Excellence* 2006 **23** (5), 11–13.

[9] Smith, P.A.C. and Sharma, M. Developing responsibility and leadership traits in all your employees: part 2—optimally shaping and harmonizing the high performance, Management Decisions, 2002 **40** (9), 814–820.

[10] Lebow, R. Freedom-based work, *Leadership Excellence* 2006 **23** (11), 19–23.

[11] Eurpoean Commission Green paper on innovation, *Bulleting of the European Union, Supplement* 19965/95.

[12] Paul, G. Mobilisihg the potential for initiative and innovation by means of a socially competent management, *Library Management* 2000 **21** (2), 81–85.

[13] Stephens, D. and Russell, K. Organisational development, leadership, change and the future of libraries, *Library Trends* 2004 **53** (1), 238–257.

[14] Rees, F. *The facilitator excellence handbook: helping people work creatively and productively together*, 1998 San Fransisco: Jossey-Bass/ Pfeiffer

[15] Moore, T.L. Facilitative leadership: one approach to empowering staff and other stakeholders, *Library Trends*, 2004 **53**(1), 230–237.

[16] Revans, R.W. *Plans for recruitment, education and training for the coalmining industry*, 1945 London: Mining Association of Great Britain.

[17] Marquardt, M.J. *Optimizing the power of action learning: solving problems and building leaders in real times*, 2004 Palo Alto, CA: Davies-Black

[18] Australian Library and Information Association , Succession planning for libraries http://www.alia.org.au/groups/libtnat/technique/2006.01/succession.html (accessed 28th March 2007).

K.G. SAUR

IFLA Series on Bibliographic Control

Barbara B. Tillett / Jaesun Lee /
Ana Lupe Cristán (Ed.)

■ **IFLA Cataloguing Principles:
Steps towards an International
Cataloguing Code, 4**
Reports from the 4th IFLA Meeting of
Experts on an International Cataloguing
Code, Seoul, Korea, 2006

2007. Approx. 676 pp. Hc.
€ 128.00 / *US$ 179.00
IFLA members: € 98.00 / *US$ 137.00
ISBN 978-3-598-24281-6
(IFLA Series on Bibliographic Control, Vol. 32)

■ **ISBD: International Standard Bibliographic
Description**
Recommended by the ISBD Review Group. Approved by the
Standing Committee of the IFLA Cataloguing Section

2007. 322 pp. Loose-leaf with ring binder.
€ 84.00 / *US$ 118.00
IFLA members: € 64.00 / *US$ 90.00
ISBN 978-3-598-24280-9
(IFLA Series on Bibliographic Control, Vol. 31)

Marie-France Plassard (Ed.)
■ **UNIMARC & Friends: Charting the New Landscape of
Library Standards**
Proceedings of the International Conference Held in Lisbon,
20–21 March 2006

2007. 133 pp. Hc.
€ 68.00 / *US$ 95.00
IFLA members: € 48.00 / *US$ 67.00
ISBN 978-3-598-24279-3
(IFLA Series on Bibliographic Control, Vol. 30)

de Gruyter
Berlin · New York

www.saur.de

*For orders placed in North America
Prices are subject to change